Eleazar Thompson Fitch

# Sermons, Practical And Descriptive

Preached in the Pulpit of Yale College

Eleazar Thompson Fitch

**Sermons, Practical And Descriptive**
*Preached in the Pulpit of Yale College*

ISBN/EAN: 9783744744218

Printed in Europe, USA, Canada, Australia, Japan

Cover: Foto ©Thomas Meinert / pixelio.de

More available books at **www.hansebooks.com**

# MISCELLANEOUS SERMONS

OF THE LATE

## REV. PROF. ELEAZAR T. FITCH, D.D.

First Series.

# SERMONS,

## PRACTICAL AND DESCRIPTIVE,

PREACHED IN THE PULPIT OF

## YALE COLLEGE.

BY

## REV. ELEAZAR T. FITCH, D.D.,

LIVINGSTON PROFESSOR OF DIVINITY FROM 1817 TO 1852.

*—He being dead yet speaketh.*

NEW HAVEN.

JUDD AND WHITE.

1871.

# PREFACE.

This volume is issued in response to the urgent request of a number of my father's friends and admirers; and its publication is doubtless looked for by many others.

The sermons selected are such as, from the subjects and the mode of their treatment, were quite generally valued at the time of their delivery. And accordingly it appears eminently appropriate to commit them to the press; not only for the sake of those persons, among whose most sacred memories their words yet linger, and who will greet them as long absent friends, returned again; but also, that productions, thus proved by the concurring opinions of so many competent judges to possess the elements of a permanent influence, may reach a wider public, and accomplish larger results of good.

It may be proper to observe, that the selection is based chiefly, upon the special mention of particular sermons in cordial and encouraging letters of friends, received since my father's death, or upon the suggestions of judicious advisors at hand.

Should this volume be favorably received, I may follow it with another series of the same general character.

LUCIUS W. FITCH.

New Haven, July, 1871.

# CONTENTS.

# GOD'S WORD MAN'S CHIEF *JOY* IN THIS PRESENT TIME.



PSALM CXIX : 54.

THY STATUTES HAVE BEEN MY SONGS IN THE HOUSE OF MY PILGRIMAGE.

FROM the lives of others we may derive lessons of practical wisdom at the very commencement of our own. While yet the morning of youth is beaming on us, and we are looking forward to a long day of anxiety and toil on the earth, we may hear from the lips of the aged the recital of their experience, or read in the volumes of the dead their yet surviving testimony; warning us of the dangers we are to shun, and pointing out to us the true paths of peace and prosperity.

I have now read to you the testimony of a pious monarch in Israel, respecting his own life, which he recorded, for the praise of Jehovah and for the benefit of succeeding generations; in which you hear the voice of experience, testifying to you the sources of happiness which exist for the consolation of man amidst the mutabilities of the present world. This monarch, near the close of his eventful life (as it has been generally supposed), surveys the past; recalls the events of fleeting years through which he has journeyed,—a stranger on a pilgrimage in the earth; recounts the days of affliction and prosperity that have rolled over him; and, in grateful acknowledgment, testifies unto God that his statutes have illuminated his dwelling with its brightest joys and consolations, which, in days of prosperity were prized by him beyond "thousands of gold and silver;" and without which, in days of darkness, he "had perished in his afflictions;" which had ever afforded him themes of grateful meditation;

guided him in the conduct of life; inspired his confidence and hope; rapt his spirit in the composition of devotional songs; and caused his tabernacle to resound with the glad voice of praise and joy:—"Thy statutes have been my songs in the house of my pilgrimage." The experience of the Psalmist, to which he has testified in this declaration affords to all, this salutary lesson for the regulation of their lives:—that THE WORD OF GOD IS THE ONLY GUIDE TO TRUE HAPPINESS AMID THE CHANGES OF THIS WORLD.

In inculcating this truth, I purpose to consider, particularly, some of *the sources of joy* which the word of God offers to man *amid the changes of this life.* This train of remark may serve at once to show us on what the happy experience of David was founded, and how we are to transfuse the same experience into our own lives.

In order, then, to set before you the fountains of joy which the statutes of Jehovah open to man in this life, I remark,

I. That, amid all the changes of time, they present to his meditations the same God of unclouded excellence.

Man is a contemplative being; but in his busy contemplation he finds no resting place within the limits of created things. He surveys, indeed, with pleasure, the wonders of creation which surround him; he explores with delighted vision and study, the world of his habitation and the worlds which glitter upon him from the firmament; but from all these lower objects of creation, his mind instinctively rises to that Eternal Spirit from whom they proceeded, who guides all by his wisdom and hath established over all his throne in the heavens. I say, *instinctively,*—for the disruption of his soul from God, which afflicts fallen man, is a strange violence done to his nature.

Now it is the statutes and testimonies of Jehovah, which present to the contemplations of man the brightest exhibitions of his infinite glory. While we gaze on the astonishing exhibitions of his power and intelligence which meet us from the works of his creation and providence, his word comes to address us more fully; to explain his designs; and to make known, beyond a doubt, the attributes of his will. Benevolence, righteousness, mercy, truth, in one unclouded sun of glory, beam upon us from his throne; and assure us of his perfect claims to the veneration, homage, praise, obedience, and confidence of all on earth and in heaven. In the law which he has ordained for his moral kingdom, in conformity to which he conducts all his works of providence, government, and redemption, we read his heart of benevolence; and find him a being worthy to be contemplated with supreme delight during every stage of our endless existence,—a being with whom the spirit can hold a communion in intelligence and love, forever improving and brightening.

What a fountain of joy is here opened to man amid the changes of time! Whatever events betide him, from the mount of prosperity or the vale of sorrow and trial, he may look up alike to the unclouded excellence of his God and King. Leaving out of view his own humble interests, he may look to him who is unchangeably glorious on the throne, conducting all things with a goodness, righteousness, and purity forever untarnished, and, absorbed with delightful contemplations, be lost, as it were, in the glory of his Maker. Whether the cup of joy or affliction be administered to him, he opens the statutes of Jehovah and sees the same God of Glory on the throne, worthy as ever to be loved and praised by his creatures; and he can mingle with every blessing and trial of his earthly lot, as did David, the song of praise: "the Lord reigneth, let the earth rejoice."

Man, I say, may derive this joy from the statutes of the Lord. They place before his meditations, the unchanging and untarnished excellence of his King; and assure him, beyond all the darkness and doubts that might otherwise hang over this life's pilgrimage, that God is just and good and pure, in all his doings in his kingdom.

How much joy and peace and consolation, derived from this source, have cheered and brightened this vale of tears is fully known only to the eye of Omniscience. But if you would learn its exalted nature, go to David, Isaiah, Paul; Newton, Bacon, Locke, Hale, Edwards; rapt with the inspiring contemplation: and see what themes have illuminated and expanded their minds beyond all the discoveries of the heathen, and which have mingled with their earthly lot the joys of brighter worlds! The language of one is the language of all: "O how love I thy law, it is my meditation all the day."

Another fountain of joy opened to man by the statutes of Jehovah, I mention,

II. That amid all the changes of time, they administer to him one *perfect rule of action.*

Man is an active being; formed to resolve and execute, and to affect himself and others by the course of his conduct. But in his conduct he finds not his rest in attempting to please himself and his fellow-beings merely. In order to his highest happiness he needs to commence and terminate his activity in God, the fountain of all being; to be directed and quickened by the authority of that wise and perfect Being who watches over his own glory and the good of his kingdom with ceaseless care, and to be employed in fulfilling the plans of his goodness and mercy.

Now it is through his statutes that he uses his wisdom and authority in guiding the conduct of men; and that he employs them as his servants in executing the works of his benevolence. These statutes comprise every requirement of men in one grand, perfect and unchangeable law of doing good,—in glorifying the Creator, and in blessing mankind. In this law, the activity of man is directed by the Best of Beings to the best of ends. Towards God it is the reverence, homage, worship, obedience, gratitude, trust, of perfect love; and towards man, the justice, truth, compassion, long suffering, meekness, forgiveness of perfect love,—the perfect precept that sweetly binds the soul to moral purity,—perfection in seeking the glory of God and the welfare of his kingdom: and it is a law to inspire joy in the obedient during the ages of an endless existence.

Here then is an unfailing fountain of joy opened to man during the changes of this pilgrimage! Jehovah undertakes by his statutes to guide him in the paths of righteousness. On the basis of these statutes man may become his servant, and attempt, through every scene of this life, to follow the will of his Lord! Whatever providences betide him (in this mutable state,) here may he gather the peace of those who love the Lord and his kingdom. Though in the actions of life he should not attain a perfect conformity to the will of his Father in Heaven, yet he would not have that will any the less perfect, less pure, or less holy. It is its unchangeable perfection and purity that renders it desirable and transforming; which, while it humbles him for every failure, sweetly keeps him to exalted aims and purposes worthy of immortality. And if, in this changing state, this pilgrimage of life, the events which befall him, seem joyous or grievous, he still sees Jehovah by the quickening influence of a perfect law of action, conducting him to the peace and purity of the undefiled in heart! Oh it is a joy beyond the reach of the agitations of this world, which the obedient gathers from following the law of his God! In secret it is the *consciousness* of holy purpose and filial communion, which awaits the soul in friendliness to Jehovah and his cause, and which no storms from without can assail: in public, it is the *effort* of holy purpose, which allays the miseries, calms the contentions, and heals the moral maladies of this guilty world; and which spreads around it the peace and serenity of a new creation.

Wherever he goes, and whatever befalls him, the statutes of the Lord invariably direct, quicken, and support him in this peaceful course of action. They would elevate him above the covetousness, lust, pride, rancor, jealousies, rivalries, of this sinful world, to the peace of holiness and purity and love; and while the days of his pilgrimage are blessed with these quickening and purifying statutes of the Lord, he unites in the joy and song of the psalmist: "Thy testimonies that thou hast commanded are righteous and very faithful. Thy word is very pure, therefore thy servant loveth it."

Another source of joy which the statutes of the Lord offer to man, and one which springs only from these, I mention,

III. That amid all the changes of time, they administer to him the same perfect *assurances of divine favor.*

Man is a dependent being, affected in his welfare by the feelings and conduct of others, and most of all by the feelings and conduct of Jehovah. His personal interests as a dependent being are all cast upon God, who if he favor, or frown, carries the weight of all creation, and providence, with him, to attest his kindness or his indignation.

Now in his testimonies, this glorious Being has put into our hands the solemn assurances of his favor towards offending man. Though our apostasy had provoked his just indignation, and might have separated him at hopeless distance from us forever, yet in the benignity of his grace he has here given us assurances, strong as his own oath, and the humiliations of his Son, that he is ready to be reconciled to us and with more than parental care to manage for us all our interests. We here read the covenant of his mercy and care; assured that we shall find in him a Helper ready to uphold and guard and guide us in the steps of this pilgrimage. Here is the basis of firm confidence.

These assurances lead man to the joy of reconciliation with God. With a conscience burdened with the apprehensions of guilt he is ready to distrust his Maker, and cling to his rebellion: and it is only on the firm assurances of his published word, that he can believe, and enter into the joys of reconciliation.

These assurances encourage him to seek continually the blessing of God. On the basis of these he bows his knees in humble and suppliant confidence before the Father of Mercies; and founds the expectation of that grace which is sufficient for him in all the circumstances of this life.

The joy derived from the personal friendship of God is thus communicated to the soul. Here the assurances ever stand written, and unchanged, in all their length and breadth of love. His Almighty Finger has engraven the engagements on everlasting tablets. They are faithful and unfailing promises. Here then we may build our faith unmoved; revive it when it decays; strengthen it when feeble; and sustain it through every change of an outward providence.

And what a fountain of joy is this, to see through every external change, the changeless eye and front of love still beaming on us from the heavens. To know that whatever untoward circumstances may come upon us from his providence, or whatever griefs men may occasion us, he still maintains, beyond these clouds of sorrow, a heart to do us good, and is ready to be sought of us in all our necessities. Through all the changes of this state, weak, erring, sinful, and dependent man thus descries the same unclouded throne of grace open for his resort ; and in the strength of faith in the promises, may visit that throne with his wants, as did David : " Thou art my hiding place and my shield. I hope in thy word."

One other source of joy which the statutes of the Lord present to man, and which he can gather from no other source, 1 mention only,

IV. That, amid all the changes of this life, they administer to him the *hope of a nobler existence in eternity.*

Man is an immortal being, sojourning on the earth but a transitory season, ere he enters on an eternal dwelling. With the mind of an immortal, he instinctively looks for that permanent good which can come only from him who is on the throne of immensity and eternity. He will, now and then, even in his farthest alienation from Jehovah and his busiest devotion to the world, feel the impulses and desires of an immortal spirit within him panting after the nobler and more substantial joys of immortality.

The wants of man as an immortal being, Jehovah has consulted in his testimonies. Here he testifies, in a voice that puts to rest the agitations of doubt and unbelief, that the kingdom of holy subjects which he is rearing will share in the vision of his glories, the cheerful obedience of his commands, and the light of his favoring love, for eternal ages before his throne. The joys which his word administers to his servants on earth, the same word assures them shall be perfected and continued forever beyond the grave. And it sets before man a practicable way of obtaining this nobler state. Here he pledges his own grace, in a method of effectual redemption through Christ, to lead and uphold those, who cordially seek him, through the snares of this life, to justify and accept them in the day of final trial, and to elevate them to the crowns and the thrones of the righteous in his kingdom.

Now it is on this word alone, assuring him of the triumphs of Christianity and of the unfailing love of God, that man founds the cheering hope of a glorious immortality. And he who, guided by this word, delights in meditating on the glory of God, in following his commandments of purity and in seeking his favor, is prepared to feel the inspiring joys of such a hope.

And how suited to administer to him consolation and joy, amid all the changes of this life, is such a hope! All that is afflictive, all that seems untoward here, are but the trials of a short pilgrimage, and all beyond is one eternal day. Whatever events befall him here, whether his paths be lighted with prosperity or shaded with adversity, the statutes of the Lord direct him to look beyond them all to the glories of immortality. This hope sustains, comforts, elevates; lightens and alleviates the woes of earth; purifies and enhances its joys. From life it removes its disappointments; and from death extracts its sting. Man stands forth rejoicing in the liberty wherewith God hath made him free. Disenthralled from the fetters and bondage of sin, and led forth by his Saviour from the prison-house of eternal death into the glorious light of day, he breathes the air of immortality; and even while he walks this earth, he is enrolled a denizen of the Heavenly Jerusalem, and claims a kindred with the saints and a fellowship with angels in the transports of the skies. The testimonies of the Lord have enkindled within him these glowing hopes. They have introduced into the house of his pilgrimage these songs of immortals. In days of health, vigor and activity, when his dwelling on earth seems most fixed and durable, he repairs continually to these walls of salvation for his sweetest hopes; and when he stands on the verge of life—his heart and flesh failing him—he leans upon the ark of the covenant and the word of the testimony; and as the shadows of death thicken around him, with the last ray of feeling he breathes out his soul unto God: " Let thy mercies come unto me, O God, even thy salvation, according to thy word. So shall I keep thy law continually, forever and ever."

I have attempted, my brethren, to set before you *the Scriptures as the only guide to true happiness amid the changes of this world;* and have illustrated the truth, by showing that they administer to man through all the events of this life an exhaustless theme of cheering meditation, a permanent law of beneficent action, a fixed basis of confidence in God, a firm ground of hope.

Your attention is now invited to a few remarks suggested by the subject of our present meditations.

1. We see how far the Scriptures elevate man above the changes of time.

The changes to which man is subject in this life are many and great: changes in condition, in station, in possessions, in friends, in prospects, in health, in enjoyments. If the sun of prosperity gild his skies to-day, the clouds of adversity may obscure them on the morrow. To-day the son of Jesse is exalted from the sheep-cote and anointed on Hebron king of Israel amid the transports of his people; to-morrow his rebellious son rends from him the kingdom and the hearts of the people, and he retires from the sacred city, ascending Olivet with a few adherents, destitute, barefoot, and weeping. Nothing here is permanent; nothing stable and sure. The mutabilities of this world have ever agitated the minds of men. Nor has man, unguided of God, relying on his own wisdom, ever been able to exalt himself in his feelings above these changes, or to rise above the wide spreading curse that afflicts and desolates humanity.  The thoughts of the wise have been vain, the counsels of the prudent foolish.  What can the boasted light of heathenism do for me?  One sage would make me a Stoic, and attempt to soothe the ills of this life by rendering me insensible to both the good and ill.  But instead of leading me to some permanent good that might cheer me amid the trials of this state, he has cruelly told me to relinquish the hope of every good, to attempt the spiritual suicide of extinguishing all my sensibilities and retiring in apathy from all the glories of God's creation.

Another would make me an Epicure: and tell me to seize each joy that meets me, and revel while I can in all the delights of sense, and blot the future from my thoughts.  But while I gather around me the pipe, the tabret, the harp, the dance, the feast, the wine, and fill my senses with the delights of earth in a day of worldly prosperity, I cannot annihilate the morrow nor the evils that may come with it, and when the days of calamity come, all my good is gone and my griefs are insupportable.  I asked for something that would exalt me above these changes, and he sets me on the vain attempt of annihilating the evil.

Another would make me an Ascetic: and by self-imposed privations and self-inflicted tortures, attempt to purchase, beyond this life, some high gradation in glory.  But he denies me even the little good that beams upon me in this world, and gives me no security that I shall not be disappointed in my hopes of good hereafter.  From a land where some peace and sunshine dwells, he has embarked me on a rough and tempestuous ocean without assurance that I shall ever reach a happier shore.

But when from the darkness of this world, I turn to the testimonies of the Lord, I see a God illuminating this world with the radiance of his glory, employing me as his servant in labors of beneficence and purity and peace, attending my paths with the guardianship of his Almighty Grace, and pouring into my breast the joys of immortality.

Here Jehovah descends to transfuse into the cup of mortals the joys of paradise.  These testimonies exalt man above the mutabilities of this state by yielding him a good, great in itself and abiding: a good which far transcends the joys of time, and which remains the same rich fountain to cheer and to sooth in days of the greatest worldly affliction.  It is here that the good man ascends the mount of converse with God,—high above the storms and tempests which desolate the world below,—where all is sunshine and eternal peace.  And while he looks down on a ' world that is to pass away with all the lusts thereof,' he knows that his joys have the firm footing of immortality, and that 'he that doeth the will of God abideth forever.'

2. We see how the Scriptures combine the peace of man on earth with his welfare in eternity.

They who are of sensual and earthly mind, often think that the joys of the future world demand the sacrifice of all true happiness in this life.  The reason of their judgment is easily seen in their own supreme attachment to the joys of time and inexperience of the joys of the soul that is united to its God.

But the testimonies of the Lord require not the relinquishment of any real good.  They demand indeed the relinquishment of a supreme and absorbing regard to the things of this world; but it is that man may participate in a good immensely greater and more enduring.  They would lead him from the objects of creation, amid which his errant and rebellious soul has been wandering in disappointment and grief, for its good back again to its Creator and Shepherd to receive in his returning favor and presence and his holy service the high joys for which it instinctively pants.

This, to an erring soul, is the joy of redemption; a welcome to the friendship of God and a place in his household to cheer the days of his pilgrimage below and to last through the coming ages of eternity.  Here then, at the sacred oracles, the heavenly art is learned of combining the happiness of time with that of eternity.  The joys which these testimonies inspire, are the very joys of heaven. They mingle that world with ours. They connect its happy family with the family of the saints. They inspire in the redeemed soul in the house of this pilgrimage, those songs of redemption which are struck but with higher rapture in the realms of everlasting day. This life is rendered the dawn of heaven; its paths a happy pilgrimage to the world of glory.

3. Finally, we learn the duty of depending for our well being in this life on the published word of God.

The testimony of David is the testimony of the whole host of the faithful who have walked before us in the counsels of the Lord—that these statutes have yielded them the sweetest joys and consolations which they have experienced in this pilgrimage. They open before us, my brethren, the same fountains of joy that they have done to others—the same ennobling views of divine glory —the same converting and purifying precepts—the same assurance of assisting grace—the same path to immortal blessedness.

But in order to reap this joy, we must in faith repair to these sacred fountains. We must accept the good which they tender us for an inheritance. We must meditate on that glory of God, and walk in the precepts of that law, and bow before that throne of grace, and make sure that calling to eternal life, which are revealed to us on their pages.

Are not the joys which they are ever ready to administer to us then, sufficient to claim this from us as our sacred duty? And do we not need, amid the trials and changes that await us in this uncertain state, to be guided by the unerring testimonies of our God?

This duty, however, I would on the present occasion more especially commend to the attention of those of us who are now to leave these walks of science, and soon to enter upon the vicissitudes and changes of active live.

My Friends,—this life the Psalmist has expressively termed a pilgrimage. You have just commenced the existence of intelligent, active, dependent and immortal beings under the dominion of Jehovah. He has placed you in this world but for a transitory season on trial for eternity. You are strangers in the earth. Its fleeting joys and sorrows are but the rapid incidents of a journey to the everlasting world. The past—how like a dream appear its fleeting changes now, from cradled infancy to this eventful hour of manhood! The future—its uncertain joys and sorrows will soon be past, and on the confines of eternity the whole will appear indeed the pilgrimage of strangers here.

To render your course in this short life truly happy and prosperous, you need a good that is above earth's changes, enduring as eternity ; and this good is brought near you and offered you in the testimonies of the Lord. Go then in every scene of this short pilgrimage, and meet him at his holy oracles. Repair constantly to these fountains of knowledge, holiness, grace, and immortality. Here you may establish and cultivate a friendship with the High and Holy One, that shall be in days of prosperity your highest joy, and the solace of your hearts in the darkest days of affliction.

The time is now at hand when you will be called to act your parts in life alone. Away from your parental homes and the guides of earlier years, you are to contend singly with the duties, temptations and afflictions of the present state. And to whom or to what as you turn to us the eye and press the hand, in parting affection, can we better commend you than to God and to that word of his grace which is able to build you up in holiness here, and to give you an inheritance among the sanctified in the world of glory ?

Have you already felt the power of this word to draw you near the Lord, and do you at this hour feel the sacred impulse of that faith that casts all its cares for time and eternity upon his grace? Go forth, ye servants of the living God, go forth at his call, in peace. Your confidence is founded on the Rock of Ages, and will abide, unmoved, the storms of earth. The counsels of the Lord will guide, protect and bless you; and yield you many a song of praise while on your way to join the fellowship and higher joys of immortals!

Or are you still estranged from God? Seek you no higher joys than can be gathered in this short pilgrimage, and in the objects of this transitory world? Shall those immortal spirits of yours, cultivated and refined by science, turn away from the themes that employ the highest and holiest of the creation? the laws that purify and exalt them? the favor that guides the humble to their joys? Come then, ye unhappy aliens from Jehovah, and at this hour, around the ark of his covenant, on the basis of his offers, settle your controversy with your Maker. Establish with him the peace of an endless reconciliation. Shall not the grace that calls you, touch and move your hearts?

You have heard of the stubborn son, perhaps, whom neither the bonds of parental nor fraternal love could restrain from his froward purpose; who left in alienation the home of his earlier years; who, when on the billowy deep, or in some foreign clime, he was surveying his little stores, cast his eye on some memorial of a mother's or a sister's undying affection, and conscience awoke; his heart relented; the expiring rays of filial feeling were re-kindled in his bosom; and he returned in dutifulness to the once agonized but now overjoyed family. And is it not so with erring man? Is he not roving in alienation from Jehovah and his holy family, in quest of some portion among the distant objects of his creation? And, as in grief and disappointment and shame he surveys the emptiness of the good he finds in this estrangement, amid the memorials of heavenly affection that yet surround him the ark of the covenant meets his eye—over which the angels bend in admiration—containing the archives of a Savior's love, the love that through humiliations and tears and groans invites him back to the happy family of God. Conscience awakes; his heart relents; he drops his idols; he submits to God, and seeks through the pilgrimage of life the world of his presence. And all heaven joys over his return. O may this heavenly influence reach and subdue your hearts!

My Friends, whatever purposes you entertain in your hearts respecting the future, I have presented to you the only path to true prosperity in this life and beyond the grave. And now, in view of the vicissitudes of this pilgrimage and the unchanging states of happiness and misery that lie beyond the grave, we commend you to God and the word of his grace, while we affectionately bid you, *Farewell.*

ISAIAH V : 20.

WOE UNTO THEM THAT CALL EVIL GOOD AND GOOD EVIL.

ONE of the artifices by which the grand adversary deceives mankind, is that of calling things by wrong names; and, as it is his grand design to keep up the empire of sin in the world, he does this more especially by reversing the names of moral good and evil. For he knows that, as Eve in Paradise, his first victim, had,—so all her fallen posterity have, such an innate sense of the beauty of virtue and the deformity of sin, that he must needs put on the form of an angel of light and deceive them by names of virtue to gain a conquest.

To many the artifice might seem very shallow and little likely to deceive. For, say they, is not holiness as distinct from sin,—benevolence as distinct from selfishness, as light is from darkness; and can any one possibly mistake things in their nature so opposite on account of any misrepresentation or misnomer? But it is not holiness and sin in the general and abstract to which he directly applies the artifice, or in which he attempts to deceive men. These he leaves untouched by any direct assault. It is enough for his purpose to assail them in the concrete and merely accidental forms which they assume in conduct, in action. He did not attack Eve on the general notions she entertained of holiness and obedience to God, and attempt at once to subvert these ideas by an exchange of names. That were but to strip himself of his mask, to throw off his robes of light, and appear before Eve the fiend of darkness without ability more to deceive. No. He converses simply about a

4

given conduct—the act of eating a particular fruit in the garden. Now, as that external act itself seems not in its own nature holiness or sin, independent of its connections with other things, the field is open for his artifice to present that specific action as connected with high and holy ends—with good rather than evil. And so he does. He represents it by his plausible and fair speeches as desirable to render her wise in knowledge and virtue. He thus surnames the evil good and the artifice succeeds.

Now, as it is true of the great adversary and tempter, so is it true of all who are enlisted in his work on earth and are sustaining his empire of sin, that one of the most effectual weapons they wield is that of attaching by sophistical reasoning and argument wrong names to conduct, and thus subverting to common minds its proper moral classification, calling what is evil good and what is good evil.

The text denounces a woe on all who originate by their sophistry, or give currency by their consent to, this misrepresentation of the names of moral qualities by which those which are morally evil are classed with the good, and the morally good with the evil.

In order to set forth to you the grounds of such a denunciation, I will present the evil done by him who gives currency in society to this misapplication of terms on moral subjects. To this end I will attempt to show—

I. That all conduct has its classification into moral good and evil before God, according to its tendency, which classification is unchangeable: and

II. That notwithstanding this, the wrong names which are applied to it exert a powerful influence to deceive men, and thereby as a consequence to effect vast evil.

1. In the first place, then, all conduct has its classification into the morally good or the morally evil before God, according to its tendency, which classification is unchangeable.

By this proposition, I mean that all the conduct of man in the circumstances in which it is performed, is necessarily clothed with the attributes of moral good or moral evil, and takes its rank accordingly in the view of God. The same specific action outwardly, may be either innocent or constitute a crime, according to the particular circumstances and conditions in which it takes place. As for instance, the taking the life of a man, if the act of the proper officer and done in the execution of a proper judicial sentence, may be innocent; while the taking of it, if by the act of a private individual, and done to advance his own personal ends, would constitute the crime of murder. But though a specific act in different circumstances and under different conditions, may vary in moral quality; what I mean to assert is, that conduct is always so related and conditioned that it must have a moral character of some kind attached to it, and that, where the attendant circumstances and conditions are the same, it must always have the same character.

That conduct must always have moral character of some kind, is evident for two reasons: one, that all conduct must have its general tendency to good or evil; the other, that the law of God takes cognizance of man in all his conduct.

All conduct must have its general tendency to good or evil. For man always has some ends of good or evil in view when acting, which lie beyond the action itself. He never acts for nothing, however near his actions seem at times to terminate in it. He has some design, some end in view, some object on which his heart is set, some motive for his conduct. And every such intention proves that the act itself, whether he rightly interpret it or not, must redound either most to himself alone or most to the general good; it must be either selfish or benevolent; either morally evil or good.

It is evident also that all conduct must have moral character of some kind attached to it, because the *law of God takes cognizance of man in all his conduct.* His law, we know from its general tenor as requiring the whole heart and strength, and from the interpretations of it in its application to the specific circumstances of the life, is so exceeding broad as to reach to every action, requiring man in each thing he does to do what redounds to the honor of God; and constituting him responsible at the day of judgment for all his deeds done in the body. Every act, therefore, must not only be in its own nature and its necessary tendency benevolent or selfish, but must be one of obedience or disobedience to the lawgiver, and consequently in this relation morally good or evil.

But not only must every action have moral character of some kind attached to it, as appears from these considerations, but also the same species of action, where the attendant circumstances and conditions are the same, must always have the *same moral character*. For the tendency of the action is the same, and by its real and true tendency to natural good or evil is it classed in the law as right or wrong. The general tendency of the same action performed in the same circumstances and under the same conditions, must always be the same invariably, whether it be to the side of good or evil. For this is but repeating, in another form, the plain axiom that like causes produce like effects. For example, if to take or to use an article that belongs to a neighbor, without his consent, tends to injure him and to encourage such injuries in the community, then to take or use an article at any other time when the same conditions exist, viz: that it belongs to a neighbor and his consent is not given, has just and precisely the same tendency. And as is the tendency of an action to good or evil, so is it ever to be classed in morals as right or wrong. That which tends to good is invariably right in form and can never in itself be wrong, whatever be the character of the actor; and that which tends to evil is invariably wrong, and can never be made right by any force of character in the actor. On these principles which determine what species of actions in the abstract men ought to pursue and what they ought to avoid, moralists have proceeded in classing various specific actions with their limitation and conditions under the names of virtues and sins; the scriptures too have presented to us on such grounds and upon the authority of God, a great list of specific actions as right or wrong in their own nature and tendency—as commended or disapproved in his sight. The names are given, and that species of action to which the name attaches, stands forever on the moral list as he has himself enrolled it among the things which are right or are wrong.

And this classification I said is unchangeable. Whenever a being does an act which in its kind and circumstances classes it under any of the names attached to the specific forms of moral evil, the name and the odium of the name attaches to it forever in the court of conscience and of heaven. If it is theft, if it is lying, if it is slander, if it is oppression, if it is any other species of sin, the indictment is made out in that form ; and the proof of the specific kind of action taking place in those circumstances which bring it within the limits and conditions of the statute, is enough to establish the verdict of guilty. Nor can the indicted criminal plead that the opinions of mankind varied from the statute book, or that his own opinion differed, or that, like Eve intending to gain wisdom, he intended anything good. He is bound by law in the court of conscience and heaven—his voluntary commission of what was prohibited in the statute book, and prohibited as a thing necessarily tending to evil, is enough to sweep away, as vain, all those flatteries of a surrounding world or of his own heart which, in the day of temptation deceived him, and emboldened him to the crime.

But I proceed to show,

2. That notwithstanding this eternal distinction in the court of conscience and heaven of actions into morally good and evil according to their tendency, the wrong names which are given them exert a powerful influence to deceive man and thereby as a consequence work out vast evil.

To set the truth of this proposition more clearly before you, I will present to you the origin of the misapplication of terms, which is made among men on the subject of morals, the great influence these misapplied terms have to deceive men, and the vast evils which are consequently effected by it in the world.

The origin of that gross perversion of terms in the world which represents evil as good and good as evil, lies in that spirit of libertinism which is natural to the heart of man.  Man does not well brook the restraints of a pure and sound morality.  His own nature furnishes a conscience, and revelation presents a God, enacting a strict, unpliable, unchangeable code of morals; before which man must bow with willing submission and conformity, or be crushed in anger.  Before the list of duties and sins presented in this unmitigated code, sin trembles and fears to advance ; and its libertine spirit seeks to hold up another and more accommodating list before its eyes.  The more to sustain itself in a world where the light of the true code is still shining, it seeks to advocate its own perversions before men, and, by arraying around it a party of adherents with their countenance and protection, thus to entrench itself in a kingdom of darkness, too deep, if possible, to be penetrated by any rays from the kingdom of light.  Here then this libertine spirit, instigated to such boldness no doubt by the grand adversary, enlists her public advocate.  She has now a tongue to speak and a plea to make in the world.  And that advocate she introduces into society under the different characters of the proud sophist and the vulgar scoffer.

The proud sophist miscalls evil good and good evil by his perverted and false reasonings.  He takes the more elevated stand in society of the eloquent reasoner : and from his more lofty station looks down with pride on the vulgar crowds he would gain over to his conclusions and attach to his standard.  He discourses, back, of the great principles which lie at the foundation of morals.  He argues against Christianity with its revelations, or against the eternal sanctions of the righteous government of God, or against the being of God himself, the grand support of morality, or else against some of those principles which are essential in themselves to a sound code of morals.  The name he would affix to any species of action is not directly advanced, but follows rather as a conclusion from the fine web he spins of sophistical reasoning and casuistry.

He is not willing that an action and the moral classification made of it in the Scriptures should pass for its worth. His common sense and that of the world might see too clearly that the name and the thing correspond. By going back therefore to take up and sustain some false principle, or by starting with a correct principle and moving forward on a false track, things in his view have come in the result to change sides. Though the same titles of virtue and sin remain to head the two lists, the actions enumerated in the lists are wonderfully revolutionized by the process. The old-fashioned sins enumerated in the Bible have disappeared as mere foibles or are gilded over as virtues. Its old-fashioned virtues have faded away as weaknesses or are blackened over as sins.

To the sophist in this work of moral perversion, succeeds the vulgar scoffer. He acts in society the double part of the flatterer and the scorner. Taking the conclusions that are furnished to his hand by the sophist, he goes forth in society with the signals and watchwords of his leader and party, applying titles of flattery furnished him for the wicked and of scorn for the godly.

He is the flatterer of the wicked. He seeks to soothe their disturbed spirits with the smiles of commendation, and to blind their eyes with the glare of great swelling words of vanity applied to their conduct. Their unbelief in God and his word he calls, perchance, the triumph of reason over prejudice, their impiety a spirit of lofty independence; their sins and lusts the dictates of a true, large and free nature; their indifference to the sins and impieties of the world around them, a generous liberality to those who differ from them in opinion; and their servility to him and his flatteries, the offerings and evidences of a good heart: names properly used to signify things which are good, but applied by him to things which are evil.

He is the scorner of the godly. In his quiver are the arrows of detraction. They are tipped with the venom of scorn. They are shot with the laugh of boasted triumph. For their firm belief in the word of God, he derides the godly as weak and prejudiced enthusiasts;

their calm and serious frame of devotion to God with its full and tranquilizing joys, of which he knows nothing, he scouts as mere gloom and melancholy ; their deep reverence of God and holy fear of sin, is entitled, in his vocabulary, dark and harrowing superstition : their strict obedience to the scriptural precepts of morality, blackened as the bondage of Pharasaical austerity and hypocrisy ; their zeal for the progress of divine truth and the reformation of mankind, stigmatized as narrow-minded bigotry, or blind fanaticism : and their faithfulness in reproving him for his sin, resented as the venting of a spiteful and malicious heart :—names which signify evil things, but applied by him to good.

Such then are the arts of misrepresentation used in the world on the subject of morals : used to a greater or less extent in every age and country—arts, which every one must expect to meet ; a trial which every one must encounter. The great power of this misrepresentation to deceive mankind; we are now to consider.

That there is in this artifice great power to deceive will appear from facts, and from the nature of the case.

Facts abundantly show us the power of falsehood to deceive. Every day presents us with the spectacle of its sad victims. Men are daily carrying on the work of representing the good as evil and the evil as good, and their arts of persuasion too often succeed. Men are thus deceived and defrauded out of everything good. They are deceived and betrayed into everything evil. There are commercial cheats and those who believe them ; social cheats and those who believe them ; political cheats, and, worse than all moral and religious cheats, with their believers and followers. None stifles his conscience and turns knave, but is sure to make some his dupes. Nothing more fully attests the power of the deception used in the world than this its success. Its success began even in paradise ; it has gone forward to this day, and so it will continue, we have reason to fear, till the whole process is arrested and broken up by the trump of the Archangel and the appearance of the Final Judge.

But the influence it exerts with respect to moral good and evil among men will be better understood if we examine the nature of the case—that while the arts of deception which we have been considering are well adapted to have influence upon men, men on the other hand are greatly exposed to their power by their weakness, their ignorance, their inconsideration, and, more than all, by their inclinations.

The arts of deception we have considered are such in kind as are well adapted to have influence upon man. A fellow being like ourselves on the stage of life with us, having the same great interests at stake, in time and eternity, appears the champion of what he calls good, the opposer of what he calls evil: himself so much the dupe of Satan as to believe in the false cause he advocates. He (or she, for in these last days we have seen even woman to head the band of the scoffers) stands up before us with the attributes of apparent wisdom and philanthropy to command respect and attention. He speaks with an impassioned earnestness, involving himself and 'his eternal interests in the cause. Attention is summoned. Decision is called for. His net is cast over and around many minds, and his proselytes stand ready to drag it on shore. They go forth to secure decision and consent; to gain an open avowal from the consenting; to bind them, by public committal, to their own ranks. They take up the terms and cant phrases that embody the results of their leader's arguments. He has coined for them some word that in their mouth covers up sophistry: a word that shuts out argument: a word that is the badge of honor in their ranks: a word that is flatteringly offered to the acceptance of the hesitating with a smile of offered friendship. Will he accept it, is the demand: yes, or no? If still hesitating, they are ready to ply him with the alternative their leader has furnished them in the false phrase by which he has blackened the cause of good. It is presented as a thing of scorn in their ranks. It is tossed at him with an air and frown betokening triumphant contempt for the one who should accept it, with the demand, Will you take that? Assailed by such arts and weapons of sophistry, surely it would require firmness in man to withstand them.

But the art of false persuasion appears greater still in degree when it is considered relatively as bearing on the weakness of man.

Man is exposed by his ignorance. Men begin their existence as babes; and often, in the moral sense, they never advance beyond childhood: not having their moral senses exercised, by reason of use, clearly to discern good and evil. They have very little acquaintance with the system of practical ethics given in the Bible, with its limits and grounds. They know them, as they do most of their fellow men, by name only. They are far better acquainted with the desires of their own hearts, and with the objects of the present world. They know more of the relation of their actions to things which are temporal than the relations they bear to the unseen God and the issues they are to have in an unseen eternity.

But again, men, whatever is their knowledge, are *inconsiderate.* They are inconsiderate about *preparing themselves for the onsets of temptation.* They are hesitating and wavering on the point of any fixed principles that would arm them with strength. They do not take it into consideration and decide, whether they will accept from God the Saviour, the armor which he offers them in his word by which they might be able to withstand all the wiles of the adversary. And as they are not fixed, trusting in God, they are exposed to put too much trust in man. And *when the hour of assault is come*, they are still inconsiderate. They take into consideration indeed the whole that is offered them in the temptation; but, in that hour of their utmost need, how often do they fail to take into consideration the counsels and persuasions that are offered them to the contrary in the word of God; and to make up their minds at once to follow a faithful Creator and reject their tempter. How, then, with no consideration to meet and with none to repel their tempter, can it be expected they would escape?

But still again, and worse than all, men are inclined at heart to welcome their tempter. Their hearts are not set right about good and evil. Their estimates of temporal good and evil are higher than their estimates of spiritual and eternal. They love and fear the one more than they love and fear the other. By this strange perversion of feeling, their real and worst enemies come to appear in their view as their friends, and their real and best friends to appear as their enemies. Their tempters are soothing flatterers who exact no change, who impose no cost of reformation and self-denial: while God and the good are severe reprovers that in their faithful love exact both. Is it strange that they whose hearts are thus perversely inclined should say, Prophecy unto us deceits, speak smooth things, cause the holy One of Israel to cease from before us;—that they should be ready to turn the eye and ear away from God and open them both to their tempters?

Is it strange then that men, amid all the spiritual ignorance they suffer themselves to remain in, which seems hardly competent even to say which be the first principles of the oracles of God ;—that men, too inconsiderate even to decide whether they shall trust in God or men most, and thus ready to exalt men over all on the throne of their feeble reason ; that men so in love with the world and estranged from God in their hearts, as to fear the costs and self-denials of religion more than the pains of eternal damnation ; should be carried away by the deceptive arts of the ungodly wise men and disputers of this world, when pressed with all their sophistry and assailed by the clamors, the boasts and the scorns of their adherents? Is it strange that they should come to believe a lie, when it is so acceptable and so strongly enforced— that they should commit themselves, enroll with the party, and unite with them thenceforth in calling evil good and good evil?

We come now to consider the vast evils which are effected by this process of deception in the world.

Its evil consequences are to be judged of by their nature and extent.

Their nature is unfolded in the fact that the distinction between moral good and evil which God has proclaimed to his creatures—a distinction forever true and unchangeable—is made by him the basis on which he reposes his own honor as the Ruler of the Universe; on which he establishes the peace and joy of his kingdom; on which he secures the salvation of souls. Against all these high and endless interests therefore, the blow is leveled which seeks to destroy that distinction between moral good and evil which is the foundation on which they all rest.

He, therefore, who aims to pervert the distinctions between good and evil, does injustice to God, to the interests of society, and the spiritual welfare of individuals, and the more and farther he prevails, the wider is the extent of the mischief.

He does injustice to God. His great name is dishonored and blasphemed as the author of falsehood and confusion: his government, with its laws and sanctions, is rebelled against and invaded: the kingdom of light and holiness and peace which his grace has set up among us by his Son in the midst of our rebellions, is hindered in its progress.

He does injury to society. The foundations of its security are shaken. Rapine, lust, fraud, deceit, violence, are sent forth by him to fatten on their spoils; and justice, integrity, truth, the fear of God, are hunted and cried down as enemies: till lands, fitted to rejoice as the garden of God, are desolate; and heaven weeps, and earth mourns, over innocence slain and equity prostrate.

He does injury to the spiritual welfare of individuals. He meets the ignorant, inconsiderate, worldly wanderer from God whom a Saviour is inviting back to forgiveness and to rest. He commits him, and enrolls him, the son of perdition. A lie is received, and grasped in his right hand as his treasure and defense. His way to destruction is made easy and sure. Onward he goes to the gates of death. He dies an outcast from God. The pangs of a just condemnation seize upon his soul. He finds out the cheat too late ; deceived by false names of virtue and of evil, he is forever fallen. O, that any, charmed by false names of wisdom, should forever part with the substance ; that any for fear of being called fools in the scoffs of the ungodly, should make themselves such in reality to all eternity !

To how wide an extent this mischief is carried on in our world may be seen by a survey of the kingdom of darkness : a kingdom which has its oldest and firmest seat in the lands of idolatry, which extends over the adherents of the false prophet, and embraces all within the light of Christian lands who retain the mark and the practices and worship the images of the great Beast of Idolatry in the earth—a kingdom built on error—sustained by sophistry and deception—in which evil is called good and good evil. What hecatombs of ruined men, of ruined nations, lie before us : whom Satan the god of this world hath blinded and deceived in person and by his emissaries, and whom he will continue to deceive till Christ shall come, in the brightness of his spiritual dominion over all, to drive him away and enchain him, that he go out to deceive the nations no more.

I have thus set before you, as I intended, the ground of the woe denounced against him who calls evil good and good evil—that the distinction between moral good and evil, set up by the Creator being founded in the necessary tendency they have to promote the natural good and evil of beings, is in its own nature true and unchangeable ; and that the wrong names and sophistical reasonings set up by men which confound this distinction have yet great power to deceive and as a consequence work vast evil.

The use which I would make of the subject as I conclude, is that of caution against deceiving and being deceived, against employing the arts of deception and falling under their power.

We have been looking on the world abroad to examine the operations of deceit that are in it in reference to moral subjects, and to behold the vast evils it works among men.  Every man is not living abroad in the large world, but every one is living in a little world of his own : and influences are in thousands of ways coming in from the larger world into the smaller one in which he resides, and going out from his circle again into the wider circle of humanity.  Every one is therefore capable of exerting a wider influence upon others than he now sees.  Every one is exposed to a wider reach of influence from others than he fully apprehends.

Beware then (1) Against deceiving others.  Be not the advocate of error.  Advocate nothing at any time, in any place, which your conscience or revelation condemns.  Your words of error and sophistry may fall on the ear of some soul in spiritual ignorance, inconsiderate of safety, inclining to evil, and enlist and secure him in error—error that shall keep him from Christ and holiness and land him in the region and shadows of eternal death.  Nor does the evil stop here.  The evil of sin is as the plague of leprosy.  The soul you infect goes forth and spreads the infection in the wide world.  There are atheists and infidels and men of lax morals enough in the world already.  Why should you increase the number?  You have sins enough to answer for at the tribunal of God already.  Why should you go on to add sin to sin and heap to yourself greater condemnation?  No; enlist rather at once under Christ, the great Supporter of Truth and the Author of Salvation, that every past sin may be forgiven you.  Be the firm and unflinching advocate of truth and holiness.  Represent things as they are.  Call evil evil, and good good.  Uphold the honor of God, the kingdom of Christ and holiness, advance the good of mankind and the salvation of souls, and take your reward with the faithful in heaven.

Beware again (2) Against being deceived by others.  Fall not the victim of error.  Be not over-confident in your own wisdom, lest it prove your folly and ruin.  There is ignorance and inconsiderateness and perverseness of feeling enough cleaving to the best, to expose them to deception ; and the sophists and disputers of this world, meet you at every corner and turn of life. If you are not armed for safety, you will be ensnared, deceived and ruined for ever. Fix your heart then forever on God the source of life and safety, trusting in Him as a child. Take the plain instructions and precepts of his word as your guide, its promises and threatenings as your strength. Learn them, consider them, love them more and more from day to day. Hold them fast, amid all the sophistical arguments or vulgar ridicule and abuse of an ungodly world. Be not afraid of the result. Be ye sure the fear of the Lord is the beginning of wisdom, its principle and support, and will one day so appear to his whole kingdom. If you cannot answer all the arguments of the subtle, if you cannot be indifferent wholly to the flatteries and scoffs of the wicked, still believe in God, estimating his wisdom above their sophistry, prizing his promises and threatenings above all they can offer. Be firm, and you will find much to encourage you in this world. The public advocates and hearty friends of God's truth and cause are many to strengthen you ; and they are advancing forward continually in the earth from conquest to conquest. Be firm in these days of assault and trial, and when the day of God shall burst upon the world, you will see his wisdom triumph gloriously over all the machinations of the perverse, you shall be crowned as his faithful and confiding servant before his kingdom.

---

ECCLESIASTES, IX : 18.

ONE SINNER DESTROYETH MUCH GOOD.

THIS is a truth attested by universal experience. Its
importance is apparent, even when applied to him who is
a sinner only in *heart;* who is destroying his own soul,
and all the influence of the counsel and care bestowed
upon him by Jehovah and the pious. But the truth assumes a higher importance when applied to the *open*
transgressor; who not only destroys himself but becomes
the corrupter of those around him; spreading as he goes,
a wide waste of moral pestilence and death. Applied to
such an one, it assumes an importance corresponding with
the stations which he occupies in life, and the means and
facilities which they give him for approaching others with
his polluting society and example. Witness him in a
family; it is there he infects the springs of domestic order
and happiness. Witness him in the intercourse of friends;
it is there he comes, as a fiend of perdition, to destroy
some confiding associate. Witness him in the hall of
legislation or on the bench of judgment; it is there he
poisons the fountains of justice as they flow down into
the community. Follow him into every station; he appears in all, the same fiend of ruin, destroying everywhere the good exposed to his polluting touch.

But I shall not call you to dwell upon what the open
transgressor may do to destroy, in merely imagined circumstances; I would bring the truth much nearer home
to you, and apply it to a reality often witnessed within
the precincts of this College. I would ask you candidly

6

and seriously to hear me, while I attempt to portray the truth: that *one open transgressor, in an Institution like this, destroys much good.*

This power in a single sinner to destroy what is good is manifest even in this sacred retreat of science. You are here assembled in a miniature world of your own, withdrawn from that outer and larger world that surrounds you, and even here you see operating on a scale of less extent the very evils in their germs that you can see grown rife and mature in the wider circle of the world that surrounds you.

Will you not allow me then as one who has long been conversant with the interests of this little college world, and as one who still wishes and prays for the welfare of its members, to set the truth of our text before you, as it is exemplified in such a circle as yours—the society gathered within the walls and occupied in the peaceful pursuits of a College.

Let me show you that one sinner here has great power to destroy, and that the good which he destroys here is peculiarly great.

I. *One transgressor among you has great power to destroy.*

He comes with his habits of dissipation, intemperance, debauchery, gambling, into a society which, in some respects, is very open to his influence. For he unites himself here to a circle of the young and inexperienced; open in their confidence; absent from parental restraint, and surrounded by many facilities and encouragements to lead them into the practice of all these vices. He uses his enticements and example with companions whose peculiar circumstances strongly favor him in obtaining a victory over their minds.

He enters here into the circle of *the young and inexperienced.* Youth and inexperience, it is well known, are circumstances always favoring temptation. Youth is sportive; buoyant in its feelings; bright in its hopes; eager after its pleasures; unestablished in its principles. Experience has not yet come to trace out actions with faithful hand, to their remote results and consequences;

to instil her sober views of life; to mould the character into distinct and stable form. Is it strange that minds thus quick to receive every impression, thus open to every influence, should be an easier prey to the contagion of a vicious companion? When I see one person of dissipated life and habits—living and moving in your circle, I feel that he has great facilities for carrying on the work of destruction among you. He is not easy in sin without companions; and his polluting enticements he spreads before those who, though not in extremest youth, are in that middle stage between it and manhood, which combines all the quickness of youth to receive impression and habit, with all the strength of manhood to retain it; and I fear that he will achieve at once, an easy and a permanent victory.

Again, such a transgressor within your circle is conjoined to a *fraternity most open in their confidence.* The person who has never been united to such an institution, scarcely conceives what strong bonds of confidence are intertwined amongst its members. Equal nearly in age, engaged in the same general pursuits, daily associated in the same public exercises, hourly sharing in the same trials and enjoyments, they view each other only in this common relation. The distinctions of wealth, family, character even, disappear. All hearts are interwoven into one common woof. An openness and familiarity of all-reposing confidence, renders every heart accessible. Classmate is but another name for brother. Even the little feuds and strifes that occasionally arise, dissolve under the power of its charm. Is it strange, then, that in a society so open and unsuspecting in their confidence, he who comes as a destroyer should easily obtain victims to his sins and associates with him in vice? Into what room may he not enter and sit down with you as your companion? Into what ear may he not whisper his corrupting persuasions? And who that is not steeled with that fortitude of moral principle which says at once, like the Saviour, to every temptation, come it from whom it may: "Get thee behind me Satan;" who else will not feel the strength of that bond which unites him to a class-mate, and be drawn by it to listen to his suggestions and to consent to his guilty proposals.

Again, such a transgressor here is united to a society of youths who are *absent from parental restraint and watch-fulness.* What power has a father's friendship, and a mother's pure and deep love, to check the waywardness of youth and to guide it with the wisdom of experience! I have seen the youth dwelling under their roof; nurtured by their care; watched by their eye; guarded by their love; and have felt that next to the bond of heaven's authority and love, theirs is the strongest, the purest. What, when they place the son of their hopes in an institution like this, remote from their eye, shall supply the place of their watchfulness? Its appointed guardians may exert a parental watchfulness over him; but it shall not touch his heart like the eye of father and mother. When the seducer of his morals comes to meet him here with his enticements, his father may be thinking of him with deep solicitude, his mother may be praying for his welfare with heart-broken agonies. But he is far from their presence. The eye of a father bent on him in its sternness, or of a mother beaming upon him in its love, might nerve him to say 'no' to his enticer, to refuse uniting with him in his unworthy proposals. But the corrupter assails him afar from the parental roof. The tempter here finds him, removed from the watchfulness of those hearts that would bleed most deeply over his downfall. And the temptations which youth and confidence favor, are thus strengthened by the absence of parental restraint.

Again, the destructive power of the transgressor here is increased by *the facilities and encouragement for dissipation which surround the Institution.* Were all those who surround our literary institutions as faithful as their officers, or the parents of their pupils, to withhold from them the means and discountenance them in the practice of dissipation, the transgressor within their walls would not have that power which he now has to lead others with him into polluting and forbidden pleasures. Without a haunt to which he might lead his victims, inspected by eyes which would frown upon him with indignation; his polluting influence would be checked; and youths, otherwise exposed, be rescued from his grasp. But ah! it is a sad story that here the young and inexperienced, confiding in each other, and removed from parental inspection, are drawn and lured away by the facilities and encouragements to dissipation which are brought around the very walls of their habitation. How many for the sake of receiving the money of the young, will administer to their guilty pleasures and vices; see their morals debauched; encourage their enticements over one another, and be accessory to this progressive ruin of souls! When was there ever an institution like this planted any where, but these harpies of ruin hovered around it on their filthy pinions? "Through covetousness and with feigned words" "they make merchandise of you,"—the dreadful traffic of your souls for their gains. What power do these give the person of dissipated habits among you to destroy. Money only is needed; and the pleasures to which he entices you, however guilty and polluting, are readily administered. The transgressor is thus often countenanced, encouraged, animated, in his work of temptation and ruin, by external accessories, who are interested both to aid in sin and to screen from detection.

Such are the circumstances relative to college life which show how great is the destructive power of a single corrupt and vicious student over his companions; that he brings his temptations to the young and inexperienced; who repose the utmost confidence in him; who are far removed from the watchful eye of their parents; and who are surrounded from without the institution by those who favor the pleasures of vice and guilty dissipation.

Let me show you now,

II. That *the good which a transgressor succeeds to destroy here, is peculiarly great.* He always destroys much good:

in the immediate victims of his corruption ; in the Institution of which he is a member ; in the families to whose sons he has access ; in the community among whose rising hopes he dwells.

1. He destroys much good *in the victim of his corruption.*

The youthful student here, bright in talent, high in hope, presents a spectacle, to all, of no ordinary interest. He is justly regarded as one who is to participate in higher responsibilities in life, and to engage in wider and more efficient spheres of action than the companions whom he has left at the plough, at the anvil, at the counter. At any rate he enters upon great privileges which are denied to them, and for which he must give account.

The dissipated youth, who seduces a companion here to unite with him in his vices and guilty pleasures, seizes on a victim of no ordinary interest, and brings upon him no ordinary ruin.

He is the destroyer of *literary attainment.* The inebriating cup, the noisy revel, the lewd debauch, hold no communion with the room of sobriety, the table of study, the lamp of diligence, the page of learning and lore. Intemperate and guilty pleasures debilitate the body, clog the mind, indispose both for study, reduce the whole man to the indolence and apathy of the brutes. The victory of a sinner over his companion here, is a victory over his attainments ; the defeat of his diligence ; the perversion of his privileges.

He is the destroyer of *character.* The victim of his enticements is led to pleasures which scar the conscience ; stifle each generous sensibility of the heart ; eradicate the principles of virtue ; and reduce the man in subjection to their imperious power. The misled youth has entered into the haunts of guilty pleasure ; he has enrolled his name among her votaries ; he has dedicated himself at her altars ; she will never give him a discharge from her dominion ; he will never satiate her with his offerings : he must surrender to her his conscience, his principles, his *character.*

He is the destroyer of temporal *prospects.* What hopes

might have dawned upon the youth before he fell into the fangs of his destroyer! The prospect of entering upon life, with health, with attainments, with reputation and character; opening before him the avenues to the confidence, the respect, the love of his fellow men! But ah! his destroyer has blasted these hopes; and delivered him over to his parents and the community, without attainment and without principle, an idler and a sot, to be henceforth bloated and deformed by his lusts; with no other prospects for life than those which the wise man assures us belong to him "that loveth pleasure"—"he shall be poor"—the prospect of poverty in character, in estate, in reputation, in public confidence, in peace of mind; until he reach the grave.

He is the destroyer of the *soul*, for the drunkard is disinherited from the kingdom of God. Earth has no language nor any similitude adequate to describe a ruin like this. An immortal mind debased; its endless aspirings disappointed; its recreant energies recoiling in anger on itself; a heaven of glory lost; a hell of speechless agony forever endured; these are the melancholy parts of such a ruin. Oh how little apprehended and known in this world! Is it not enough for any one of you to go alone into these everlasting burnings? Must you take with you some hapless companion? Will you select him from this group and bear him away from these high privileges to take the lowest place in hell, and endure the fiercest flames of wrath?

Such destruction does the sinner here bring upon the *victim* of his corruption: But,

2. He destroys much good *in the Institution of which he is a member.*

An institution like this, founded in piety and prayer, nurtured by the wise and the good, consecrated to Christ and his cause, and embosoming in it the hopes of the Church and the State, is an institution of most sacred character; which calls upon all who are in any way connected with it to guard it from injury, to further its design, to aid in its prosperity. The stealthy transgressor who becomes a member of it, who brings the polluting and destructive influence of his vices into the community, vitally assails its welfare. Though bound, in entering upon its privileges, to unite with its instructors, its official guardians and its pupils in securing the great and good ends of its establishment; he comes not to build but to destroy.

He destroys *the influence of its instructions.* Here men are stationed by Providence in the laborious office of imparting instruction. They are laboring to communicate lessons of knowledge and wisdom and piety for the good of the community. With pains, with watchings, with prayers, they open to you the fountains of human and divine knowledge; and never do they reap a richer reward than when they see their instructions distilling on the mind with fertilizing influence as the dew, ripening youth into the glories of an intelligent, wise, and virtuous manhood. But the open transgressor sets at nought these counsels and instructions: he leads the victims of his corruption to unite with him in passing them heedlessly by; and his heart and tongue are enlisted in destroying widely around him the moral and religious bearing of these instructions, on the mind of his fellow students.

He destroys *the prevalence of its laws.* Those salutary regulations and restraints which its wise and faithful guardians have enacted to secure that order which is vital to its welfare, are bonds as light to his conscience as the web of the spider: for pleasure, intemperate and polluting, knows no law; abides no restraint; breaks through every wholesome regulation; and riots in her own lawless sportings..

He destroys *the health of its morals.* The morals of a community are composed of the morals of its members; and he and the victims of his enticement are dissolute. Every such member therefore swells the amount of sins and transgressions in this little community. He also does much to lower the general tone of moral sentiment; for that dread of vice never too quick, that aversion to it never too strong, which are necessary to guard the morals, are in his presence and daily familiarity relaxed and softened down by the power of sympathy. One such sinner shall do much to weaken in almost every breast the sentiment of abhorrence and indignation felt at vice. If they "embrace" not "the monster" at the first, yet,

> "familiar with her face,
> They first endure, then pity, *then* embrace."

He destroys *the vigor of its piety.* I would hope that no such transgressor could ever prevail on one of this little flock, named after the name of our Lord Jesus Christ, directly to follow him and unite with him in his guilty pleasures. Yet, relaxing the tone of moral sentiment as he goes, he prowls around the sacred enclosure of the Church; and if he obtain no victims from it he often inspires, in the less established and the less vigorous, the fear of assuming an unpopular firmness and decision of religious character. Even the most established and the most vigorous in the body, at times, witnessing the immoralities without and the decay of religious sentiment within; find their hopes discouraged, their ardor dampened, their faith weakened and almost yielding to despair.

He destroys *the soundness of its reputation.* For what deeper wound can he inflict on its honor than that which is aimed at its instructions, its order, its morals, its piety?

Such is the destruction which he brings into the *institution* of which he is a member; But,

3. He destroys much good *in the families to whose sons he here has access.*

The thought is full of interest to every one who is a member in an institution like this, as he looks around on his fellow students, that he is admitted into the confidence and bosom of almost as many families, scattered over this extensive country. Each student with whom he is in the habit of daily and familiar intercourse, has a father or mother; perhaps, some friendly brother; or affectionate sister; who contemplate, in him, the son of their hopes, or the brother of their pride and joy. Each youth here should feel that his influence has this extensive bearing on relations so sacred, so touching. Every one, be it remembered, who is dissipated in his habits and corrupt in his morals, brings a moral pestilence into the bosom of all these families scattered throughout the length and breadth of our vast country. He carries, into all these sacred enclosures of domestic love, a heart more cruel than the grave, to destroy their peace, their counsels, their hopes.

He destroys their *peace.* For they feel that the sons of their prayers and hopes are exposed to the polluting venom of his example and enticements. A thousand anxieties crowd around their hearts as they watch over the course of their absent children ; as they receive from time to time intelligence of their progress : for they know that a pestilence is near them that may give them its deadly contagion, that an enemy is nigh them ready to devour. How would it relieve the anxieties of these households, what peace and confidence would dawn on their again happy circles, were it known to them that no such wolves were prowling in ambush among their sons ! that every individual of corrupt habits here, were searched out, reproved, humbled before all in deep repentance, or else excluded from all ; and that the hearts of all this body were set, as a munition of rocks, against the inroads of every vice and iniquity !

He destroys their *counsels.* The parents of these youth, many of them, have instructed and warned them from their infancy. In tears and with many prayers, they have often administered to them the counsels of faithfulness and love. But ah! what shall become of all their admonitions ? Their son is far removed from their presence ; and nigh him, in the garb of confidence and friendship, dwells the destroyer ; ever ready to distil into his ear his polluting enticements ; and to lead him, with the basest ingratitude to forget his father and the mother who bore him, and trample on all their counsels.

He destroys their *hopes.* Come, go with me to the family whose son the corrupter has here led astray into intemperance. It is the house of mourning; but not for the dead—for the worse than dead—the living buried in his pollutions. See, as we enter it, what mortification, what grief, what despair, are depicted on the countenances of the family group: for he whom they loved, whom they labored and prayed for, they have heard has fallen a victim to intemperate and polluting pleasures; such as ruin his diligence, his character, his prospects, his soul. Let the corrupter go before us; and in our presence, deliver over to this afflicted family their ruined child, his victim. Let his eye meet the father's brow of burning indignation; the mother's lip of quivering anguish; the brother's, the sister's eye, swollen with agony! Listen, while the father, in behalf of this afflicted circle, pours forth the language of despair, over hopes for ever blasted, a child forever lost! The love, the cares, the labors that from dawning infancy had showered their blessings on the child, rush to his heart; his future course of increasing shame and infamy, fill his apprehensions; and on you, the corrupter of his child, he fastens the stigma of that deep ingratitude and ruin, which are to fill his heart and the hearts of his household, with sorrow, on their future journey to the grave.

Such is the destruction which the sinner here brings into the *families* to whose sons he has access;

But, once more,

4. He destroys much good, in *the community at large among whose rising hopes he here dwells.*

Need I remind you that they who dwell together here, will soon vacate these seats; and, bidding one another farewell, disperse everywhere over the face of this country : that on them will devolve many important stations in life, many weighty concerns in the community. To these retreats of science the state looks, the church looks, for their supports, their pillars, their ornaments: for here dwell the hopes of our country, the youth of her pride, disciplined and trained for her future service. Your influence here, therefore, extends beyond the companions with whom you associate; beyond the institution which fosters you; beyond the families who have introduced their sons to your confidence—it extends to your wide country and the world. Every one whom you lead into ways of wisdom and virtue here, you deliver over to the community of your fellow men as an angel of mercy and blessing: every one whom you pollute with intemperance and lust, you hand over to it, as a demon of wrath and cursing. You have led a companion into intemperance: see how far that destruction extends among your fellow men.

You have *disqualified your victim for every useful station.* Is he to be a husband? Bloated with intemperance, he takes his lovely and confiding partner, only to wound her with his cruelties and to burden her with his disgrace. Is he to be a father? The children whom God hath given him, unblessed by his counsels or prayers, live to witness his infamy, to bear his rage, to be corrupted by his example. Is he a neighbor? The families which surround him have no enjoyment in his presence; but dread him as a monster, shun him as a pestilence. Is he a magistrate? Alas, if any can so elevate him, his intemperance, if it corrupt not justice, gives sway and currency to the same desolating vice in the community.

You have *withdrawn him from every good work.* His intemperate pleasures demand his time, his attention, his property. On these will he wait, though every work of religion and humanity in the world around him should cease. What will he do on the earth for Christ? That much loved name, the fountain of our hopes for eternity, his lips of pollution praise not. What for the Church? Redeemed and adorned by Christ, she stands forth the pattern of religion, the expectant of glory: but he comes not himself, he brings none within her sacred portals of salvation. What for ignorant, oppressed, or suffering humanity? The calls of intemperance are too loud and urgent for him to turn aside to bless the needy!

You have *devoted him to the work of ruin.* He came here a sober and lovely youth; you have sent him forth into the community of your fellow-men, a drunkard, a prowling enemy, ready to devour. What will he not do in his fits of intoxication? Without reason; without conscience; a delirium is on his brain; his passions are dark and wild as the whirlwind. As well uncage the monarch of the forests, and send him forth to dwell in amity with men. What is he, in more sober moments? An idler at best; without employment; free to be occupied with schemes of evil. A vagabond, perhaps; disgusting all with his presence, wearying all with his wants. A gamester; enticing others to the card or billiard table, that he may gather spoils from the wreck of their fortunes. A seducer; leading by his falsehoods the hapless female astray to mourn, in unavailing agony, the ruin of her virtue. A robber, become desperate through want. A murderer, rendered furious by resistance, The picture is not too deep and melancholy to be realized; even by those who are elevated to the advantages of this favored spot, who take to their mouths the inebriating cup and enkindle in their appetites an unquenchable flame. I knew a student once, my equal and companion; (others might select examples to fill out other shades of the picture ;) who here began to unite with companions only in occasional acts of intemperance. His appetite raged; it became imperious; he relinquished every useful station; he abandoned every good work; he roved a vagabond over the face of the land ; and a burden to society, while living; he died, if I am rightly informed, by the way-side, neglected and alone !

From the thoughts I have now presented to you, is it not obvious, that the good which a transgressor destroys here, is peculiarly great? He deals his blows at advantage, against interests most precious. Impressed with this momentous truth, I feel myself impelled to speak out its admonitions to you with the utmost candor and plainness.

Is there any youth here *who has been enticing his companions into scenes of dissipation ?*

Young man, whoever thou art, I charge thee before God and this youthful assembly, consider, seriously, what thou hast done. You have approached a youth in his ardor and inexperience. You have come nigh him in the garb of confidence and friendship. You have met him at distance from the eye of parental watchfulness, and with opportunities surrounding you to screen his guilt and yours. And what have you done? You have led him to quaff deep the inebriating cup ; to enter into the polluting embrace of the harlot. You have kindled a fever in his appetites that shall burn as hell. You have sprung a mine, whose devastation shall spread far and wide, carrying grief and desolation to many hearts.

Come, face the account that lies recorded against thee in the book of God. The account shall meet thee at another day, in an assembly far more solemn and imposing. Meet it now. Stare at each item in the dark catalogue of ruin, till it make thee tremble. Let the arrows of the Almighty, the Avenger of the injured, pierce thee, now, with salutary smart. Repent of this, thy wickedness. Humble thyself before God and all those youth, who may have witnessed thy faults. And like an angel of rescuing mercy, flee at once to thy victim. Pluck him, if thou canst, from the devouring flame. Unbind from his hands and feet, the manacles and fetters of sin. Restore him to himself, to this institution, to his aggrieved family, to his injured country ; a man of sobriety and virtue, the benefactor and not the curse of mankind. And instead of the sorrow and mourning that now fill so many hearts, a wide jubilee of joy shall be proclaimed over thee, in heaven and on earth.

Is there a dissipated youth here, *who is determined to continue in his course of dissipation ?*

I would hope that considerations, suggested by a subject like this, would break down such a determination in every mind ; would lead such an one to serious reflection, to a better resolution, to a thorough reformation. But, if he will persist in his dissipation ; if, in defiance of every motive which can be urged of religion or humanity, he must continue to riot in his polluting pleasures ; I know not what counsel I can better give such a pupil than that he abandon his vices at once, and seek healing at the fount of mercy; or, if he will not do this, that he withdraw at once from this retreat of science—this depository of most sacred hopes. If he must be dissipated, he would better be anything than a student. Let him go, and choose, from the laborious occupations of society, his employment; it will be honorable for him to labor, and safe to withdraw himself from temptation. The truckman at his dray, the oyster-man at his barrow, pursues an honest employment and deserves the respect of the community. But the dissipated student is an useless idler; who well needs blush before all for his unprofitableness and tremble at his increasing responsibilities and sins.

If he must and will be dissipated, better be anywhere than here. Let him labor in the fields: for the beasts thereof that plod with him and the tenants of the air that sing to him, he cannot corrupt. Let him traverse the billows of the ocean, with companions corrupt as he; for the fish of the sea who sport around him, cannot drink in his iniquity. Let him immure himself in the shop or counting room; for there the eye of a master will be constantly over him to restrain, and a surrounding world be more excluded from his contaminations. But let him not dwell in a community so open to his enticements as this; let him not blast, with his corruption, these sons of promise,—the pride of our country—the hope of the church and the world.

One word of direction only to *those in this community who are youths of seriousness and sobriety.* On you, my friends, devolves a most sacred duty. You know what precious hopes are deposited in this body; and what devastating ravages are made upon them by every member of dissipated and vicious habits. Be it yours, then, not merely to shun every pollution yourselves, but to do more: to oppose its destructive progress in all around you. With deepened abhorrence of the evil, stand forth to stay its ravages. Gather like a sacred band of sentinels, around this depository of the hopes of the Church and your country. Guard it from the attack of every

invader, however specious, apparently however friendly.
To the counsels and labors of its instructors and guardians, lend your countenance, your efforts, your prayers
to God.   Above all, take to yourselves the  whole armor
of God :—the girdle of truth ; the breastplate of righteousness ;  the shield of faith ;  the sword of the Spirit :—
that you  may resist every enemy that invades this nur-
sery of the Church, with boldness and with success.   Our
interests and yours are but one.   Let one high aim inspire
the hearts of all : and that aim be to keep this sacred
fountain pure.

And O, Thou Spirit of Light and Joy, Guardian of thy
Church, Inspirer of every Grace, come, with thy sacred
fire : consume, in every breast, its destructive lusts: that
they who go hence, may be sons of light, heirs of promise, angels of soothing and rescuing mercy, in this guilty,
polluted, bleeding, weeping world.

------

LUKE X : 42.

MARY HATH CHOSEN THAT GOOD PART WHICH SHALL NOT BE TAKEN AWAY
FROM HER.

THIS commendation was passed by Jesus while visiting
at the house of Martha in Bethany. On this visit, it
seems that Mary, desirous above all things to receive the
gracious instructions of her guest, sat humbly at his feet
to hear his word. But Martha, though, as appears from
other parts of the history, she was a friend and disciple
of Jesus, was so anxious to spread her table with a pro-
fusion of dishes to gratify the bodily appetites of the
social circle, as that she lost in a great measure to her
soul the spiritual advantages which she might have derived from the word and presence of her divine visitor.
This worldly anxiety, as is its usual result, betrayed her
into impatience: and she came into the presence of Jesus
and Mary, interrupting their holy communion with this
querulous language: " Lord, carest thou not that my
sister hath left me to serve alone? bid her therefore that
she help me." But as is usually the case with one who is ·
censorious and petulant, she was herself the person most
needing reproof. Jesus, in order to call off her attention
from her sister and fix it on herself, repeats her name:
Martha! Martha! and then briefly contrasts her worldliness with the spirituality of her sister. " Thou art careful and troubled about many things "—the things you will
prepare, the manner of preparing them, your own hard
service, and what you think your sister's sloth and indifference—things relating to the wants of the body ; " but
one thing is needful "—to beings who have a soul there is

one thing of which they have absolute need ; which
forms a supreme concern ; for which they may well relinquish their worldly anxieties ;—the enjoyment to be derived from the knowledge, the favor, the service and
communion of God : and then, to remind her that Mary
on this particular occasion had acted wisely and in character, and as she herself to be consistent with her profession ought to have done, he adds : "Mary hath chosen
that good part which shall not be taken away from her."
Her choice is fixed on a better portion than worldly
things and she has manifested it on this occasion. The
Saviour calls it a good part which she chose—or, as
the Greek term may be rendered, "lot" or "portion."
For the word means a lot or portion to be enjoyed, and
not, as the English might admit, a part or character to
sustain in the conduct of life.

The example of Mary, therefore, as presented to us in
this description of the Saviour, shows us that *there is a
satisfying portion offered to our acceptance which when chosen
will never be taken away.*

In more fully treating this subject, I will attempt to
show,

I. What is that *good portion* which was chosen of Mary ;

II. The fact that it must be *chosen* by all those who
would have it as their own ; and,

III. That when chosen by any, it will *never be taken away.*

I. Your attention is first invited to the nature of that
*good portion* which was chosen of Mary.

Now if you will but observe the conduct of Mary at
the time when Jesus passed this commendation upon her
character, you will see that the thing which she chose for
herself above all others was *the friendship of God* which
was brought to her acceptance and enjoyment by the
presence of Jesus Christ. Like a sinner needing salvation and dependent for it on that Saviour who came into
this guilty world from the Father with the word of
Eternal Life, she humbly placed herself at his feet to
receive this free and bounteous gift at his hands. Dis-
missing every other care and every other thought for the

time ; and knowing that the Saviour who could restore to her the friendship of God and lead her more fully into the enjoyment of it, was near, she listened with all her heart to his word of counsel, instruction, reproof and comfort, as involving in it all her happiness for this life and eternity. His word was the means of guiding her more fully to the enjoyment of this highest object of her wishes—an object for which she postponed every other care, for which she renounced every other pleasure, and for the full enjoyment of which she was eager to improve every occasion,—and especially one so favorable as was vouchsafed to her at this time by the presence and word of Jesus, who came direct to her from the throne of God with the full offer of salvation, and whose society she could hope but seldom to receive in the house of her pilgrimage.

If this conduct of Mary shows that the thing which she chose as the portion of her soul was an interest in the friendship of the great Jehovah, the same thing is still more clearly shown by the characteristics which Christ attributed to the portion of her choice as being the one thing which to sinful men is altogether needful and which is in every respect *good*.

The friendship of God is the one thing which is altogether needful to sinful men. For by their voluntary departure from God, they have not merely deprived themselves of his friendship : they have fallen under his positive displeasure and wrath. For in going after other objects of enjoyment, and thus setting up idols in their hearts, they are guilty of despising all the goodness of God their Creator, disrespecting his high authority, trampling on his law of benevolence and holiness, and thus they fall under that penalty of his endless displeasure which he, out of righteous regard to the holiness and happiness of his moral kingdom, has affixed to the violation of his law. To mankind therefore who have fallen under condemnation by the law of God and are subject to his everlasting displeasure, the one thing which above all others is needful, is the restoration and enjoyment of the favor of God. For there is no being in the universe that can afford them the relief they need, so long as they remain alienated from him and subject to his wrath. Nor can they find relief in the temporary benefactions which they receive from his long-suffering goodness : which they are only abusing and provoking him to withdraw from them forever so long as they remain subject to his wrath. And there is nothing which he can himself do for them which will afford them any relief, short of their restoration back to the enjoyment of his friendship. As long as they remain destitute of this one thing, they must be subjects of his wrath. And if they continue such, the day must speedily come when they must be removed from all his abused benefits ; and, stripped of every source of enjoyment in the universe, must lie down in the everlasting burnings of shame and degradation and despair,—hopeless outcasts from the love of God and from his happy kingdom ; despairing sufferers in the everlasting torments which come from his righteous judgment. To souls then which have fallen by their sin under his displeasure, the one portion which they absolutely need ; without which they must be forever wretched and ruined ; without which all the high capacities of the soul and its everlasting existence must prove but a deeper curse,—is the restoration and enjoyment of the friendship of God.

This one portion too is the only one in the universe which is *absolutely* and *relatively* good.

This is the only portion man can enjoy which is *absolutely* good. For every other species of happiness taken in separation from the love and friendship of God, cannot afford any solid peace and satisfaction to the soul. It is alloyed, at the very time it is most enjoyed, with the reflection that it is separating the heart still farther from God and filling it more with the feelings of worldly idolatry and sin. But in seeking and enjoying the friendship of the infinite God, the soul feels conscious that it ascends to the very source of all blessing and enters into the possession of a love which commands all the gifts which are in the universe,—a love which fills the soul with a purity and peace which are satisfying to its largest desires, which will render every other inferior enjoyment doubly rich, which will extract from every sorrow of this life and from death itself the stings of an accusing conscience and divine wrath. Here in the presence of God and beneath the light of his countenance, with his love shed abroad in the heart by the Holy Spirit, the soul is filled with a peace and joy in God which passeth all understanding.

The friendship of God is a portion too which is *relatively* good. When the soul seeks this portion for itself, it invades the happiness of no other being in the universe. It stands in a right attitude towards all. Not only are its own capacities of enjoyment filled from the fountain of living waters to which it repairs, but the benevolence of the infinite God is gratified in taking charge of the soul that honors him by casting itself wholly on his love. And in repairing to his benevolent love for its happiness, the soul too is filled with benevolent sympathies for that kingdom which is deriving its happiness from the same pure source; and with deep solicitude for the sinful and guilty lost who are wandering away from it into hopeless exile and misery. The soul that with all the heart cleaves to the love of God for its own portion of joy, is thus filled with desire to imitate the love of its Father in heaven, to fulfil his sweet commands, and to aid in those works in his kingdom which redound to his praise and the welfare of his creatures.

The portion then which Mary chose for her soul was that needful and good portion which was brought down to her acceptance by the presence of Jesus Christ—even the enjoyment of the friendship of God.

II. This portion must be *chosen* by all those who would have it as theirs.

Mary, it seems from the declaration of Christ, chose the friendship of God for herself as her portion of happiness. She considered the friendship of the Infinite God as brought down by Jesus Christ to her free acceptance. She knew that she could not receive and enjoy it while she remained indifferent to it and set her heart supremely on other objects. Refusing all other objects, therefore, inconsistent with it, she chose this with all her heart as the object of her happiness, and in this way—so far as her own conduct was concerned—it became hers. She actually enjoyed that friendship which with all her heart she chose. And so must it ever be with all who would enjoy the friendship of God—they must seek it with all the heart. And there are various considerations, beside this explicit declaration concerning Mary, which show that in order to enjoy the friendship of God, men must choose it with their whole heart as their supreme portion. I observe, therefore, as evidence of such a truth:

1. That in the Gospel God proffers his friendship to men for their choice and acceptance.

This constitutes the very difference between the law of God and the Gospel. In his holy law he denounces a curse against all sin, and brings all men as sinners under the sentence of condemnation. And if he had never published to the world any other message, he would place all in a state of absolute despair and under the inevitable endurance of his wrath. But the gospel is the annunciation to men of the glad tidings that with their offended Lawgiver there is pardoning mercy and recovering grace adequate to all their need. Here he offers freely to remove from their souls the sentence of his wrath and restore to them his everlasting favor. There can be no doubt nor mistake on this point which is so essential to the salvation of guilty men. The very object for which he sent his Son into the world and consented to the pains of his crucifixion was to render it consistent with his rectitude to offer this reconciliation to the acceptance of our guilty race. On that basis the offer is now published to the world. And accompanying the offer are published most earnest entreaties, most solemn warnings, most touching expostulations and imperious commands, that they immediately avail themselves of the offered grace; that they receive it not in vain.

If therefore the reconciliation and friendship of God is thus freely offered to men, it is most obviously presented to them as an object which they must either accept or refuse. For the very fact of offering this reconciliation shows that it is not conferred independently of all choice; that so long as men refuse it, so long as they remain indifferent to it, so long as they prefer their sins and idols to the friendship of God, that friendship will not be theirs. And on the other hand, the offer shows that God is perfectly willing to bestow his friendship upon any one who does in reality seek it with the heart as all his salvation and all his desire. Let any one, I say, make the full and hearty choice of the friendship of God as his portion, and he will be permitted to enter into that source of pure and endless enjoyment. For how can God, consistently with such an offer, turn away from his throne with refusal the heart that comes to him desiring his reconciliation and favor above all idols, and sins, and all inferior joys?—a heart that gives up everything for his favor and that prefers it as its portion above all things else which God can give?

The necessity of choosing this favor, in order to have it as ours, will appear still further, if we consider,

2. That the *nature* of God's friendship is such that it cannot be taken by us without choice. The fact that it is offered would show that it is not bestowed absolutely as an object independent of our choice; its *nature* I will now attempt to show is such that it *cannot be.* And on this point, I apprehend people often indulge a great mistake by which they attempt to excuse themselves for the great indifference of heart which they feel in respect to so supreme and necessary a good which involves in it their whole salvation. Because they see that God is an infinite and independent Being, who has created them and who bestows on them many benefits without their care, they say that he can bestow on them the highest benefit, even the friendship of his heart and their eternal salvation, just as independently of their choice. But in this view they lose sight entirely of the fact that he is a Moral Being, seek-

ing, as the great object of his reign over the universe, the happiness of intelligent and voluntary beings like himself; and that there is just and precisely the same necessity, if he would do good to such a kingdom, that he dispense his favor and displeasure on his subjects with relation to their voluntary conduct, as there is that a good father should do so to his children, or a wise and faithful ruler should do so to his subjects.  If therefore it be considered that men have offended him and fallen under his displeasure in this very way by disregarding the design of his benevolent government and seeking their happiness in objects and ways which he has forbidden, it is evidently impossible that while they adhere to their wrong choice they should ever receive his friendship.  And it is obvious, that whatever else the atonement of Jesus Christ may have effected, it has not removed this invincible necessity of subjecting all our interests to the government of God by a hearty choice of his friendship, if we would take that friendship as ours.  The atonement of Christ and the offer of reconciliation made on the basis of it, shows indeed this glorious truth to the guilty,—that past separation from God and past condemnation by his law for our sins, do not stand in our way as impassable barriers to such an immediate and hearty return to the love of our Father in heaven.  But they have not removed, and never will remove the necessity which arises out of the very nature of God and ourselves as intelligent and voluntary beings, that if we would avail ourselves of the opportunity of reconciliation now granted us, we must renounce those chosen portions which have alienated us from God and choose his glorious friendship as our supreme hope and joy.  Otherwise we shall still remain alienated from him in our hearts, insubmissive to his benevolent and holy government, with our wills perversely bent on our individual, selfish and sinful gratification; and how can we expect, while retaining such feelings of opposition to his government, to receive his reconciling and saving mercy?  Do you say that with all these feelings of insubmission, you can still choose his reconciliation and friendship? But if you suppose this, you only deceive yourself. You may indeed be willing that he should remove from you his displeasure and become a friend to you, while you are still pursuing your course of sin and opposition to his holy government. But in all this, the real choice of your heart is to take the happiness which you can find in other objects than God ; and in your own ways of disobedience. You in reality refuse the joy of his reconciliation and friendship. Your wish to receive his favor is in reality no other than the choice that he would renounce the benevolence and holiness of his moral government, and leave you to go forward unmolested in your sins. To choose his friendship as your portion, you must take it as it is: valuing it supremely for the very reason that he is so good and holy ; and renouncing, for it, everything inconsistent with its enjoyment. If you will thus accept of his friendship, if you will seek it with all your heart as the thing most desirable to your soul, if you will make that hearty choice of it that, for entering into its enjoyment, you will cheerfully take on yourself all the humiliation, and renunciation of self and sin, and devotion to his service which in his holiness and grace he requires, it is yours. If he is willing to be reconciled to any of mankind and receive them to his Fatherly care and love, it is to such as thus choose to cast themselves and all their interests on his care and redemption, and to seek their everlasting all in his pure and holy friendship.

But still farther to show that his friendship becomes ours by our choosing it with all the heart as our supreme portion, I observe again,

3. That such a choice is necessary for entering heartily into the privileges and duties of his children. There can be no doubt that they who with all their heart enjoy the privileges and perform the duties of his children are interested in his forgiving and adopting love. And in order to see that a hearty entrance and continuance on these privileges and duties depends on choosing the love of God as our portion, you need only to look at one very simple and plain principle—that the heart can cleave

only to one supreme portion : and that portion must be,
either the selfish happiness derived from the world, or the
happiness found in the favor and benevolent service of
God.  From this principle it is clear that either the world
must be renounced for Christ or Christ must be renounced
for the world; there cannot be any compromise in the
real choice of the heart between them.  And in choosing
to derive your happiness from Christ himself rather than
from things around you in his creation, you cannot possibly be wrong, unless it be wrong to take happiness above
all things in the love of Christ and the benevolent service
to which that love leads us.  And with this hearty choice
of the friendship of Christ, that renounces all things for
the sake of his love and cleaves to his love as all, every
Christian privilege is entered on and every Christian duty
is performed with a devoted and cheerful heart.  The
Scriptures are read and the throne of grace is resorted to
in prayer, with constancy and delight as the very means
and privileges which are designed to bring Christians
more fully into the enjoyment of that grace of God on
which they rest their hearts.  And duties are performed
and sin is resisted with a full and cheerful purpose of
heart, for the sake of continuing and advancing in the
enjoyment of that benevolent and holy love of God which
is chosen as all the happiness of the soul to eternity.
There is no other way in which a sinner can enter heartily into the privileges and duties of a child of God, or go
forward with the strength of grace in the Christian conflict with temptation and sin, than by renouncing as a lost
and humbled sinner that portion in the world that has
withdrawn his heart and all his powers from God, and
choosing God in Christ as the Friend in whose love and
under whose benevolent government he would find his
portion of joy for ever.

But I proceed to show you,

III. That this is a portion which when chosen by any
will not be taken away from them.

This surely is the testimony of Jesus Christ.  For the
very same portion is offered to the guilty now which was

chosen of Mary, and if it was true in her case, that in choosing this portion for herself it was secured to her forever, there is the same reason in the nature of the portion itself and the free offer made of it to others, that it should be secured to them also, on their choice of it, for eternity. And there are various considerations which go to confirm this animating truth, besides this declaration and other declarations of the Scriptures equally explicit: A few of these considerations I will now present to your view. And,

1. The expense at which God offers to sinners his friendship shows that he designs it when accepted by them for an inalienable gift. If you wish for convincing proof that his grace is thus full and ample, look to the sacrifice which he has freely made for us on Calvary. He has consented that his Beloved Son should leave the throne of heaven, and that, taking upon him the load of our sins, he should go to the cross and bear the indignation for us which we deserved, in order that the endless penalty of his law might be freely removed from our souls, and we be restored to the joys of his friendship as dear children. Could the heart that voluntarily endured all this trial in order to remove from us the penalty of death and restore us again to his friendship, design any less a gift than our restoration to his endless love? Could he leave us, after reconciliation and after the restoration of his love, to fall back again to endless condemnation? Could he, by his own act of the withdrawal of his fatherly love, render the cross which had reconciled us of no effect? The thought of such a withdrawal of his favor, is totally inconsistent with that strength of desire which he has manifested for our recovery in the mission of his Son and the appointment of his crucifixion. No! The heart that conceived such a gift, was full of desire for our recovery from endless death and our enjoyment of his blessed favor and reign to all eternity. He surveyed the full length and breadth of our wants ; and, in his benevolence, determined fully to meet them. In the cross, we have full testimony that his benevolence and grace are

thus large and free. " He that spared not his own Son but delivered him up for us all, how shall he not with him also freely give us all things?" What can ever overcome such intense love? What can ever alienate it from those who repair to it with all their heart and make it all their desire and hope for eternity?

He will never take away his friendship from those who choose it as their supreme and everlasting portion; because,

2. They will need it for their happiness through all eternity. There will never be a time during their immortal existence when he can withdraw from them his friendship and care without depriving them of the happiness for which their very natures were designed, and leaving them desolate and wretched and hopeless forever. And why should he voluntarily withdraw his friendship from such dependent and needy creatures who have sprung from his own creating hand, when with all their heart they throw themselves on his care? There is no need now of executing upon them the penalty of his law in order to maintain his authority. He can freely dispense with their punishment on account of the atonement he has accepted at the hands of his Son. And the very fact that he once enters into reconciliation with them and receives them to the enjoyment of his friendship, is a full acknowledgment on his part that he is not bound by such a necessity. There is nothing therefore to hinder his consulting the everlasting wants of their souls. And will he not as freely bestow his friendship for eternity as for a limited time? The very act of coming forward to seek their reconciliation, shows that he desires their welfare. And when they come with all their hearts to receive the gift and seek to share in the largeness of his mercy to the guilty, will he ever think of turning them away empty, and driving them from his presence and love? Would not this be a needless neglect of their wants? Is this the goodness of the infinite and all-sufficient Creator? Will he treat thus the souls that he has made? Will he, when on his invitation they come to him

for their soul's salvation, knowing that he is the only being on whom they can depend for it, and that he can grant them their desire without injuring any in his kingdom,--will he receive them merely for a day or a few years, and then cast them off from his love to destitution and hopeless misery forever? The heart that calls us back to his love and kingdom has surely felt for our deep necessities as immortal beings and dependent creatures, and is more bounteous than to forsake us in all our need, when self-abased for our sin we put all our confidence in him for an endless salvation. " I will not," says this High and Lofty One, to sinners who are broken off from all self-confidence and self-sufficiency and who look to Him alone for their eternal hope and joy,—" I will not contend forever, neither will I be always wroth, for the spirit should fail before me, and the souls which I have made." He feels an interest in lost sinners as deep as their endless wants, and he would not invite them back to the care of his friendship and love without a perfect willingness, and even an ardent desire, that on their return they should freely share in his holy friendship to all eternity.

I will only add,

3. That to such as choose to enjoy his friendship and live under the care of his holy government to eternity, he has granted already all the means necessary to their everlasting continuance in his love. He has placed his word of instruction, counsel and authority in their hands, accompanied with the free offer of his grace, to which they can resort through all the pilgrimage of this life, and rest their souls on his promises. He has elevated his Son to the throne as their living intercessor, through whom they may freely repair to his throne of mercy in all their wants. He has sent his Holy Spirit as a friend to their spiritual welfare, on whom they can rely at all times to help and guide them in the way to heaven. And with all these aids to help them forward to the chosen object of their heart—the everlasting enjoyment of his love,—what is there in the universe that can separate them

from this love?  God is for them, and who or what can be against them and prevail?  Shall sin again have dominion over them?  But they are not under bare law which condemns them, but under the care of a grace which is sufficient for their victory, and to it they may constantly repair for strength.  Will Satan or the ungodly prevail over them?  They have a Friend mightier than all their foes, in the shelter of whose love they are strong and bold to resist.  Will the joys or sorrows that come upon them in their earthly lot, withdraw their hearts from God?  But the Lord in whom they trust, is the dispenser of every earthly providence; and no temptation will he suffer to come upon them which they are not able to bear, and in all he opens to them a way of escape in their free access to his all-sufficient grace.  Will death separate them from the God in whom they hope?  But in that hour he is as near as ever to take care of the body and spirit which they resign to his disposal.  Will the day of judgment bring upon them any sentence of separation from God?  But the God who offered them the pardon of all their sins and to whom they fled for reconciliation, will confirm that pardon before his whole kingdom.  Nor can impenitent men or fallen angels in their envy and malice, bring any accusation against them which will prevail over his pardoning mercy.  They, therefore, who really renounce their sins before God, and choose an interest in his love for their immortal souls, have the portion of their choice secured to them through life, at death and the judgment, and to all eternity in heaven.  Nor shall life or death, things present or things to come, or any creature, all which are under his control, be able to separate them from his love.

Such, then, is the evidence I have presented to show that there is a satisfying portion which may be chosen by us, which will never be taken away.

I remark, in closing,

1. That God is fully willing that sinners should secure their own everlasting happiness.

He is not willing, indeed, that they should be eternally

happy in departing from him in their affections. His benevolent regard to his moral creation requires that, if they continue in that course, he should abandon them to destruction. But although men have wilfully and perversely entered on that course, he has met them in his grace with the offer of a free remission of the penalty and the everlasting friendship of his heart, as their inheritance of joy, if they will return to him in true repentance. And now nothing remains but that you take with your whole heart the portion he offers.

This responsibility he casts upon you. But in casting this responsibility on you, he shows a perfect willingness that you should secure that happiness. For this responsibility is a necessary result of his creating you rational and voluntary beings. And unless you were such beings, he could not possibly bring you into the blessedness of a communion in his love and friendship. And with this responsibility lying upon you, and when you had forfeited the care of his government by forsaking him, he has not only brought that friendship down to your choice at all the expense of making an atonement for your sins, but he urges on you the choice of it with all the solicitude of a true Friend to your everlasting happiness: saying, "turn ye, for why will ye die?" And his Spirit often strives for the very purpose of inducing you to renounce all things for a portion in his love. And now when nothing remains but your own choice, is he not fully willing? If you will now with all your heart renounce your supreme attachment to the world and choose the friendship of his heart as your supreme joy, if you will thus turn to God in your hearts in true repentance—if you will forsake all things for Christ and his love, the Spirit of grace who strives with you to bring you to that very choice, will lead you forward in it to all eternity. The God of grace to whose redeeming love you cleave, will conduct you up to one height of grace after another through the temptations of this life, and convey you safely through the vale of death and beyond his judgment seat, and place your purified and happy spirit among the ransomed in heaven.

And will you complain now, that he is unwilling that you should find eternal happiness under his government? Will you stand cleaving to this world as all your joy— renouncing the service and friendship of God ; and at the very time you are refusing his endless love, will you complain of him as an enemy to your welfare? Will you throw on him the blame of that very separation from him, to which with all the heart you yourselves are clinging? Will you find fault with him for giving you souls capable of endless happiness and misery, because you are tearing them away from the blessedness of his government? Treat not thus that God who is love, and who meets you in the midst of your wilful alienation and unjust complaints, with the offer of endless reconciliation through Christ. He is not the God of hatred and injustice which you pretend. But you are the unjust and ungrateful rebels against him which he declares. And if you will not confess it and renounce your sin, while he offers you his grace, he will roll on you before his whole kingdom the everlasting shame and contempt of despising his love, and will leave you to your own choice of separation forever to eternity.

Once more ;

2. The everlasting interests of your souls urge you to choose immediately for your portion the friendship of God.

The Lord who made your souls, who knows that all their happiness depends on their union to his love, has brought down his endless grace with all its benefits and offered it to your acceptance through Christ Jesus. And the great and practical inquiry arises: will you accept this happiness as the portion of your souls? Will you betake yourselves to the Lord Jesus Christ; and renouncing every other dependence, choose him as your Redeemer and Lord for eternity, surrendering all that you have and are to him, expecting henceforth all your happiness from his friendship and love? You must come to this renunciation of all things for Christ, or remain unreconciled and at distance from him cleaving to your sins. There is no dispensing with your own choice in this matter. There is no influence of the Spirit of God that will ever take you out of these circumstances of responsibility, or that will or can ever lead you to salvation in any other way than through your own hearty choice of communion and friendship with God. The everlasting interests of your souls then are suspended on your choosing the good portion which Christ now offers.

And why should you not choose it with all your heart? God is willing. He is desirous. And is not the happiness to be found in his favor and communion, the most exalted to which your souls can aspire? Is it not worthy to be chosen by you with all the heart? Is it so? May you bring that soul of yours under his fatherly love and care to all eternity; and will you despise such a gift? Will you tear that soul away from those everlasting blessings, which are to come from his benevolent reign? And why? What causes are there that you will permit to operate so far as to keep you away from the love of Christ? Are they the possessions of this world — its wealth, pleasures, honors? But he only forbids you to cleave to these as your supreme portion, and to pursue them with all your heart. He calls for your heart himself, and will still leave many of these possessions with you as his steward. Or is it regard to the favor of man or to the fear of man's displeasure? But what can man do for your soul, if for his sake you should refuse the portion it needs in the infinite God? And if you should cast your soul on the care of Almighty grace and have God for your helper, what need you fear what man can do unto you? Or shall pride hinder you? Shall a dying sinner who is on the brink of endless ruin, feel so self-sufficient that he will not seek after God?—a poor, guilty and condemned criminal, who is about to be consigned to perpetual darkness and pain, be ashamed penitently to accept deliverance before all from his offended God?

And now will you not make the wise and happy choice to which the Gospel calls you? Will you refuse a portion in the love of God, and cleave to the base and momentary pleasures of the world and sin? Will you go forward to eternity an alien from God, and wilfully deprive that soul of yours of all the joys of God's eternal kingdom, and place it irretrievably and beyond redemption in all the degradation and anguish of eternal punishment? Look up to the glory of that God who made this mighty universe and rolls the spheres through the boundless firmament. See that heart of love ready to receive you as a child, and conduct you forward to the holiness and joy that are to flow on his kingdom from his benevolent government through the eternal ages to come. He knows what a boundless good he is preparing for the immortal minds he has made; and he invites you to come up and take your portion in his love and kingdom. Christ who died for you, is willing. The Spirit who strives with you, is willing. The angels who welcome back the penitent, are willing. The Church who plead with you and pray for you, are willing. You need not perish. Cleave then no longer to the world and sin and perdition. Moved by the grace of God, say from the heart, "I will arise and go to my Father." Let his righteousness receive its honors in the cross. Let his grace receive its honors in your salvation.

PSALM CXII: 7.

HE SHALL NOT BE AFRAID OF EVIL TIDINGS: HIS HEART IS FIXED, TRUSTING IN
THE LORD.

THIS, the Psalmist testifies, is the happy lot of the righteous man. With a heart throbbing with all the sensibilities of life, exposed to all the sources of evil that are overwhelming others, he has found for it a point of rest, that is exalted above every evil: he has anchored it firm and fast in the haven of immortal security, forever beyond the raging tempest: and with a heart thus fixed and established, he can triumph over the power of evil: in view of the unseen and untried future, he is not afraid of any tidings of overwhelming evil. This happy lot is secured to him by trusting in the Lord; by looking to the Lord alone for his welfare, surrendering all his interests for time and eternity implicitly to his disposal; submitting everything to the decision of his will; owning him with childlike dependence as a wise, forgiving and faithful Father alike in days of prosperity and adversity; and expecting from him steadily a complete deliverance out of all evil and an exaltation to endless joy in his kingdom.

That we may secure this happy lot of the righteous man, let us consider his act of trust, and its power to strengthen and establish his heart for a triumph over evil.

The act of trust in God I will however first describe, and then show its efficacy thus to establish the heart.

I. To trust is to commit some interest of ours into the hands of another, in the belief that he is competent and willing to manage it for us, and with the expectation that he will make it good.

II. It must be some interest of ours—that in which, directly or indirectly, immediately or remotely, our welfare or feelings are concerned—otherwise we have nothing to trust.

III. We must believe the trustee capable and willing—and expect him to be faithful,—to secure the interests we commit to him; otherwise we squander them rather than trust them for security.

An estate, for instance, falls to you in your minority, which you are incompetent to manage with safety yourself; and which, as you are deprived of the natural guardian of your youth by the decease of your parent, must, if kept from running to waste, be entrusted to the care of some other person. Now in your act of trust you choose some individual, willing to take that care upon him, as your guardian and trustee, to whose management you commit it, in the belief that he is worthy of the trust, and with the expectation that he will keep it safe unto the day for your complete possession. Thus you are not to trust without committing some interest of yours to the keeping of another, nor without believing the trustee capable. For to place your interests in incapable hands, would be to throw them away to the sport of mere chance. Nor are you to trust without expecting the guardian to be faithful. For to put your interests into the hands of the faithless, would be to squander them away on the support of injustice or crimes.

The act is essentially the same when the guardian to whom we commit our interests is God. We commit them to his care, in the belief of his competency and willingness, and with the expectation that he will keep them safe for our possession. Only the trust is distinguished from all others, by the *extent of the interests enumerated in our deed of trust*, by the qualities of God our Guardian which fit him to take them in charge, and by the solemn forms in which he conveys his promises and engagements that he will be faithful to secure them for us to eternity.

Before God we are all minors, incapable of securing to ourselves the estate of immortal glory and blessedness which is the original birthright of his rational creatures. Nay worse: we are perverse and rebellious children, who have taken the chief management into our own hands, and refused it to him, our natural Guardian : and thus by our unnatural separation and our unrighteous rebellion, have forfeited our whole estate in his love and kingdom, and are in imminent hazard of final and utter disinheritance.  In this situation we all are when the good tidings of promise reach us—a promise essentially the same in all past ages and the foundation of trust to all his righteous servants, but which is more amply set forth and more widely published in these last days, in the Gospel of his Son—the promise that he will, notwithstanding the past, act as the Parental Guardian of all who will return to him and entrust the management of their immortal interests to his hands ; and that he will see them put into the full and happy possession of an immortal inheritance in his kingdom at the last day.

Many, indeed, who hear the tidings refuse the offer. They persist in venturing all upon their own management still ; and, in continued alienation and rebellion, they either—like the prodigal—squander every remaining gift and bounty of God on their own lusts, careless and unregardful of the future ; or—like the Pharisee—while equally estranged from God in heart and abusing to equal perversion all his gifts, vainly attempt to build on their hollow ceremonies that over-stock of merit with which to purchase from God, after they have squandered their earthly portion on sin, that heavenly one for which they have rendered themselves unfit, and which they have scorned to receive as his gift.  But—unlike the thoughtless prodigal worldling, or the deluded victim of self-righteous pride,—the righteous man accepts the proposal of God made in Christ Jesus : returns to him submissively, chooses him as the Guardian of his well-being, entrusts all to his keeping, with unshaken belief in his faithfulness.  He has learned, from the little he has seen of himself and his fellow men, from the teachings of his own nature and of providence, the utter vanity of cleaving to an earthly portion in separation from God: how the heart is all disturbance and agitation, from the conscious sense of ill desert, ingratitude and unworthiness; from the insecurity of the portion to which it clings; from the temptations it offers to increasing sin; from the brood of evil passions it engenders: and he is sick of its emptiness. He has learned too, that he cannot possibly manage by himself to secure true and lasting riches in the kingdom of God—the heavenly portion. The evils of unworthiness, dissatisfaction, temptation, malicious passion, which are the only abiding fruit of his course of separation, are crowding upon him with ever greater force, and must make his everlasting portion forfeit, and forever detain him under their power, —an exile from the happiness that reigns in the holy and immortal kingdom of the Creator—unless he return to him and seek the help of his mightier power.

It is with these heartfelt convictions, troubled and dissatisfied with his erring courses, conscious that he is astray from God and must lose all if he continues so, and yet hardly daring to think that his Creator can forgive the past or do anything for him in the future, that his eye meets the written promise of God, which assures him that there is yet a way to secure the birthright of a child in his eternal love and kingdom; that if he will make Him his Guardian, and come, committing in good faith and in well doing all his welfare to his disposal, all his sins will be readily forgiven him, and he shall have kept and made sure to him an eternal portion in heaven. He reads the word of God. He is convinced that the record has been made by his eternal Creator; that it has been published by him in good faith; that he is disposed and able to make it good. He believes the record. And now his trust begins. In the resolve of a trusting soul, he says within himself, ' I will go to my offended God with this sorrowing and bursting heart. I will ask his forgiveness for the past, and implore him to be the Guardian of my immortal interests.' He makes out, in his mind, his deed of trust. He includes in it his whole being with all its capacities and powers. He surrenders all, he commits all, in good faith, to the care of the faithful Creator. He goes with it into his presence; declares it to be his free will and deed; subscribes it before him with his own hand; and lodges it with him for a testimony.

And now his joy begins. His heart is fixed by this deed of trust to the source of safety and rest. And he keeps it fixed, by *continued* trust—by *holding on* to his Guardian, to his word and throne of grace: submitting all to him and receiving all from him, in good faith. So it is by *trusting*—by the act of trust *continued truly and in good faith*, that he keeps his heart fixed amid all the changes of this life; through duties and trials, privileges and privations, joys and sorrows. By trusting, he hides himself within the secret pavilion of the Almighty for defense and repose, unto the day when he shall enter on the immortal inheritance purchased for him in heaven and receive his birthright as a child of God,—a life estate of holy joy in his eternal kingdom.

II. But we will consider now more particularly the effect of his trust, to fix and establish his heart, to exalt it to an ascendancy over evil.

The righteous, with his neighbor, is embarked on an eventful life, with all his interests in the future at stake. Exposed to many sources of moral and natural evil, which seem ready to devour, neither can fix the heart in immovable repose by resorting to apathy and indifference. The sensibilities of the heart cannot be extinguished; nor be stifled so far as to need nothing for joy, as to bear every thing without anguish. There is to every heart some loss which, if incurred, would be insupportable; some evil which, if inflicted, would be beyond endurance. No heart therefore is steadfastly fixed in repose, that does not rest for its happiness on something that is beyond temptation, guilt, disappointment and sorrow.

Now the righteous, by trusting in God, fixes his heart to such an object, and establishes its happiness on an immovable foundation exalted above all evil; because in his trust he anticipates a full and perfect inheritance of joy in heaven: he assures his heart of securing it beyond failure: and he arms his heart with patience to endure every temporal loss or suffering which may come upon him before he is put into its full possession.

1. He anticipates an inheritance in heaven that is fully and forever satisfying.

He has set his heart on God, his reconciled and gracious Father in Heaven. His treasure is in God himself, the ever holy, the ever blessed; the full and overflowing fountain of good. It is laid up in the inexhaustible stores of his wisdom and goodness and power: from which he supplies the holy in his heavenly presence with fullness of joy: by which he places them in an estate of perfect glory and blessedness; exalted, like his own, high above the reach of every evil; firm and enduring, as his, to eternity. This inheritance in heaven will be enough to feed his capacious mind and heart with fullness of joy forever more; and in the anticipation he now rests with calm and settled delight.

He doubts not that his Father in heaven has abundant riches to settle forever on all the children of his adoption, the heirs of promise. He trusts in his word, with unshaken confidence that there is such an inheritance in heaven worthy of all his toils, and there his heart fixes its desires and affections. Nor is he afraid that the evil tidings will ever reach him that he has fixed his heart on vanity and delusion. There are indeed in the world those who publish tidings of evil—who announce that there is no immortality for man—that there is no Creator enthroned in the wealth of eternity to own him as a child and endow him as an heir of immortality—and who, in their atheistic blindness, call upon him to seek his happiness solely in the objects of this fleeting world. But what authority have they for the evil tidings they publish? Have they traversed the vast provinces of this creation and the regions of immensity beyond, and made the discovery by actual searching, that there is no God nor any world of his immortal children? The servant of God, while he sees in the atheistic around him, those who are confined to the same world with himself, and who have no more knowledge by actual vision than he, will still go on with unshaken heart, to trust in the existence of the invisible God and his invisible kingdom, and await the issue of his trust after death. In the mean time he has seen within him and around him too many of the works of God to doubt his existence; he has experienced too much of his care already to doubt his grace. He has proved by experience that there are depths in his own nature which none else can ever fill. At distance from him he has encountered the stormy ocean of selfishness, temptation, guilt and passion; and has passed by the wrecks of those who have sunk in utter disappointment and wretchedness and despair. He has himself tasted deeply of all those ingredients of agitation and anguish that cleave to a worldly portion taken in alienation from God. And now, since he.trusted in God and submitted his destiny to his disposal, he has tasted some of the first fruits of his grace: the foretastes and earnests of the promised inheritance. He has felt the tempests of temptation and sin subside within him at the command of Christ. He has felt the love of God taking possession of his heart more and more as he has trusted, and strengthening him in the ways of holiness. He feels that the God in whom he trusts, in communion with whom even now his heart at times takes in a measure of joy that is unspeakable and full of glory, is all sufficient to his endless joy. With the witness of the Spirit in his heart that he is a son of God, with the earnest of the future inheritance now in possession, he trusts on, undisturbed amid the evil reports that are circulated in the world around him respecting his heavenly Father. He trusts on, rejoicing in the delusion, if it be one, that so ministers to his present holiness and joy and to his hopes of futurity. He trusts on till death, willing to abide the issue in eternity.

2. Again, by trusting in God, he assures his heart of securing that heavenly inheritance beyond failure. The

promise in which he trusts assures him, not only that there is an immortal inheritance in heaven for the obedient sons of God, but that the guardianship offered to the guilty and needy on earth through Christ will, to those who in good faith rely on it, secure the possession. The securities upon which he proceeds in his trust, are firmly settled to the satisfaction of his own mind. He acts on the word of God which he is satisfied is genuine. He has risen above the fear that the record is counterfeit. He sees upon it the known signature of God—the marks of his omniscience, omnipotence, holiness and love. He is not afraid to rest in it as genuine, to come with it before God and plead it in his presence, and to make it the basis of all his welfare for eternity. His heart is at rest on that point. With a genuine promise from God in his hands, he is satisfied too that the Promiser is good beyond all deceit or failure. He wishes no better security than that of his name. The promise is backed with the weight of his character, and it can be by no higher security. And to this promise his Father has bound himself with an oath ; and because he could swear by no greater, he sware by himself; that by these immutable pledges in which he could not lie, strong consolation might be given to the heirs of promise who have fled to him for refuge. With these securities settled to his satisfaction,—that the promise is genuine and the Promiser good beyond failure, —his trust places his heavenly inheritance secure in the keeping of God. He knows in whom he believes, and is persuaded that he is able to keep that which he commits unto him against that day. Nor while committing his cause to God, resting on his word in good faith, does he fear that anything will be able to cut him off from his final inheritance.

He escapes in this way the dangers that lurk within his own being. Does he hear the tidings published, that the heart of man is deceitful above all things ? And does he see the melancholy wrecks of those around him who are led by their own lusts into confirmed iniquity and guilt, and are become the suffering, helpless, despairing captives of evil?  He knows indeed that he carries within his own breast such tendencies to evil as render him unfit to manage his interests alone—enough of pride or covetousness or sensuality to make utter shipwreck of his welfare were he to trust in his own heart.  But he has fled from this danger which once threatened his utter overthrow.  His own weakness and exposures as a sinner he feels, and for this very reason, unwilling to trust the cause of his welfare to his own hands, he has betaken himself to the immediate care and supervision of an Almighty God and Saviour.  In him he trusts for deliverance from all the evil that is still lurking in his heart.  He goes as a trusting child into his immediate presence and pleads in prayer his gracious promise for deliverance from the power of his sinful inclinations.  Nor does he fear, while resting on his word and feeling the sanctifying power of his love already in his heart, but that his Father will present him holy and unblamable in his sight at the last day, an inheriter of eternal joy.  He thus escapes from his own weakness and sin by hiding himself in the arms and upon the bosom of his Almighty Guardian, and taking to his heart the sanctifying power of his truth and love.

Nor does he fear that fellow-beings will cut him off from the promised inheritance.  For the Lord in whom he trusts is high and infinite, over all the foes that can rise up against him in the creation.  If evil spirits in this universe are allowed to come near him, or if his fellow-men ever gather around him to assail his welfare, he puts his immortal interests beyond their reach by committing them as a child to the care of the Almighty.  He goes up to him who controls all.  He calls upon him as his Guardian, for defense from the assaults of temptation.  He pleads before him with confidence his own promise.  He knows his word is sure.  On it he is willing to rest.  And while binding his heart to the Almighty in unshaken trust, while cleaving in steadfast faith to the love of God in Christ Jesus, no assaults of enemies in the creation can break the bond.  None can divide between him and God.  His heart and treasure is above all, bound fast to the throne of the Infinite and the Almighty.

Nor does he fear that God himself will cut him off from his heavenly inheritance. He expects to behold him on the day of judgment, and to hear his lips pronounce on multitudes who appear before him, the sentence of final and endless exclusion from his kingdom. But in view of that coming day he is not afraid of such tidings of evil to himself. He now betakes himself to God and commits his cause to his management in season. He knows that he has merited as a perverse and guilty creature a disinheritance from his love and kingdom. But he has been brought nigh to God in reconciliation, and has accepted his gracious proposal to justify him and admit him to his birth-right in heaven. He pleads that promise now as his defense. He is willing to abide the issue, on that fearful day. He trusts in his word that it is he who justifieth the ungodly, who believe that his Son has died and risen again to make intercession. Clinging to a Guardian whose sole prerogative it is to pronounce final sentence on mankind, and who engages to justify his righteous servants, he fears no condemnation. He sees his immortal interests safe in the keeping of his Father in Heaven. He trusts on till death; assured of receiving beyond failure the immortal inheritance, for which he pants, of a child in his kingdom of glory.

3. Once more; by trusting in God he arms his heart with patience to endure every temporal loss or suffering which may come upon him before receiving the inheritance. For having his heart fixed on a pure and unfading inheritance in the immortal kingdom of God and a title secured to that inheritance which is beyond failure, there remains no evil for him to encounter but such as affects his temporal interests: his happiness in this life merely, while on his way to eternity. The worst tidings that he can expect to hear are such as respect temporal disappointment and loss, or temporal sufferings. He knows not indeed, precisely how much temporal loss or suffering may come upon him in consequence of his own imprudence or the encroachments of fellow-beings, or the more direct dispensations of Providence. Yet by casting all

his care upon God, he is preparing his heart to endure the utmost that may come upon him. He surrenders all his mortal interests into the hands of God ; assured that his providence is over the wide creation ; that every temporal good, by whatever secondary almoner administered, is his gift ; that every temporal evil by whatever hands inflicted, is his rod of chastisement : and he trusts in the word of God his Guardian, that he will order the bounty and discipline of his hand according to his wants, and act toward him, in all his earthly course, as a wise and kind Father ; consulting his highest welfare—intent to render him a partaker of his holiness and blessedness. Having from the heart committed all to the orderings of his wise providence, he is prepared to receive every earthly gift with that spirit of thankfulness, and to endure every earthly trial with that spirit of patience, which the wisdom and love of God inspire in every truly trusting heart.

Why then, in a world which his Father superintends, and in which his Father is training him up for the holy joys of his eternal kingdom, should his heart be overcome with the fear of evil tidings?

He is in a world indeed that is full of evils. Many hearts around him are sinking with forebodings of what is to come or fainting under the evils which are already upon them. They cannot bear their earthly losses and disappointments and cares, and, if they do not suffer themselves to pine away the lingering death of inconsolable grief, vainly attempt to stifle their own sensibilities in intemperance or rush upon utter annihilation. But all these are embarked on the stormy ocean of mere self-adventure, wilful wanderers from God, with none but a worldly portion to feed their panting hearts. He has escaped ; and is fast moored to the Rock of Eternal Strength, the Citadel of Eternal Joy.

And now, what evil tidings does he fear shall come to affect him at this anchorage ground? Shall he hear of the death of beloved friends? or shall disappointments and losses as to worldly good assail him? or shall pains and sufferings announce their presence in his decaying body? But in all these, even at the worst and when inflicted by malicious foes, he sees the hand of God in whom he trusts. Though accumulated upon him at once as they were upon the righteous Job -though messenger after messenger arrive with evil tidings—he still clings to the God of his hopes. He casts himself with all his burdens afresh in prayer on the love and sympathy of God, and arms his heart with patience to endure. It is the Lord; let him do what seemeth him good. The Lord who gave hath taken away; blessed be the name of the Lord. If some spirit of impatience and evil suggest to his heart that he curse God and die, he repels the blasphemous suggestion that would tear his soul away from the anchorage of its hopes. He still clings in trust to a bright reversion in the love of God. His tribulation even now worketh the patience of filial love, the experience of divine compassion and faithfulness; and hope grows stronger in a heart into which are flowing these fresh and increasing measures of God's love. And whether his afflictions pass over him wholly in this life or not, they are but the faint clouds and gentle ripples of the dark and furious tempest that is raging out on the broad ocean he has escaped; which lie awhile over the harbor of security he has reached; and which skirt a land before him of eternal brightness and joy.

What tidings of earthly evil then shall he fear? Is it the tidings of temporal death? But that is his last enemy. All the malice of his foes in the whole creation, can reach no farther. And the God in whom he trusts, disarms even this enemy of his sting. By whatever means the evil shall be inflicted, he sees in it the messenger of the Lord. He fears no evil from the Lord his Shepherd, who summons him into his presence. ' Though he slay me, yet will I trust in him,' is the language he returns to the message. And now as he leaves all things earthly forever, with the heavenly inheritance full before him, the foretastes of its joys in his heart, the covenant of promise in his hands, he goes down, at the bidding of the messenger, to cross the narrow passage which yet separates him from the citadel of his King, the land of his inheritance. At that hour he clings to the promise of the eternal covenant that has fed his heavenly hopes and affections during the vicissitudes of former days. That promise of his Creator and Saviour is now the joy and rejoicing of his heart. That promise binds his heart to God and attunes his lips to the praises of victory. And venturing his all upon it as he goes forth to the shores of eternity, he escapes the terror of his last enemy. He passes away in the full expectation to meet face to face the Creator of his spirit, to hear him own the promise as genuine and good, to receive from him, the Redeemer of the lost, the inheritance of an adopted child in his holy and immortal kingdom, and to be exalted forever beyond all approach of evil.

I have thus set before you the effect of trust in God to establish the heart of the righteous in the repose of an invincible strength ; to establish it firm against the overcoming fear of future evil :—that it does this by setting the heart on God and thus administering to it joyful anticipations of a satisfying inheritance in his love and kingdom : assuring it of entering into the possession beyond failure : and arming it with patience to endure every evil that will be permitted to assail him while on the way to that full inheritance. " The righteous shall not be afraid of evil tidings : his heart is fixed, trusting in the Lord. His heart is established, he shall not be afraid."

And now, to conclude, I would, as a practical improvement of the subject, propound two questions for serious consideration and decision. Is not the lot of the righteous in this kingdom of our Creator more excellent than that of his unbelieving neighbor ? And is it not wise to imitate him in the trust by which he secures that lot ?

1. Is not the lot of the righteous in this kingdom of our Creator more excellent than that of his unbelieving neighbor ? Whose condition bids fairest for happiness in the unseen and untried eternity to which both are hastening ? Who is most likely to fare well in the endless ages

to come? I speak as unto wise men,—able to discern between good and evil; judge ye what I say.

You see the unbeliever living without God, trusting to the devices of his own heart for his happiness, seeking his portion in the pleasures he can find in mere worldly things. He is out on the uncertainties of this life, venturing his whole welfare on this trust. Yet even now temptations are thickening upon him, the evil passions of pride and sensuality and selfishness and malice are occupying his heart with intenser sway; and disappointments, losses, sufferings and fears are crowding upon him a more inconsolable burden. He goes forward to eternity the captive of guilt and sorrow; and we see him no more.

You see the righteous,—once embarking his welfare on the same course,—alarmed and dissatisfied; turning to the promise of this book and recognizing it as the promise of the Creator; renouncing before him his former trust and submitting himself and his whole welfare, as this book directs, to the disposal of his wisdom and goodness and power. Now does he wash his hands in innocency, and compass, as a filial servant, the altar of God his joy and refuge. He enters into holy communion with him, filling his heart with richer assurances of immortal joy in his kingdom, and arming it with patience to endure and overcome every sorrow that meets him on his way. He passes from us in this state of triumph: and we see him no more.

I say, you see the righteous on this triumphant course. For in the portrait I have drawn, I have but described the case of well known individuals who have existed in the world and passed before us into eternity. Not that every righteous man is equally exemplary and constant in his filial trust, or attains equal degrees of hope or equal degrees of exaltation over natural and moral evil. Nor that there are not those who profess their filial trust in God when in works they deny him, who utterly fall in the day of temptation and trial. But the existence of the true believer, and the effects of his filial trust in this life, are facts too clear to admit denial.

You see then both on their course in this life, and venturing their well being on their different trusts. They have now entered on an untried eternity, and what, judge ye, is the issue? Say not, you have not seen eternity—that it is hid in the darkness of futurity—and you cannot judge. Look to what you do see: this word that is with us; and the believer in it, here on his way, and the unbeliever. Judge from what you do see, as to what you do not see. Which, think you, is likeliest to fall the eternal prey of natural and moral evil? Which is likeliest to rise to an eternal exaltation over both, in this kingdom of our Creator? Whose prospects are the fairest for inheriting a blessed immortality? Are both alike to fail? Are both alike to succeed? To bring the question to a test: whose condition would you prefer? Were your Creator at this moment to render himself visible, and, setting aside in your case the general rules of his government, were he to assure you, that a mere word from your lips should decide it—that, as you said it should be, whether to take your place in eternity with Paul the apostle, or with Nero his persecutor, with the believing Baxter or with the infidel Voltaire; what would you say? Ah, is there a heart which ever came near the light of this word or the example of its trusting believers that, when brought to the test, would not say, ' Let me die the death of the righteous; let my last end be like his; let my lot in eternity be cast with his.'

2. I ask again, Is it not wise to imitate the righteous in the trust by which he secures his lot? I address the question more particularly to those who have not yet returned to the Lord in repentance and put their trust in his promises of grace. Is it not wise for you to imitate the righteous in his faith and trust?

The word of promise, with its conditions, is before you; the word on which he ventures his eternal well being, and by trusting in which he rises so far ascendant over the moral and natural evil which is pressing upon the world, as to appear before you the joyful child of God and to convince you that it shall fare well with him in eternity. Is is not wise then to do as he does—to renounce dependence on that which leaves you under the power of evil, and venturing all on this word of promise to choose, as it proposes, the Lord for your Shepherd?

You are to act of choice in your trust, and not by force. Your eternal well being is at stake, and you are to trust it somewhere. You must venture it all upon something. Do you think it wise to rest it where you now do, in your own hands, in alienation from God, in subjection to the power of evil, and trust on and wait the issue? Is it not better to rest it on the promise of this word and to come, as this word proposes, a lost creature to God, surrendering yourself to his care through all the vicissitudes of this life and seeking of him through Christ Jesus forgiveness, holiness and endless redemption?

Do you object that this is not a matter of folly or wisdom, reproach or praise, but of necessity; that belief is involuntary, depending upon evidence? But you can trust where there are very slight grounds for belief, and you can refuse to trust where the grounds for belief are the strongest. It becomes you therefore to search impartially for the truth, and that right early. But that you are not even now kept from trusting in this word of promise by mere want of evidence, is proved by your present conduct. You are now actually trusting all the interests which this promise calls you to venture upon God, somewhere else; you are now willing to stake all in your own hands and upon your own management. Have you then as much evidence for believing your interests secure where you now stake them as you would have were they staked on God and his word of promise? Say ye who think of future repentance; say ye who, determined to brave it out as ye are, still admit in your hearts the superior prospects of the righteous? Would you not, if brought to the issue at once in the visible presence of the Creater, prefer rather that your trust were staked upon revelation than upon its present basis? And if now you are trusting your immortal interests where you *believe* there is the *less* security of the two, could you not trust them, if you chose, where you believe there is the *greater ?*

The gospel bids you forsake your false refuges of lies and sins, return with submission and love to God your Creator and Redeemer, and secure your immortal interests at his hands. The record has his signature. They who trust in it are living proofs of his faithfulness so far as the eye can trace them on their course. If then you would be wise for eternity do as they do. If you see ground enough to render it wiser in your view to trust your immortal interests upon God and his promise, than where you now trust them, do it: nor wait another moment. If you wish for increasing light, that will dawn upon you the more, as you walk with God and study his word on your future way. If you wish for actual vision, that will not come till each one takes the issue of his present courses in eternity. You must trust, you must venture all, beforehand. Be wise then now, to enter with the righteous on his *life* of filial trust, and thus secure his happy inheritance beyond the grave.

———

GENESIS XXII: 1—19.

THIS portion of sacred history informs us of a trial to which Abraham was subjected, at a time of great peace and prosperity, by the express appointment of God. The time and origin of the trial are made known in the introductory remark: v. 1,—" It came to pass after these things that God did tempt Abraham."

After the things already related—when the former trials of his life were past; when his anxieties about Hagar and Ishmael were relieved by the express promise of God in regard to their future lot; when the difficulties with Abimelech were settled by a covenant of perpetual amity; when he and Sarah, amid temporal prosperity, were rejoicing in the constant presence and society of Isaac, now arrived at the years of opening manhood; and when at the altar of devotion which he had erected in the grove of his planting at Beersheba, not far from his shaded dwelling, he, with his rejoicing household, was wont to call on the name of Jehovah, the everlasting God;—in this time of profound peace, he is suddenly called to undergo this severest of all his trials.

The trial came upon him by the express appointment of God. At the midnight hour probably,—for he " arose " " early in the morning," it is said, to fulfil the appointment—the Lord suddenly appeared and, by a severe command, " did *tempt*," as our translation renders the Hebrew verb, or as the word is more properly rendered, did *try* or *prove* " Abraham." The old English translation was more exact upon this clause, and should have been preserved : " The Lord did prove Abraham." The same word is so rendered in our version in the passage, Exodus xvi : 4, in which the Lord speaks of granting Israel food, in the quails and the manna, to attract them to his service by his bounty—"that I may *prove* them whether they will walk in my law or not." For God by bounties or afflictions, by gifts or their withdrawal, to put men to the *trial* and *proof whether* they will *obey or not*, is but employing on his part a necessary means to advance his honor and their welfare : though, unavoidably, it may afford an occasion for men to be *tempted* by their own lusts, or of the devil, to *do evil rather* than obey. But God tempteth no one neither is tempted, *to evil.*

But let, us look at the trial which, at this time of profound peace, the Lord suddenly appointed his servant.

Following the guidance of the history, which presents the distinct parts of the subject in their true order, we will notice,

I. The command of God imposing the trying sacrifice;

II. The obedience of Abraham in performing the command ; and

III. The gain that resulted to both at the close,—both God the Ruler and Abraham his servant.

I. The command of God which imposed the trial upon Abraham, is introduced and stated in these words : v. 1,— " God said unto him, Abraham : and he said, Behold here I am.  (v. 2.) And he said, Take now thy son, thine only son—whom thou lovest—Isaac " :—I give, in this reading, not the order of our translation, which introduces the name before the description is finished, but the order of the Hebrew which with fine effect, keeps back the name, Isaac, to the close :—" Take Isaac, and get thee into the land of Moriah ; and offer him there for a burnt offering upon one of the mountains which I will tell thee of."

Before giving the trying command, God summons the presence and attention of Abraham, that he may give ear to some order which he is to receive and that he may be ready to execute it : " Abraham," 'my servant, whom I have called ; with whom I have made my covenant ;

whom I have charged to walk before me and be perfect: hear my voice.' Abraham, like a ready and attentive servant, at once replies: " Behold, here I am." 'Speak, Lord; for thy servant heareth.'

The order is now pronounced in words and tones which fall with deepening terror on the heart of this father, and this inheritor of the promises; and which put to the utmost task his faith in the goodness and in the covenant of his God.

" Take now thy son." The patriarch, I imagine, at the first mention of his son, startled as with some strange apprehension, might have kept back his heart from the worst awhile by wavering between his two sons, after this sort: ' I have two sons, Ishmael and Isaac:' take "thy only son "; ' but both are only sons of their mothers ': ' take the one ' " whom thou lovest"; ' but I love them both :' 'take ' " Isaac"! ' ah! it is he, whom I feared; my darling one, the child of Sarah ; the son of most precious hopes and promises. Yet, doubtless, God will not suffer any evil to befal the child. I have trusted in his wisdom and goodness; I cling to the express promises of his covenant; and what he says I will do, nothing doubting. Well, I will take Isaac: but *where* shall I take him ?'

The word from God proceeds: " And get thee into the land of Moriah." ' Well ; it is a long journey from Beersheba to Moriah; sixty miles, perhaps, through wilderness and over mountain tracts ; there may lie on our path no tent of any hospitable shepherd with whom we may find entertainment ; there may be perils from wild beasts of the wilderness or from robbers: but God commands; I will trust in his providence, and take Isaac to the land of Moriah: but what shall I *do with him* there?'

The order from heaven proceeds: " Offer him there for a burnt offering upon one of the mountains which I will tell thee of." ' Can it be? Do I hear the order aright? There is no mistake. The command is on the ear, distinct as the tones of heaven.' " Offer him there for a burnt offering." What a multitude of thoughts rush upon the heart of the father to crush it, how many suggestions against such a deed are ready to spring up, to prevent obedience : which nothing but unwavering faith in the wisdom and goodness of God can surmount, and render that heart free to obey. ' Can I endure to make such an offering? It would be hard to part with this beloved son by death, even in the usual course of providence by disease; it would be harder still to have him taken away from me by the hand of violence, were the blow struck by a stranger : but to have this arm inflict the death-wound,—the arm of the father—the arm that has so often clung around him with affection—the arm on which he has always rested for safety : how can my heart be nerved to the deed? But God commands : and shall I not hush every distressing emotion with the thought that his infinite wisdom and goodness are back of me, giving direction, by explicit command, to my will and my arm. I have been wont to yield implicit obedience, trusting in his wisdom and goodness, and in his word of promise : and shall I not do it now? Yet never before have I received from him any command which seemed so contrary to his character for wisdom and goodness and so contradictory to his own promises, as this. What possible honor to God or pleasure can be derived from a human sacrifice? How will the nations be shocked at so unnatural a deed on the part of a father, and reproach the God whom I serve for his cruel exaction? What too will become of his promise to me : " In Isaac shall thy seed be called?" Shall posterity arise from the ashes of the dead? I am now left with a bare command from God; a severe command : no explanation accompanies it, no assignment of reasons, no promise : it is sole and simple authority. He seems purposely to have withdrawn from me every support out of himself and left me to lean on himself alone : as if to see what is the respect I have for his will. I know that he commands the sacrifice. I cannot question his right to dispose of the temporal life of men. Nor is it my place to wait till I see *how* he will defend his honor and my character, or *how* he will fulfil his own promise to me, before I obey his known will.

His command is upon me: and I know that I am safe, and safe only in obeying his voice. His command is upon me: and I know that he can and will defend his honor and protect my character and fulfil his own promise when I obey. Whether I can see the particular *way* in which he will do it or not, I know that he *will* do it in *some* way. I resolve, therefore, to leave all in his hands, and follow his will. I will take Isaac, whom I have *received* from God as one raised up from the very dead, and, in the land of Moriah and on the mount which shall be shown to me, I will *offer* him *to God* as a burnt-offering; trusting that the same power which has done so much to. fulfil the promise already, will, in this last extremity, raise up his life from the dead, if needs be.'

But to resolve on obedience is easier far than to perform: and the spirit of obedience is proved to exist, and is ripened into full strength, only as it is carried out into execution in the particular deeds of the life. Let us, then,

II. Consider the obedience of Abraham, as made manifest in being carried out to the full in the performance of the commanded offering.

His respect to the will of God was clearly made manifest to rise supreme above every opposing consideration; because he not only resolved in his heart to obey that will when it required the greatest temporal sacrifice he could make, but he began at once to put the resolve into execution, and carried it forward through every obstacle to the accomplishment.

He began at once to put his resolve of obedience into execution: as the history, immediately after reciting the command of God, proceeds to say (v. 3): "And Abraham rose up early in the morning and saddled his ass; and took two of his young men with him, and Isaac his son: and clave the wood for the burnt offering." At the earliest dawn of day, this prompt and faithful patriarch provides the necessary means for accomplishing the offering. He orders his faithful beast of burthen to be made ready for carrying provisions and relieving him in his old age of the tedious foot-walk, in which the rest of the party in the vigor of their youth are to engage. Two of his young men-servants are selected to accompany him on the expedition with their services, and these, with Isaac, form the party. By his orders wood is taken, probably from a seasoned pile near his tent, and cleft for burning :. that everything may be ready on his arrival at the mount of sacrifice. While this work of preparation is going forward, no suspicion or alarm, it would seem, is awakened in Sarah or in any of the numerous household. The only interest which she or they appear to take in this little group, with their patriarch head, in their preparations for departure, is that of an absence for a .few days on some ordinary expedition. Doubtless Abraham revealed not the dreadful secret even to Sarah, but kept it locked up in his own breast, that she and all he loved might, with him, abide the issue. With what a cool and deliberate purpose of obedience, then, must he have gone through this work of preparation before his household, not to betray, by any outward signals of look, tone or action, the unwonted emotions at work in his heart ; not to excite any suspicion in others of the dreadful task he was preparing to accomplish !

All things being in readiness, he now proceeds to carry out his purpose of obedience through every obstacle to its accomplishment. The history thus mentions the departure (v. 3) : He " rose up and went "—*i. e.*, started to go, for it is the journey begun, and not the journey accomplished, which is here spoken of—" unto the place of which God had told him." The moment of departure is one of deep interest ever to both fragments of the parting household. The oneness that unites all hearts seeks expression, at the time of separation, in farewells and blessings ; in pledges of remembrance ; in hopes of re-union. But now one heart—that of the patriarch head of the household— bears on it a load it must not express, it must not betray. But there is faith in God to bear up, at this hour, that heart with all its load. He is on his course of obedience to God. So, as the party take leave of their friends at

Beersheba—Isaac of his mother and the domestics—the young men of their fellow-servants and their mistress—the patriarch, with manly composure, pronounces his benediction on the household ; then mounts his animal to lead the way ; and the party, turning their faces northward, depart for the land of Moriah. (v. 4.) " Then on the third day Abraham lifted up his eyes and' saw the place afar off." For two days the party had been advancing. Isaac and the wood are constantly in sight of the patriarch ; the dreadful work appointed him is ever in prospect ; yet with deliberate purpose he moves steadily forward. There might have been bright and beautiful scenes of nature through which they passed during these days, which Isaac and the young men in their freedom from care admired, and called upon the patriarch to admire with them : and though his heart was charged with graver cares, yet doubtless he refused not to admire with them the glorious works of God. They may talk of other days and of the friends they have left behind them : yet does he not refuse to turn from the painful prospect before him to hold communion in their feelings and joys. His heart is fixed, trusting in God ; and so he has leisure to mingle in the interests of others; and does not betray to them the dreadful object of his solemn and deliberate purpose. But now, on the third day, a mountain range is seen, loading with its green wooded domes and its grey masses of rock the northern horizon. On one of these mountain tops appears the signal of heaven—the cloud of light and glory—noting it as the place chosen of the Lord for the offering. It is that mount Moriah on which in after times the temple of Solomon was built ;† that mountain elevation on which Christ, the Only Begotten Son of the Father, the promised seed of Abraham, was offered up for the sin of the world that he might extend the blessings of salvation to all the families of the earth. But now, overlooking the hills and valleys far around, it raises its lofty and rocky summit into the sky, in all the

---

† 2 Chron. iii: 1.

silence and rugged grandeur of nature. No voice of man is heard, no mark of his industry seen, on this vast altar pile in the temple of creation.

But the place is approached: and now the patriarch must set himself, more seriously and exclusively, to accomplish the sad duty before him. (v. 5, 6.) "And Abraham said unto the young men, Abide ye here with the ass: and I and the lad will go yonder and worship, and come again to you. And Abraham took the wood of the burnt offering, and laid it upon Isaac his son: and he took the fire in his hands and a knife: and they went both of them together." Another step is now taken towards the execution of his purpose. The young men-servants would be in his way at the serious hour of sacrifice: they might disturb his composure or effectually resist the offering. They are left, therefore, to wait till his return. But what mean these words of Abraham at parting: " *We* will come again to you." Had the dead ever returned to life? or did he now yield up his purpose, and resolve, after all, that in the last extremity he would spare the lad? No. But he believes in the promise of God; "In Isaac shall thy seed be called"; and the hope of a resurrection to life has sprung up in his heart. So he goes forth to ascend the heights of Moriah, Isaac, the unconscious victim, bearing the fuel, to be consumed together with it; he carrying in his own hand the knife and the fire, the weapons of destruction. Oh! as on that lonely walk they pass through the forests at the foot of Moriah and clamber up its sides together, will not the father relent and give way? No; the command of God is upon him: that command nerves his heart to obey and to cast all its anxieties and cares upon God. Up as they ascend from one elevation to another, his purpose remains settled on faith in the wisdom and goodness of God, firm as each pinnacle of rock on its everlasting basis. But the silence of their walk is, for a moment, interrupted by this short dialogue. (v. 7, 8.) "And Isaac spake unto Abraham his father, and said: My father: and he said, Here am I, my son. And he said, Behold the fire and the wood: but where is the lamb for a burnt offering? And Abraham said, My son, God will provide himself a lamb for a burnt offering." The loving and confiding eye of Isaac, striking upon the eye of the father, and sending such a piercing question to his inmost soul, must have overpowered a mind that was not immovably fixed in its purpose. But Abraham remained unmoved : and, not to disclose as yet the real victim, referred the whole matter to God to provide a lamb for a victim—the innocent lamb before him, that had been nurtured in his own bosom. (v. 8, 9.) " So they went both of them together. And they came to the place which God had told him of." The place where he had seen the signal of God resting—the cloud of light and glory. Here on the table land of the mountain top ; on some open area where the altar may rest, and upon which the sun is pouring down his meridian rays; surrounded by the darkness and thickets of the forest ; in this temple, built of God ; stand the father and son, to make ready for the sacrifice. (v. 9.) " And Abraham built an altar there, and laid the wood in order." Sad task, indeed ! Each stone which they bring to the structure, each piece of fragrant turf which they lay upon it, appears to the patriarch already to teem with the blood of Isaac, and puts a load on his heart heavier far than it does upon the earth. Yet he is fixed immovably in purpose : the structure is completed : the wood laid upon it in order, suited to the burning. The hour of sacrifice has now come. The victim must be taken, bound, slain. The purpose of Abraham can no longer remain concealed from his son. How now will he advance to his task? in silence and with force? will he suddenly lay hands upon his son, and, in his haste and violence, appear unto him as the frantic maniac? What then will Isaac do? In the solitude of the forest, far from his loved mother and her household, beyond the hearing of the young men, no stranger nigh, despairing of any pity in the breast of a father, so alienated and maddened with delirious phrensy, will he seize a billet from the altar, and with equal fury rush to disarm the father, or take life for life? No: the mind that is fulfilling the will of God, is ever calm and rational; and seeks, in accomplishing its purpose, the methods of wisdom. No doubt, avoiding every show of force, in a cool and rational manner, Abraham disclosed the dread secret so long laboring in his breast, by entering into free and serious conversation with his son. There in the deep solitude beside the altar, in the presence of God, he tells him, doubtless, of the command which he has received; to fulfil which, he has taken the journey with him and brought him up the mount. He may reason with him, from the signal of divine glory which both had seen that morning, hovering over the place, that truly God *had ordered* and *was superintending* the strange and trying sacrifice. He may reason with him on the obligation that now rests upon both alike to comply with this most trying will of God; on the faith which it becomes both to put, notwithstanding this season of darkness, in the goodness and in the promises of God, and the expectation which both may cherish that, after the hour of sacrifice, there will be a resurrection to life again, and a happier meeting than now. For it could not be, that Abraham would have refrained from inculcating upon his child the duty of submission, at the hour of death; nor would he leave the matter, if it could possibly be settled thus peaceably by voluntary submission, to come to a violent contest of physical force. Isaac, too, whether he had ever yielded his heart to God before or not, doubtless at this solemn hour bowed in submission to the trying will of God; and consented, like his great Archetype, the Son of God, to surrender himself a voluntary victim for the sacrifice. For he resisted not: and though called a lad, he might, with that title as then used, have been of full age; and, in his vigorous youth, have proved a match for the physical strength of the aged patriarch. Gently then, we may believe, the hand of the father winds the cords around his yielding son: and so " he bound Isaac and laid him on the altar upon the wood." The agonizing moment has come. The trembling victim lies, expecting the pangs of death. The heart-aching offerer of

the sacrifice stands ready to slay.  (v. 10.) "And Abraham
stretched forth his hand and took the knife to slay his son."
He grasps the deadly weapon; he raises his arm; the fatal
blow ——— is arrested by a voice from heaven. (v. 11, 12.)
"The angel of the Lord called unto him, Abraham,
Abraham : and he said, Here am I.  And he said, Lay
not thine hand upon the lad, neither do thou anything
unto him."  The sacrifice is thus prevented at the last
moment, by the same authority which had commanded it.
For it was enough.  The trial of Abraham was complete;
and his obedience finished.  But one muscular effort of
his arm remained; and that was kept back in mercy.  For
it was not *blood* that Jehovah sought, but *obedience*.  The
command is obeyed, to the very last act, in the spirit and
intention of Abraham.  All who ever hear of it will
acknowledge that he would have struck the blow, and
have completed his task, had it not been for this sudden
stay put on the whole proceeding by an order from the
Lord.  The trial is closed; and God has secured the
result at which he aimed; a result to Himself and his
servant full worthy of the whole trial.  But let us, more
particularly, consider,

III. The gain that resulted from the trial to both parties—God the Ruler, and Abraham his servant.

The history shows us, that, without any evil resulting
to Isaac, Abraham obtained, through his persevering
obedience in the trial, the approving testimony of God;
the joy of a thank-offering for delivering mercy ; and an
assurance stronger than ever of an interest in the
promises.

No evil has befallen Isaac.  The order from heaven,
" Lay not thine hand upon the lad," has saved him harmless.  The sharp trial, too, of the moment when he
learned the will of the Lord and submitted himself as a
victim, has passed away forever; while the consciousness
of his own submission, and thankfulness to God for
deliverance, remain as permanent sources of satisfaction
in his future life.

Abraham, by means of the trial, secured to himself the *approving testimony* of God. The Angel of the Lord, calling out of heaven to stay the procedure of Abraham, pronounces the testimony : (v.12.) " For now I know that thou fearest God, seeing thou hast not withheld thy son, thine only son from me." God has witnessed the patriarch on all his way of obedience. He has seen him in his faith and obedience persevering through every obstacle to the last, putting honor on his character, increasing his own holiness; and now the hour of his testimony is come. He is pleased : and gives out a testimony of approbation that will abide a source of joy to the patriarch long after the pangs of his three days of trial are gone. " Now I know " is the heavenly testimony, " that thou fearest God." ' I know that thy respect is supreme above every opposing consideration :' " seeing thou hast not withheld thy son, thine only son from me." ' The evidence is out, in thy favor and to my honor. I can now speak to all with certainty about Abraham. I can point to him as having gone through this trial with honor to me : and say to any one in my kingdom; That is the man that truly respects me. I can now publish the evidence given in this trial as an example to my kingdom. That man I can always trust to obey my orders. The fruits of righteousness abound in him to my glory. I am honored greatly, and my servant Abraham advanced in his faith and obedience.' And so at the close of the trial God and he rejoice together in the approving testimony obtained by faithful obedience.

To this approving testimony there was added the joy of a thank-offering, provided by the delivering grace of God. (v. 13.) " And Abraham lifted up his eyes, and looked, and behold behind him a ram caught in a thicket by his horns: and Abraham went and took the ram, and offered him up for a burnt offering in the stead of his son." As Abraham stood with Isaac by the altar, and beheld the substitute which the delivering mercy of God had provided, what a tide of thankfulness rises in his heart! The love of God that seemed hid awhile behind a passing cloud has broke forth in full luster upon his soul : and in the smoke of the sacrifice substituted for Isaac, he wafts up to heaven the lively breathings of joy, the glowing emotions of thankfulness ; for God and he rejoice together more sweetly than ever in the sun-light of deliverance. (v. 14.) "And Abraham called the name of the place Jehovah-Jireh: as it is said to this day, in the mount of the Lord it shall be seen,"—or, as the Hebrew is better rendered, "In the mount the Lord will be seen or appear." His grateful testimony for God he left for-ever there in the name he put upon the place : and to the day of Moses, and to this day even, it is a proverb among the faithful, that in the mount of difficulty and trial to his people, God will appear ;—that their extremity of want is God's opportunity to come with delivering grace.

In addition to the approving testimony of God and great joy in his delivering grace, Abraham obtained also a fuller assurance than ever of his interest in the promises. His hope is caused to abound the more in the certainty and joy of their fulfilment. There might, as a conse-quence of the teachings of a resurrection during the trial, have sprung up in his mind more enlarged views than ever of the extent of the promises, and, in consequence of this deliverance, greater confidence in the purpose of God to accomplish them all. But he was not left to reap hope from experience alone. The Lord, for his great pleasure and joy in his servant, comes nigh to give him direct assurance. (v. 15.) "And the Angel of the Lord called unto Abraham out of heaven the second time, (v. 16) And said, By myself have I sworn, saith the Lord, for because thou hast done this thing and hast not withheld thy son, thine only son : (v. 17) That in blessing I will bless thee, and in multiplying I will multiply thy seed as the stars of heaven, and as the sand which is upon the sea shore ; and thy seed shall possess the gate of his enemies. (v. 18.) And in thy seed shall all the nations of the earth be blessed : because thou hast obeyed my voice." These promises which were first announced to him at the time of his extraordinary call : which were repeated to him and sealed as a covenant by the rite of circumcision, at the annunciation of the birth of Isaac : are now re-pronounced, as made sure by his having stood the trial faithfully, and are now prefaced, as never before, by that highest and most solemn of all assurances which can be given—an oath : the Lord, as he could swear by no greater, swearing by himself : " By myself have I sworn, saith the Lord." So Abraham, as it is represented in the epistle to the Hebrews, " after he had patiently endured, obtained the promise " : and both God and he rejoiced together over greater security obtained on earth to the plans of good included in the promises.

(v. 19.) " So Abraham," bearing these new and permanent spiritual treasures within his joyous heart, " returned " with Isaac " unto his young men, and they rose up and went together to Beersheba."

Such is the close of this extraordinary trial of character. The life that God, the Supreme Disposer, might have taken, and over which the dark cloud of trial hung, is spared. Abraham, for the faith and obedience which he has strengthened in his own heart, and by which he has publicly honored the authority of God, takes with him, to his dwelling at Beersheba, and to his altar of devotion in the grove, for his after life, the approving testimony of God ; a heart made grateful by delivering grace ; and a hope made strong by two immutable things—in which it is impossible for God to lie—his utterance of the promises and his oath for their fulfilment.

This trial of Abraham, the history of which has engaged our attention, is fraught with instruction to the people of God in all ages.

I observe,

1. That this trial, besides its design of proving the character of Abraham, serves to illustrate, by an analogy near to our hearts, the great love of God in making the offering of his Only Begotten Son. No one, who observes how God began and carried forward in those early ages his school of spiritual instruction, by setting up in outward forms typical analogies and illustrations of the spiritual, as in the very institution of sacrifice ; or who notices the striking peculiarities attendant on the burnt-

offering assigned to Abraham, will fail to see shadowed forth in it the great offering made of that seed of Abraham, greater than Isaac, who has come to bless all the families of the earth, the Only Begotten Son of the Father. A father called to yield up his only son in sacrifice—the stroke of death to be inflicted by his own hands—the mount of Moriah selected as the place—the voluntary submission of the victim at the time of sacrifice—all serve to set forth the trial of that hour when the sword of Jehovah was lifted up against Him that was his Fellow, bowing meekly to receive the stroke on this very mount : while the change of the human offering for the ram that the Lord provided, serves to set forth the love that made that great offering on Calvary, a substitute for the penalty of death incurred by man for his sin. Whether God made such a thing known at the time to Abraham or not, whether Abraham saw in it any typical teaching of the future or not, he has lived to see it in his heavenly abode : and to all Christians on earth, it has set forth an illustration, clear and affecting to the heart, because most near and intimate to themselves in their own parental and filial relations.

And, Oh ! what a day to Abraham in heaven was that when Jesus, his son as to the flesh, God's Son as to his Eternal Spirit, walked upon those same rugged heights bearing the heavy load of his cross ! It is not now the solitary mount, without inhabitant, and covered with the thickets of the forest. The splendid temple of Jehovah, and the palaces of the kings, with their lofty towers and gilded domes, occupy those heights : and the soldiers of Cæsar and the rabble of Jerusalem accompany, with clamorous tread, the walk of Jesus. Yet onward he goes, deserted of friends, surrounded by the din of the thought-less or the reviling : and submits to be nailed to the cross and to die, an offering to God substituted in behalf of the believing for the eternal fire-offering, which the law exacted of guilty man. If tears could flow in heaven, must not that venerable patriarch, touched with fellow sympathies gained in his school of trial, have wept that

day at the thought of what was passing in the hearts of
the Eternal Father and his Son.  There could now be no
exchange in the victim, as was made in his case; yet a
resurrection to life was in prospect to this Son of Promise:
and the patriarch could rejoice that, on that rising to life
again, He should have a seed that should prolong their
happy days to eternity.  Such thoughts have often come
into the minds of Christians on earth, as they have read
the history of the patriarch's trial, and aided their fellowship with Christ in his sufferings; and caused their hearts
to abound with thanksgivings to God, for his great love
wherewith he hath loved them in providing this Lamb
from his own bosom as a sacrifice to take away their sins.

But looking to the more immediate design of the trial
of Abraham as a trial of character, I observe,

2. That God appoints trials to his people, out of faithful
regard to their highest welfare.

The welfare of his people depends on the cultivation in
their own hearts of a spirit of faith and obedience towards
God; for by this spirit only can they honor him before
his kingdom, or receive to themselves the benefits of his
wisdom, power and goodness.  But in order to improve
and strengthen such a spirit in man, it is not well that he
be left to uninterrupted prosperity in all things.  His
heart is so inclined to be its own master, to follow its own
devices, to rest on temporal possessions and joys for all,
that if no trial from the hand of God come to cross and
thwart its perverse tendencies, it withdraws itself almost
insensibly from supreme trust in God and implicit obedience to his will.  Had he been left in his prosperity without this trial, Abraham might have found his heart, even
at the very altar of his devotion in the grove, withdrawing gradually from God and settling down on the gifts
already accumulated around him as his portion.  Faithful
regard to his welfare moved God to appoint a severe
trial, which would hedge up his way against the idolatrous love of anything, however dear, which he might
call his own; and bring him to such straits, as that he
should cast himself with all his possessions and wants

afresh on the care of God in faith, and submit all to the will of God in implicit obedience. The appointment therefore was not arbitrary and gratuitous; but dictated by faithful regard to Abraham, that he might be made to partake more fully as a servant in the joys of the divine holiness.

The people of God therefore should ever account the trials, which come upon them on their path of duty, as his wise appointments. Though they may not see the wisdom and goodness of just such trials and afflictions as befal them, yet that is precisely the discipline which a faithful God sees them to need: to be put to the proof by trials, the wisdom and goodness of which they do not particularly see at the time: trials, the wisdom and goodness of which lie concealed, as yet, in the breast of God: trials, which call off their hearts from self-reliance, and dependence on creatures, that they may rest alone on God, the fountain of spiritual happiness. Should not the people of God then, whenever a trial meets them on their path, confess in it the hand of faithfulness, and without murmuring at the allotment, gird up their whole strength to the work of endurance? Shall not they who see the necessity of the discipline of their earthly parents, much more confess the wisdom and goodness of the discipline appointed by the Father of spirits? Should they not regard his allotments, even when most painful, as evidences of a Father's heart and a Father's care?—as proof that he is training them as sons and daughters for honor and glory in his eternal kingdom?

I observe,

3. From the trial of Abraham, the people of God may derive encouragement in the hour of trial to endure patiently the will of God.

For each trial, however severe or protracted, being appointed by faithful love, in · order to benefit and not destroy, will come to a close: and when God appears to bring it to an end, then to meet him with a spirit that has held on to faith and obedience to the last, will bring a harvest of delight to the soul, in possessing the approbation of God, and sharing with him in the gains of obedience and the joys of deliverance, which will overbalance, far, all the pains of endurance.

Though his trial was not such as is common to man, Abraham had to endure it but three days: and the faith, with which he rested on God in those days of darkness, satisfied his heart more at the time than the pleasures of sin could have done: and when patience had completed its work on the mount of sacrifice, what blessed results arose to his soul at the coming of God! There was the consciousness of having done the will of God, at the greatest earthly sacrifice: there was a feast of joy partaken with God in his testimony to faithfulness and in the sweet experience of delivering grace: there was the sunlight of hope casting its happy radiance over the future: that made the very mount of sacrifice an emblem of the heights of heavenly blessedness. Nor are the spiritual results, which are gained by patient endurance, momentary. They are treasured up in the ever living spirit; deposited among its memories, stored with its affections, commingled with its joys forever.

Be encouraged then, child of God, whatever trial he appoints thee, to endure it, with firm and patient submission to his will. If it seems severe; if it seems protracted; if thy heart is almost ready to faint within thee; hold on in faith and steady submission. The path he appoints thee may seem dreary. There may be mountains of difficulty to ascend. But trust in the Lord who leads thee. Trust him for his wisdom. Trust him for his kindness and mercy. Not beyond what thou art able to bear, not without any way of escape, will he make thy burthen. Hold on with patient endurance. The hour of deliverance is to come. On the mount the Lord will appear. And at his appearing, hope, love, joy, shall be shed abroad abundantly in thy heart as the results of thy patient endurance.

> "Ye fearful saints, fresh courage take,
> The clouds you so much dread
> Are filled with mercy, and shall break
> With blessings on your head."

"Be patient therefore, brethren," under all the earthly trials which may be appointed you, "unto the " final "coming of the Lord." On the ways of this life, the will of God made manifest in his precepts or his providence, will appoint you trials, more or less severe. You may pray that he would not lead you into them; and while they are upon you, that he would deliver you. You may use all lawful and suitable means to avoid their occurrence; to shorten their continuance; to lighten their burthen. Still, if you are his beloved children whom he is training for heaven, you cannot avoid them utterly. He will appoint them for discipline, and you must bear them with patience. Think, whenever they come upon you, of the faithful love that appoints them, and of the encouragements to endure. "Behold," in the examples of those who have lived before us, "we count them happy which endure." Their faith, though tried as gold in the fire, is a treasure far more precious than gold, and, through the refining, "will be found unto praise and honor and glory at the appearing of Jesus Christ."

And now, children of the apostasy, who have not yet obeyed the call of God, and put yourselves under the care and discipline of his grace, hearken to me. If severe trials are thus appointed to those who accept the call of God and walk in his ways; if judgments must invade the very sanctuary of his grace for the correction of his people; if the sons and daughters of the Almighty, whom he has adopted forever into his household, cannot be saved without scourging: what will the end be of those who obey not his call of mercy; who refuse to take shelter in his sanctuary; who persist, as aliens and enemies, in despising and trampling on all the orderings of his authority?

Oh! there is, one day, a burnt-offering to be made greater than was commanded on Moriah! The wicked who refuse to return to God, who continue to despise the orderings of his righteous will and to oppose his obedient servants, shall all be assembled in his presence. Before the great multitude of his saints, who have made their peace and covenant with him through the great sin-offering presented on Calvary—before this multitude of his saints, will he show himself true: and, as for ages he has forewarned the world, will he institute the great burnt-offering that is to honor his long insulted justice. He will whet his glittering sword. His hand will take hold on judgment. No voice of mercy will on that day arrest the stroke. His sword will devour the flesh, and be drunk with the blood of the assembled hosts. A fire will be kindled in his anger, which shall burn to the lowest hell. And upon these flames, which are never to be quenched, shall they be thrown, and the smoke of their torment shall ascend as a perpetual burnt-offering before his kingdom, to exalt his justice forever.

Will you pursue the pleasures of sin for a short season, to be devoured in these flames? Will you not choose rather to obey the will of God and suffer affliction with his people for a little, that you may partake of their eternal triumphs at his coming?

Behold he has set up his standard of salvation in the midst of you. He is now calling to himself a people. That call is resounding in your ears. Why linger ye? Gather yourselves together now to the Lord of Hosts, the Saviour of Israel. Fashion yourselves no longer after your former lusts. Be holy, as he is who calleth you. Put yourselves under his direction and care; and go forward with his people, on the path of obedience and trial, to their triumphant joy in his heavenly kingdom.

RUTH 1, 15: 16.

BEHOLD THY SISTER-IN-LAW IS GONE BACK UNTO HER PEOPLE AND UNTO HER GODS: RETURN THOU AFTER THY SISTER-IN-LAW. AND RUTH SAID, INTREAT ME NOT TO LEAVE THEE, OR RETURN FROM FOLLOWING AFTER THEE: FOR WHITHER THOU GOEST, I WILL GO; AND WHERE THOU LODGEST I WILL LODGE: *thy people shall be my people, and thy God shall be my God.*

THIS resolve of Ruth's was fixed: fixed in an iron will; a will not to be bent or broken from its purpose; yet conducting a gentle and affectionate heart to its chosen fortunes with the people and into the service of Jehovah.

This resolution of hers was intended to put away from her all further entreaty or plea to the contrary; and was uttered as final: "intreat me not——my God."

To estimate her resolution aright, we need to see what thoughts were crowding upon her heart at the time she uttered it, the thoughts that came rushing to her from the history of her past life. Ten years before this period, Naomi, with whom she was now journeying, had come to Moab, having migrated thither with her husband and two sons from the land of Judah, bringing with them the knowledge of the true God. Elimelech, the husband of Naomi, soon died: yet by the marriage of her sons with Orpah and Ruth, two of the daughters of Moab, the widow rejoiced in the affectionate hearts that were joined to her family circle. Yet this happy scene was soon broken up by the hand of death. Mahlon and Chilian were gathered to their father, Elimelech, in the grave: and over the last resting place of the father and sons the widowed mother and her two widowed daughters-in-law mingle the tears of bereavement and bitterness.

In this state of bereavement, Naomi resolved to return to the home of her youth; when Orpah and Ruth, with truly filial affection, resolved to accompany her and share with her the fortunes of life. When they commenced their journey, Naomi, out of regard to the temporal welfare of her daughters, besought them to go back and remain with their kindred and friends: and kissed them in token of bestowing her blessing and love on them at parting. But they lifted up their voices and wept; saying, surely we will return with thee unto thy people. Naomi again strenuously besought them not to accompany her in their destitute and unprotected widowhood, but to return to their acquaintances in Moab. The thought of separation grieved them, and they lifted up their voices and wept again. But Orpah, though grieved, now acceded to the proposal of her mother; and, sealing her friendship at parting with a kiss, went back unto her idolatrous countrymen. Ruth still clave unto her mother, refusing to return; and they proceeded on their journey. But Naomi, as even pious parents are prone to be, was so solicitous to ensure what appeared to be the temporal interest of Ruth as to hazard her spiritual welfare, and again urged her to return to her idolatrous countrymen, beseeching her to unite herself to the society of her now absent sister. But this last and strong appeal to the affectionate heart of Ruth was not sufficient to move her from her resolution. "Intreat me not," says she, "to leave thee or to return from following after thee, for whither thou goest, I will go; and where thou lodgest I will lodge; *thy people* shall be *my people*, and *thy God* shall be *my God*."

There was much of filial affection, doubtless, in this strong unyielding resolution of Ruth: but may we not believe there was also the deep desire of spiritual improvement? She resolved to give up her portion in the land of idols and find it in the land of God. I will give up the vain gods of my youth and the society of my idolatrous countrymen, even that of my sister; and go and unite myself to God and his people, asking a reception into the privilege of worshipping and serving him in the congregation of his people, even though it be as a proselyte of the gate in the outer court of the Gentiles.

This noble resolution of Ruth to unite herself in resistance to all entreaties and pleas to the contrary to the people and to the God of Israel, and cast in her lot immovably with theirs, is worthy of the imitation of all to whom, by the knowledge of the Lord Jesus Christ and the presence of his Church, opportunity is given to form the union. For in covenanting to take the Lord as our God, and his people as our spiritual associates, as they are offered to our acceptance, we enter into a union which ensures our spiritual and perpetual well-being, while withdrawal from such union necessarily subjects our whole being to the endurance of evil. Our subject will be the grounds which justify such a firm resolve, as they are set forth in the blessings of spiritual fellowship with God and his people, and the evils necessarily consequent on withdrawal from that fellowship.

1. Holy fellowship with God and his people is a source of the purest friendship: that of God and his saints. In the weakness that attaches to us as finite beings and the dangers that surround us from temptation and sin, what a value is there in pure friendship! In this selfish world the possession of a single friend who is pure in his love, who is devoted to our spiritual welfare, and who will adhere to us in all the changes of our condition, is a greater blessing than all earthly treasures in comparison. What an unspeakable blessing then is it, to enjoy the friendship of God and his saints! Yet if we unite ourselves to the people of God, they are our friends. They pledge themselves to be our friends in all circumstances of our condition. We are sure, as one with them in the bonds of Christ, of receiving their sympathy in our trials, the aid of their counsels and prayers in our wants and dangers, and their countenance and coöperation in our labors of benevolence. If we unite ourselves to God, this glorious Being is our Friend and Father. He pledges to us in sacred covenant his holy and unchangeable friend-

ship. His eye of omniscience is ever on us for good, his ear is open to our cries, his hand of power is around us for our protection, his wisdom instructs and guides us, his mercy blots out our iniquities in free forgiveness, his grace sanctifies and saves our souls. His heart of fatherly love is intent on our welfare, his Son is our advocate and head, his Holy Spirit is our gracious indwelling Comforter, the witness and seal of his love.

Is not the very possession of such a sympathizing friendship, flowing to us from the heart of God, and the hearts of his people, a rich treasure of joy? The very feeling that God, and that, as far as they know us, his spiritual household, are not only at peace with us, but tenderly sympathize with us in our hopes and fears, our joys and sorrows, —throws a sweet solace over the trials of the present state, sheds full joy into the cup of present blessings, and is one of the elements of the cloudless and overflowing pleasures of heaven.

2. Holy fellowship with God and his people leads to the most *exalted employments of benevolence*. What a rich field of benevolent employment is set before us in fellowship with God and his people. We are in a world that God has made, filled with immortal beings, over whom he has exercised a kind providence and righteous government, who yet have wandered from his worship and service into the ruinous blindness and perverseness of sin. In such a world God is redeeming a people to himself by his Son and Spirit, diffusing abroad the light of spiritual knowledge, the healing influence of sanctifying power. In maintaining fellowship with God and his people, therefore, it is our exalted and worthy employment to promote this work of God that redounds to his glory and human salvation. His wisdom has contrived and set before us the means on which our own faculties may be wisely employed, his grace has set before us the field into which we may enter and where we may reap a glorious harvest of good to his praise. And how is the joy of this benevolent employment heightened by conscious unity with God and his people. If by any means I am an instrument

of converting a sinner from the error of his ways or of strengthening a Christian brother in the way of the Lord, I have done it not alone, but as one with God and his people: and I know, not only that joy is imparted to the individual but that the event will cause benevolent joy to the holy brethren who hear of it, that it gives joy to the heart of the Eternal Father, and that God, from whom all grace proceeds, will be honored in consequence with an increasing tribute of praise. In this field of benevolent employment I appropriate to myself too the joy of what God and his people do in the same work. The object is one: and when I meditate on God and see the wisdom and power and goodness and righteousness he exercised in the original creation, and the goodness and super-abounding grace he manifests in the new creation by Jesus Christ, what joy his infinite heart takes in his works and what joys flow from them to the hearts of his holy and redeemed creatures, I am supremely blessed in his blessedness, I adore him for his wisdom and goodness, I praise him for the help and the blessings imparted from his throne to his dependent creatures. So, too, in this blessed field of benevolence, which is one alike in all places and in all ages, when I contemplate what any of his servants have done in past ages, or hear of what they are now doing in distant places, or see what they are doing around me, to promote in the earth the glorious cause of God, I rejoice in their joy and success and in the healing light of their example; and, for it all, I thank the God of grace.

This deep, ever flowing and ever increasing source of joy, is opened to us in that cause of benevolence for which God has associated with himself a peculiar people, zealous of good works. In the results that flow from this benevolent union, our hearts may at times overflow with joy, even here in this world, while in the field of labor and trial, while far from our Father's house, while immediately surrounded but by few of his people, and opposed by the armies of the aliens. What then shall be the joy of the benevolent laborers, when they shall have all come

in from their fields of toil to their Father's house in
heaven, bringing their sheaves with them from the four
winds, shouting the harvest home!

3. Holy fellowship with God and his people leads to
*our own spiritual improvement.* It is in union to the
Church of Christ only that we can expect to receive
spiritual edification, to persevere and grow in grace, and
increase in the knowledge of Christ. For Christ has
introduced into this body, ordinances and means of grace
designed for their use and edification. He has appointed
his holy sabbath as a day for their assembling, a day
hallowed to sacred rest and holy contemplation; he has
given them his word abounding in the instructions of his
own wisdom and love; he has given them the privilege of
uniting their hearts together at the throne of all grace in
prayer and praise; he has instituted for them the public
ministry of his word by teachers and pastors; he has
appointed their mutual watchfulness or united censure for
wholesome discipline; he has appointed the ordinance of
his supper as a memorial of his death and sufferings, at
which they may, in humble, thankful meditation, feast
together upon his love. These means, his wisdom and
love have introduced into his church for the perfecting of
the saints, for the edifying of his body, till they all come
in the unity of the faith and of the knowledge of the Son
of God, unto the measure of the stature of the fullness of
Christ.

Nor shall we fail to persevere and grow in the spiritual
graces of faith and charity, if, in spiritual union to God
and his people, we faithfully apply those means which his
grace appoints and his Spirit blesses to edification in holiness. We shall go forward to fresh victories over sin and
temptation. We shall gather fresh strength to run in the
ways of God. Our love shall abound yet more and more,
and increase in wisdom and prudence and understanding.

And how rich a source of joy is it to be transformed
into the glorious image of the Lord from glory to glory:
to grow up to him in all things who is the Head of all
wisdom and goodness and in whom all fullness dwells:

who is the pattern of all excellence and the admiration and joy of all heaven !

These spiritual attainments and ornaments will be all our own : the very habits of our souls : inwrapped with the very faculties of our natures ; which, unlike external possessions, no enemy can ever wrest from us ; and which shall be like wells of water within us springing up unto everlasting life and joy, increasing the tide of our blessedness here and forevermore.

4. Holy fellowship with God and his people conducts us to *an eternal feast of joy in the kingdom of God in heaven.* There shall we be presented faultless in the presence of God and his saints at the coming of our Lord Jesus Christ : purified from sin and all its evil inclinations ; adorned with perfect rectitude and love. There in the new Jerusalem above, shall we be gathered to the innumerable company of angels, the general assembly of the Church, the Mediator of the new covenant, and God the Judge and Father of all, and taste the sweets of their combined friendship and mingle in their exalted employments of benevolence, without a trial or enemy to disturb us more, to all eternity. There all the scattered rills of joy that pass to refresh us here below, shall meet and commingle into one unbounded ocean of blessedness. There shall the heart of Christ overflow with joy in reaping the rich harvest of his former sufferings, and all heaven exult in his joy and echo with his praise. There shall the Eternal Father rejoice with all his holy ones in having fully answered the prayer which his Son offered to him in the days of his humiliation. ' Father, I pray for those that believe in me, that they all may be one, as thou, Father, art in me and I in thee : that they all may be one in us.' And before his awful throne shall the nations of the saved and glorified bow with joyful adoration and praise. The Church of God—the bride of the Lamb—is there united in the closest bonds of love to her Lord and Saviour, and heaven becomes as it were a marriage supper of pure uninterrupted joy.

O ! what an exalted feast will this be to all the pure

minds of the sanctified in heaven! And should it not be enough to bind our hearts with steadfast resolution to God and his people here in this world of labor and trial and temptation and sin? The thought and hope of it may well yield us many a season of sustaining and refreshing joy, while involved in the conflicts of faith and bearing the heat and burden of our day of toil. It may well sustain us with buoyant hope in that hour when, called from this scene of trial, we must conflict with death, that last enemy of the saints, and lay down these bodies amid pangs and groans in the darkness of the corrupting grave. And when beyond that dark valley we lift up our eyes upon the light and glory of our Father's house in heaven, our admission into this feast of love shall fill our immortal spirits with triumphant and unending joy.

But I mentioned as grounds for cleaving with unshaken purpose to the communion of God and his people, not only the blessing to be derived from such fellowship, but the evil we necessarily incur if we turn away from that fellowship to the idolatry of the world. For if we turn away from God and his people, we do not merely relinquish all hold on the sources of good that are offered us in their fellowship : though this loss is unspeakably great, —utterly wasting to the immortal spirit, and forever irreparable. We necessarily do more. We still exist. The burning energies of life are within us. And if we turn away from this portion, we shall cleave to another. The world will absorb us. Its pleasures shall we seek. Its lusts shall we fulfill. Estranged from God through the blindness of our hearts, and aliens from his Israel, we shall pursue our way of selfishness through the world alone. Yet not wholly alone. We shall be associated with that portion of God's universal kingdom, who have gone off from him in guilty revolt ; who, having broken from the bands of his wholesome authority and trampled on his benevolent laws, and expecting to reap nothing from him but indignation and wrath, hate him, and hate the people whom he saves; who are truly hateful themselves, and who in their selfish malice hate one another.

What evils face us if we turn away from God and his people, and associate ourselves, under Satan the prince of darkness and the god of this world, with the multitude of his followers!

What is their friendship? It is not solicitous for our real welfare. It would bind us only to their selfish, sinful, malicious purposes. It seeks our subservience to sin, and in that very way plots and designs our ruin.

What is their employment? It is self-seeking, that is cursed in the doing, that is cursed in witnessing the guilty subservience of others, that breaks out in a war of mutual wrath and malice when subservience is refused, or that combines only in a greater and more absorbing passion of malice to war against God and his saints.

What is their influence? The heart is hardened yet more and more. The feelings are combining more and more into one blaze of malice. The marks of reprobation thicken upon the wandering outcast. He is fitted for wrath.

And what is the result? He and the whole body to whom he has become leagued are summoned before God the Judge; and there, as those who have made shipwreck of their souls, are they cast off from him and his people, as disturbers of the peace, a useless and mighty wreck, into the depths of hell. And there the fires of malice will burn with anguish, and burn, and burn,—to eternity.

O! is it not a weighty reason to unite ourselves to God and his people, that we cannot give up the blessedness of this fellowship, except on the dreadful alternative of taking up our final portion with the wicked? Shall we give up our portion in heaven and its feast of love, and take it in hell and its fires of malice?

From our subject I remark,

1. They who are already united to the Lord and his people, should cleave to this privilege as their highest honor and joy.

For this fellowship involves in it all their happiness, their spiritual improvement and hopes for eternity, and apart from it there is no portion in the kingdom of God, but utter perdition. And who, in such a wide alternative, should hesitate on which side to take his portion?

Are there trials attendant on your duties? But, by neglecting your duties, you will not fail to encounter trials and severer trials still: and where can you find solace and support under trials like that which is offered you in the communion of the Holy Spirit?

Are there aliens from God and his Israel around you, that would oppose you and put you to shame? Fly then to the friendship of God and his holy ones, which is one day to crown you with glory and cover all his enemies with shame, nor dare, for the sake of receiving present honor from man, to be confounded in the coming day of Christ.

Are there trials from the want of charity in the people of God? Alas! that children of the same father, in the world of their trials and labors, should ever fall out by the way or withdraw the heart from sympathy and love! Yet imperfect as Christian fellowship is in this world, it is a purer and sweeter bond than is known to the werld, and soon it will be perfected in heaven, and you and your fellow Christians will have but one heart of warm and undying charity in the house of your Father on high.

Are there chastenings from the hand of the Lord? But these are wholesome remedies which his friendship administers for our spiritual improvement, to work in us the peaceable fruits of righteousness. We are now chastened, that we may not be condemned with the world. Why then shall we not be subject to the Father of Spirits and live?

Cleave then, brethren, partakers of the heavenly calling, to communion with God and his saints. Walk worthy of him as his dear children, and of your high vocation: inviting, by your faith and prayers and Christian love, the presence of the communing Spirit. For ye are called in one hope of your calling: and there is one Spirit, one Lord, one God and Father of all.

2. The friends of God should ardently seek that converts may be gathered from the world and added to the Lord and his church.

For the world is going forward in alienation from God and his Israel, hardening in guilt and ripening for endless ruin. And the joyful fellowship in Christ to which believers cleave as their hope and joy, presents to these children of sin and error the opportunity of a complete and joyful redemption.

How then should the Spirit of their Lord—who was willing to leave his throne and joy, and to sacrifice himself on the cross for the redemption of the guilty and lost—how should the Spirit of their Lord shine forth in their example before the world, and be breathed forth in their intercourse, to win souls to salvation!

Let them go to the wandering sinner in a spirit of love that longs for him in the fellowship of the Spirit and in the mercies of Christ, and spread before him the invitation of *Christ* that he come to the free and rich feast of the Gospel, and urge on him their *own* invitation; saying, Come thou with us and we will do thee good; for the Lord hath spoken good concerning Israel.

Above all, let them seek in earnest humble prayer for the presence of God and the outpouring of his Holy Spirit. For it is when the Spirit is present with his people, and they go forth in the power of his presence and love to seek the lost, that the Spirit meets the lost also; convincing them of the righteous claims of Christ, of their sin, and a coming judgment; and by his subduing grace turns their feet into the ways of God and towards the gates of his Zion. Thus saith the Lord: "Fear not, O Jacob, my servant, and thou, Jeshurun, whom I have chosen. For I will pour water upon him that is thirsty and floods upon the dry ground. I will pour my Spirit upon thy seed and my blessing upon thine offspring. And they shall spring up as among the grass, as willows by the water courses. One shall say, I am the Lord's; and another shall call himself by the name of Jacob; and another shall subscribe with his hand unto the Lord and surname himself by the name of Israel."

Thus shall converts be gathered from the world; and Zion rejoice in the multitudes who flock to her gates of salvation.

And if there is a place in the Church where this blessing is to be desired, or to be prized, more than in any
other, that place is here, and in similar institutions;
which are the hope of the Church, the nurseries of her
future teachers, pastors, missionaries, guides, and her
ablest supporters and defenders.

3. The penitent and returning sinner should seek to be
united to God and his people in the bonds of spiritual
fellowship.

He is a child of sin and sorrow. He is in a world that
is short and fleeting. He stands on the verge of an eternal
state. He has loved worldly good as his idol. He has
wandered in pursuit of it with restless agitations, and
found his hopes ever ending in disappointment. There
has been a void in his soul that has ached for some higher
and more exalted objects. There has been a sting of guilt,
wounding him for his disobedience and disregard of his
Maker, even in the brightest scenes of his idolatrous enjoyments. It is in such a condition that the Spirit of God
meets him and opens his eyes to look on himself and on
God, on this world and eternity, in the sober light of
truth. He sees the folly of his ways and the ruin to
which they lead. The world sinks in his esteem. It is
as a barren waste to his heart, and its idolized enjoyments
are seen as the illusions of sin, that lead on to death. He
now looks to God, and the reasonable service he requires
of his creatures; and his heart begins to feel the risings
of desire and the kindlings of a new purpose to take the
Lord as his God, submitting all to his disposal and engaging all in his service. The Spirit of God thus brings him
by a new birth into spiritual life. He now begins the life
of faith and charity. But shall he pursue his way alone?
Shall he go forward to eternity as a solitary servant? No.
God in his grace has provided better things for his chosen.
He gathers them into one body, in fellowship with his Son
and with one another; that the whole body, united to
their Head and fitly joined together, may make increase,
unto the edifying of itself in love. Hither then is it the
privilege of the convert to turn, and seek in communion

with God and fellowship with the saints the sympathy,
employment, instruction in righteousness, and eternal rest,
which he needs. This is a privilege which the new born
soul has sought and prized in every age ; and for which
many a one has risked all his earthly happiness. Like
Ruth, the child of idolatry who resolved to go and unite
herself to the people of God in their worship and fellowship, they have resolved to find all their happiness in this
fellowship.

> People of the living God !
>   I have sought the world around,
> Paths of sin and sorrow trod,
>   Peace and comfort nowhere found.
> Now to you my spirit turns,
>   Turns, a fugitive unblest ;
> Brethren ! where your altar burns,
>   Oh, receive me into rest !
>
> Lonely, I no longer roam,
>   Like the cloud, the wind, the wave ;
> Where you dwell shall be my home,
>   Where you die shall be my grave ;
> Mine the God whom you adore—
>   Your Redeemer shall be mine ;
> Earth can fill my soul no more,
>   Every idol I resign.

To those who, this day, seek admission into public fellowship with Christ and this branch of his Church, I
would now say in their behalf, that we gladly welcome
you into fellowship with us in our joys and labors; and
hope that you will find in your union to the people of
God a privilege that you will not cease to prize and
cherish till it be consummated in glory.

> Come in, thou blessed of the Lord,
>   Oh come in Jesus' precious name ;
> We welcome thee with one accord,
>   And trust the Saviour does the same.
>
> Those joys which earth cannot afford,
>   We'll seek in fellowship to prove ;
> Joined in one spirit to the Lord,
>   Together bound by mutual love.

I will only add respecting the future, the exhortation that you cleave with full purpose of heart to the Lord; that from this hour you go forward in the duties of religion in the strength of Christ.  Let your future College life be spent for God, your whole life on earth and your life in eternity.  Be sure that while you live on earth, you live, and when you die, you die, in a state of true charity and fellowship with God and his people.  And then, where-ever and whenever your graves shall be prepared, they will be hallowed by the Saviour, and your name and memorial be on high.  And, at the resurrection of the just and the coming of our Lord Jesus Christ, we shall hope to meet you at that eternal feast of charity where conflict and toil and separation shall be known no more forever.

---

LUKE VII: 11—17.

THE Evangelist Luke begins his narrative of the event
by giving us the particular date of it in the ministry of
Christ, with these words: " And it came to pass the day
after, that he went into a city called Nain." If we look
back to the day referred to in this date, we shall be as-
sisted to fix on some of the circumstances of this journey.
The day before, it seems Jesus had come down from that
mount where he had spent the whole previous night in
prayer to God; *on which,* after sending for his disciples
and calling them to his place of retirement, he chose the
twelve to be the constant attendants of his ministry, that
they might hear his instructions and be eye-witnesses of
his miraculous works: *from which* he descended awhile
to the plain to heal of their diseases multitudes gathered
from all Judea and Jerusalem and from the seacoast of
Tyre and Sidon: and *to which,* on seeing the great multitudes that were assembled, he returned, that he might
give his instructions from an elevated stand to the vast
assembly; on which occasion he delivered that discourse
which is so fully recorded by Matthew, and which has so
generally obtained the name of the Sermon on the Mount.
On this day of his descent from the mount he entered the
city of Capernaum, the place then of his residence in
Galilee: and there an application was made to him the
same day by a deputation of elders from some neighbor-
ing synagogue, that he would heal the servant of a Roman centurion, who, it appears, was a devout proselyte
greatly beloved by the Jews for his piety and for his lib-

erality in building them a synagogue. The day of this healing of the centurion's servant is the date to which Luke immediately refers. It was the day after,—and consequently the day after the one on which he descended from the mount of instruction—that Jesus undertook this journey to Nain. We are to place the journey at the beginning of the second year of his ministry, soon after his return to Galilee from the Passover, during the spring or early summer.

He was not alone on the journey. A numerous throng attended him on the way. "And many of his disciples went with him and much people." The twelve, who, doubtless, attended Jesus on this first tour after their appointment, are not distinguished in this account from the "many disciples" who are grouped together as a class distinct from the "much people." The latter are remnants probably of "the great multitudes of people," who the day before were assembled at the mount, from so many parts of the country, to bring their sick to be healed, or to see and hear Jesus; who, as Matthew testifies, (iv. 25.) 'had come from Galilee, from Decapolis, and from Jerusalem, and from Judea, and from beyond Jordan;' who, after hearing his instructive discourse, and rejoicing in being healed or in witnessing the healing of others, were desirous still longer to accompany him, that they might hear more of his instructions and witness still more of his wonderful works.

The city of Nain, towards which Jesus with this throng of attendants now journeyed, lay in that part of Galilee which was apportioned to Issachar, when Canaan was originally divided among the tribes of Israel; and in a direction southwesterly from Capernaum, at a distance of more than fifteen miles. Between the two cities, but on the immediate borders of Nain, to the north, stood Mount Tabor; rising in one solitary cone to an elevation of nearly three thousand feet, with a flat area of a mile in circumference at its top, celebrated as a fortress of defense in war and an altar of devotion in peace, and afterwards made the scene, as the current tradition of the

Church has reported, of the transfiguration. Between this mountain and the city Nain, flowed the head waters of the brook Kishon, which, running west across the plain of Esdraelon to the foot of Carmel, glided along the northern base of that whole mountain range to its termination in the waters of the Mediterranean.

As Jesus goes forward to execute his purpose of mercy, instructing on the way the multitude that accompany him, this mount of Tabor rests, in elevated grandeur, before them ; concealing, behind its mass of soil and verdure, the city whither they were tending. Lifting up its lofty peak far into the blue heaven, it might well assist the Master to elevate the thoughts of the whole company to those heights above, where he had glory with the Father before the world was; whither, after he had closed his humiliating mission on earth, he would ascend again ; and to which, at the last day, he would elevate his followers, called forth from their graves, to dwell, above the sins and sorrows of earth, in his presence forever. Whether he made this a topic of his instructions on the way or not; yet, surely, he who had passed so recently a whole night in prayer on the mount near Capernaum, and was soon afterwards transfigured on such an elevation, has set forth, to all his followers, the mountain top, as an emblem of retirement from the sins and turmoils of this evil world, and of approach in devotion to the glories of the celestial King amid his worshippers in heaven. But as, with this emblem of heavenly things in view, the company listen on their walk to the discourse of Jesus, of the kingdom of God among men, the mountain is soon reached ; and, as they wind their way around its shadowy base, the city of Nain emerges to their view, with its walls and towers and dwellings, all shining joyously beneath the rays of one common sun, and resting quietly on the surface of one common world. Yet, in those distant habitations so quietly reposing among the works of God, what different characters reside, of the pious and profane ; what different scenes are enacted, of joy and sorrow ! In one habitation the guilty, it may be, are holding their impious revelry of riot and excess. In another, the pious are rejoicing in the goodness and mercy of the God of Abraham, and talking of their hopes in his promises. Prosperity is gladdening the hearts there of some happy, unbroken households. Adversity enters others; and hearts are grieved by losses, disappointments, bereavements. Yet one dwelling there, is desolate and saddened that day;—the object of special interest within the city— and which has drawn hither the all-seeing and compassionate Saviour: for death has entered it, and the inmates at this very hour are going forth in sorrow to bury their dead.

It is the house where once a happy husband and wife shared each other's joys and sorrows in that most endeared of unions: whose hearts had once throbbed together with parental joy over the birth of a first-born—a beloved son of their hopes. But that union had since been dissolved by death: and the heart-broken wife, bereft of the counselor, the companion, the friend, on whom she was wont to lean as the stay of her life, had been left in her loneliness to shed the tear of sorrow over his grave. But the son remained; the object of her affection and cares. And, faithful to the memory of the departed parent, she had watched over the child, till now she saw him, in early manhood, ready to assist her; to bear her burdens; to cheer her declining years, as onward she traveled toward the grave. What hopes were placed in this beloved son! What a solace in him had God raised up to soothe her widowed heart!

But now a bitter pang has pierced her soul. This son, her hope and solace, has sickened; and, notwithstanding all her assiduous watchings and care, has fallen beneath the power of disease. He has spoken to her the last farewell of his heart, as he died; and has left her alone in the world, parted from all her once loved and happy household. The precious body of this only son, she was that day to follow to the grave. Much people of the city were touched with sympathy for her in her affliction. The companions of her departed husband, the companions of her son, many pitying friends,—have come to her desolate mansion, to accompany her on her way to the place of burial. This mourning group were on their way, at the time that Jesus with his disciples and the accompanying multitude, drew nigh the city. As he looks towards the gate, the train appears in sight bearing out the dead to the sepulcher, situated, according to the custom of the Jews, beyond the walls of the city. The whole scene is presented to us in the following description of the historian, most beautiful for its classic brevity and its touching simplicity: "Now when he was come nigh the gate of the city, behold, there was a dead man carried out, the only son of his mother, and she was a widow: and much people of the city was with her."

What different thoughts and emotions actuate the company that move with Jesus and this company of mourners, as they meet! The disciples and the multitude surrounding the Master, have just come from the mount, where, in prayer, in instruction, and in healing a great multitude of their diseases, Jesus has drawn nigh the Father and brought down his presence and power to the earth. Many in this crowd, doubtless, are thankfully rejoicing in recovery; and all,—disciples and others—are filled with thoughts of the presence and power of God in this Galilean teacher. The sympathizing train of mourners, on the other hand, move slowly onwards. Thoughts of the happy past, thoughts of the departed dead, thoughts of the desolate survivor, are coursing over their hearts, furrowing sadness there: and from some pious sons and daughters of Abraham in that train, no doubt, prayers of the heart are ascending to Jehovah that in his holy habitation he would be the God and protecting Judge of this widow.

As the trains meet each other, the eye of Jesus, passing in its direction over the whole melancholy group, fastens on the chief mourner—the object of all this sympathy— who is overwhelmed with sadness. His compassionate heart is touched: and within it lies concealed that purpose of mercy which, in part, had brought him hither, and which would soon give back to her her lost treasure, and cause the tears of grief to give place to smiles of gladness. "And when the Lord saw her, he had compassion on her, and said unto her, Weep not." These were soothing words; spoken by one who has power to reach and to remove every source of tears. Nor did Jesus pass by with the utterance merely of words of sympathy. "And he came and touched the bier." On that support, not with coffin as among the Babylonians and Egyptians, but simply wrapped in folds of white linen after the manner of the Hebrews for depositing in the sepulcher, rested the body of the dead, borne of four. By touching the bier, Jesus betokened his wish that the bearers and procession should halt on their way. "And they that bare him stood still." All now wait in breathless expectation, to see what this famed teacher designs. They have heard doubtless of the many miracles he has wrought among the living, and how he has called back the sick and fainting from the very gates of the grave. But never, as yet, —for the resurrection of Jairus' daughter and of Lazarus took place at a later period,—has his voice reached beyond that barrier that separates between the living and the dead; between the lifeless body that remains and the animating spirit that has departed. Yet his voice of omnipotence can pierce the shadowy realms of the dead, and call back from thence the departed spirit to inhabit again its forsaken body. That voice now issues the word of authority: "And he said, Young man, I say unto thee, Arise." 'I say it,'—that all may know that with me are the keys of death and Hades; 'I say it,'—as having the power of life and resurrection in myself: 'Young man, Arise.' O, what a voice was that to fall on the heavy heart of the mourning widow! What a new train of thoughts and emotions it awakens at once within her soul! 'Can it be that my darling child shall hear that voice and come back to me again?' 'Can I again clasp his living form to this aching breast, and receive again from his lips words of respect and affection, and from his hands deeds of kindness, to cheer the remnant of my life?' That voice has gone forth. There are no shades of death so deep that it cannot reach them. The spirit of the young man has heard it, and has come back once more to the body. The dead is alive again ; and before all he puts forth infallible tokens of life. " And he that was dead sat up and began to speak": There was a muscular motion of the body, in assuming this sitting posture, that seemed voluntary, not spasmodic ; and that was proved to be such, by articulate speech, expressing the thoughts of a living, indwelling soul. What he spake, we are not told ; but, while sitting up in his grave clothes, looking on Jesus, on his mother, on the astonished and awe-struck accompanying multitude,—whether he spoke of things in the sick room he had recently left, or of the new circumstances in which he now suddenly finds himself—whether he spoke of things in this world or in the eternal—whatever were his words—he was a powerful preacher of Jesus and the resurrection.

But this recovery was not for the moment merely : to cast one gleam of joy and hope across a mourning heart, and leave it to still greater gloom and disappointment than ever. The historian adds : " And he delivered him to his mother." Jesus, who, it was now manifest, held the life of this young man in his own hand, either to dismiss it again, that the body might be carried to the sepulcher, or to retain it on earth for a further participation in the social intercourse of the living, as he gave him to his mother, assured her heart, it is probable in some form of words : ' Receive thy son : return with him to thy mansion : and let the compassion of this hour prove a blessing to thee for the remnant of thy days.' Nor was the chief mourner and her son alone, affected by this wonderful act of compassion. " And there came a fear on all." The train that followed the dead out of the city, and the train that followed Jesus on his visit to the city, are now commingled in astonishment at the mighty power of this resurrection. " And they glorified God, saying that a great prophet is risen up among us : and that God hath visited his people." Never, since the day that Elisha raised up the child of the Shunamite, had any such thing been seen in Israel. And justly did many in that multitude conclude that, in the person of Jesus, God himself was now present on some great purpose and errand of mercy, to fulfill the covenant he had made to the fathers respecting Messiah the King and the Saviour. The historian closes the account of this miracle with these words, " And this rumor of him "—or rather this story of his raising the young man of Nain from the dead, which I have related—"·went forth throughout all Judea and throughout all the region round about "; *i. c.*, Judea and the surrounding region of Galilee. This wide spread circulation of the story was to be expected. For not only were the eyewitnesses very numerous, but in the train that followed Jesus that day from the recent scene of the mount of instruction there were inhabitants of all these countries, who, with this wonderful story upon their lips, were soon to be dispersed to their several homes ; so that, wherever they went, they told their friends of the mighty power and compassion of Jesus.

Among the instructions to be gathered from this scene in the life of Jesus, I will present the following.

1. In this journey to Nain, Jesus presents to our imitation an example of beneficence. While at Capernaum, he saw with his omniscient ken the recent scene of death in that city, and resolved to visit the place, and give relief to the desolate heart of the mourning widow. Thither, to fulfill his compassionate purpose, he directed his steps. Unsolicited by any one, he went forth to accomplish the impulses of his own generous heart. He sought out this daughter of affliction in her sorrows. He went the whole distance that he might show her kindness. And when arrived in her presence, unasked by her or any of her friends, he imparted relief freely ; and, by this unexpected and surprising act of beneficence, made glad her desolate heart and the hearts of all her sympathizing friends. So Jesus went about doing good among the people ; dispensing freely to the needy and afflicted the gifts of his benevolence. In this has he left us an example ; that we

should imbibe his spirit of generous compassion, and walk in his footsteps of unwearied kindness. Not that we may enter into those works of might and power that exceed our natures and our powers to accomplish : but that, in our measures and according to our opportunities, we should seek the needy and suffering, and freely dispense the gifts and offices of our charity for their temporal and spiritual relief.

In a world of sin and trial, where guilt and suffering surround us on every side, it is not by sitting quietly in our homes weeping over the perusal of fictitious tales of sorrow, nor by waiting to be sought and solicited by the needy and suffering, nor merely by soliciting the aid of our Father in heaven on their behalf, when we can dispense substantial aid ourselves, that we follow the example of Christ, so much as when, with compassion in our hearts towards the suffering, we go forth, unasked, to meet them in their wants, and freely dispense to them the relief in our power. To this, the act of Christ that we have considered calls us, as a guiding and inspiring example, showing how blessed it is to give relief to others, and to be a fount of temporal and spiritual blessing in this ignorant, guilty, suffering world.

> Go imitate the grace divine,
>   The grace that blazes like a sun ;
> Hold forth your fair though feeble light—
>   Through all your lives let mercy run.

2. From the scene at Nain we learn, that in Jesus we have a sympathizing friend who can reach and heal every source of sorrow. When he met the weeping daughter of affliction in the depth of her sorrows, he spake those words of solace with an accompanying energy that removed the very fountain of her grief—"Weep not." These are cheering words to be brought down to this vale of sin and sorrow, and to be left with us by one who came from the heavenly throne with full powers of grace from the Father and in his own person to relieve, and who has ascended to the Father again to carry forward still his works of mercy.

And what source of grief and tears among our fallen race is there, that this Saviour cannot reach and heal? Not that he designs to remove every imperfection, every burden, every trial, every sorrow, from the subjects of his grace while they remain on the theater of this life. For, as sin is the chief inlet of all our sorrows, and as to heal the spiritual maladies of the soul and fit it for the holy joys of heaven is the chief object of his grace, it is wisely appointed, in favor of our spiritual recovery and for moral improvement by discipline, that, while we remain here, we should be subjected to trials, more or less severe. Yet those soothing words from the Saviour—"Weep not," reveal to us in the Captain of our salvation a sympathizing Friend, who is conducting his followers through every tribulation to final and complete deliverance. There is no sorrow therefore which comes upon us, in which we may not apply to him for sympathy and support, and with the hope of a final deliverance. Is it sin and guilt and remorse? Even from these his atoning blood can cleanse us, to pacify the conscience and bring the peace of divine forgiveness. Is it the moral disorders that still remain in his people, to hinder their progress and interrupt their joy in his service? To all these he is now applying the remedies of his grace, that he may purify his people, and bring them to spotless holiness in his presence in heaven. Is it the disappointments, the losses, the bereavements, the sufferings of the present time, and the uncertainties of the future, that distress our hearts and open the fountain of our tears? But in all these changing aspects of the present and uncertainties of the future, he assures us that the eternal providence of his Father is ever over his people for their good; consulting their highest welfare; conducting them in the right way to a glorious habitation of rest beyond all the storms and changes of this mortal life. What though no man is found able to unfold the book of providence and read the destiny that hangs over the future? Weep not, as though all were uncertain. The Lion of the tribe of Judah, the Root of David, hath prevailed to open the book. The fate of his kingdom on earth and of his people after they pass the tribulations of this life, he, who hath the keys of the eternal world, hath caused to be read forth to us by one of his servants. " They are before the throne of God, and serve him day and night in his temple. They shall hunger no more, neither thirst any more, neither shall the sun light on them nor any heat. For the Lamb that is in the midst of the throne shall feed them, and shall lead them unto living fountains of waters." "God shall wipe away all tears from their eyes: and there shall be no more death, neither sorrow, nor crying, neither shall there be any more pain : for the former things are passed away."

3. In this scene at Nain, Jesus revealed himself to be the *source of resurrection and immortal life to his people after death.* For the word of power which he spake that day : "Young man, I say unto thee, Arise," reached beyond the vale of death ; called back the departed spirit to its lifeless remains ; and presented that young man, in his re-animated body, on this theater of life again. This stupendous miracle convinced the astonished witnesses, that with Jesus was the power of resurrection and life. For to the mourning train who could not have been deceived as to the death of the young man, and to the train who came with Jesus, who had evidently met this mourning group without any collusion or plan formed between them to deceive others—to both, it was obvious that the words of Jesus, " I say unto thee, Arise," were accompanied with a divine energy and were the source of a resurrection to life. The conviction was fastened deep on their minds. They expressed it to one another, as they said, " A great prophet is risen up among us "; " God hath visited his people." Through Judea and Galilee, when they dispersed, they spread the report with their testimony. And this report, gathered from eyewitnesses by the diligent inquiries of the historian Luke, was published at the time and in the country in which the witnesses lived, without any denial; to make known to all lands and ages the

majesty and power of Jesus our Lord.   Jesus therefore was made manifest on that day and in this particular miracle, as one who hath visited us in this world of shadows and death with the power of life.   The promises he put forth, that he would convey his people to an immortal life beyond the confines of the grave, and collect them together, at his second appearing on this world, again by resurrection—these promises were shown at this time to be true, not by miracle merely, but by the nature of the miracle in which he triumphed over death by an instance of resurrection, and by the manner in which he claimed the power of life to be in his own hands: "*I* say unto thee."   As the Father hath life in himself, so hath he given to the Son to have life in himself.   The report first went forth from Nain, that the dead *had* heard the voice of the Son of God and lived.   Nor need we marvel at this: for it is but the foreshadowing of greater works that are to follow.   For he hath said, ".The hour is coming in the which *all* that are in the graves shall hear his voice and come forth, they that have done good unto the resurrection of life, and they that have done evil unto the resurrection of damnation."

Who then should not in these days, in which he waits on us with the opportunities of salvation, believe on him; who holds in his hands the power of an 'everlasting life': and who hath left to every believer the promise " I will raise him up at the last day "?   Who should not believe on him, and secure to his soul a spiritual life with him, even now in this mortal estate, and beyond this life a resurrection with him to immortal glory in heaven ?

4. Finally : The scene at Nain assists us to appreciate the happiness that will attend on the meeting of pious households after death.

That was a happy time when Jesus delivered the dead, brought back again to life, to the embrace and affection of his desolate parent; when the mother and son, whom death had parted amid sorrows, were thus brought together again by a joyful resurrection.   The tears of grief gave way to those of joy, and the sympathizing multitude, who beheld the re-union, rejoiced in the consolation and gave glory to God. But great as was the joy, it was not complete. They met again here on earth, amid the trials of this mortal state. They stood together before Christ in his humiliation at the foot of Tabor ; and not in his glory on its top, as did the glorified Moses and Elias.

There was joy even in this meeting again after death : but what was the joy compared to that fullness that shall overflow the heart, when pious households, who have been separated one after another by death, shall meet together —beyond all mortality and grief—beyond all temptation and sin—on those heavenly heights where, in his glorified state, Jesus the Saviour shall receive his redeemed to himself, to behold his glory and to dwell in the love of his Father forever. Happy indeed will it be for those households that shall be all gathered there, with no member missing ! And though no sorrow or fear shall ever come up to those heavenly heights—though all there will be filled with the love of God and acquiesce in all his dispensations—yet methinks there will be a less degree of joy in the heart of that parent, that child, that brother, that sister, who looks around in vain for some of their once loved circle. While sad indeed to the missing and the absent will be their eternal parting and anguish ! Let parents then, let children, let brothers, let sisters, as they are soon to be parted from all their earthly intercourse by death, and as they believe in the coming and glory of the Lord Jesus, strive together in their prayers and efforts in this life to promote each other's spiritual welfare, so that they may reach at last a happy re-union in his presence amid the unchanging glories of the heavenly state !

MATT. XVII: 1-13—MARK IX: 2-13—LUKE IX: 28-36.

EACH of these sacred historians introduces his account of this remarkable scene, by referring back to a conversation which Jesus had held with the twelve, a week previously, in the region of Cæsarea Philippi. "After six days," say both Matthew and Mark; referring to the *intervening* days: and Luke says, including the first and last day, "It came to pass about eight days after these sayings"—all of them dating from that one conversation. There would seem then to be some connection between that conversation and this scene, which brought them together in the minds of the inspired historians more closely than even this short lapse of time. They both relate to the person and impending fate of Jesus. In that conversation, Christ had asked the twelve, 'Whom say the people that I am?' And when, in answer to this question, they mentioned the various opinions they had heard expressed, he asked them again, 'Whom say ye that I am?' Peter confessed that he was Christ, the Son of the living God: upon which, Jesus enjoined silence in regard to any such confession before the public at present—it being premature; but began a language he had never held with them before, about the violent treatment and death he was soon to suffer at Jerusalem, and his resurrection that was to follow on the third day; and respecting the trials which were to be encountered by his followers, which it became them to endure if they would have eternal life when he assumed his glory : which event he assured them would take place during the lifetime of some of their number. This week was one then of sadness and misgiving, it would seem, to the apostles, in their apprehensions of the future. Peter had exclaimed, in regard to the foretold treatment of Jesus—That be far from thee, Lord—and was left sad with the severe rebuke of his Master.

At a time then when the ministry of Jesus was soon to close in death, and when his disciples were hearing from his lips sad forebodings of what they were to endure, and could scarcely comprehend what was meant by the intimations of his death and resurrection and glory, it was, that he himself and three chosen ones of his disciples were favored with this partial foretaste of his glory.

The place in which the scene was laid was a mountain; the name is not given by either of the evangelists : but Matthew and Mark call it a " high " mountain. The current opinion of antiquity has fixed the scene on Tabor, one of the loftiest mountains in the holy land. Yet many of the moderns suppose it to have been Mount Hermon, *a lofty* branch of the Anti-Libanus range; because this elevation was in the region of Cæsarca Philippi, at the head of the Jordan, where Jesus was, the week before, when he began to speak of his approaching death at Jerusalem. Yet as six full days had passed since that time, it is possible surely that he should now be two or three days journey south in Galilee, and the opinion of antiquity may still be true, which fixes the scene upon Tabor. But whether the lofty Hermon at the north, or the lofty Tabor of the south, rejoiced in this visit of its God, may remain in doubt, while we contemplate in faith this great scene of the mountain top.

Jesus, before he ascended the mount, selected from the twelve three only as his companions. He took a few, probably as more consonant to retirement from men and near approach to God—and still a number competent to give authoritative testimony. They were Peter, James and John: Peter, the first called of the whole band, whom he met on his arrival at the lake after his expulsion from Nazareth, and James and John, the sons of his paternal aunt, the wife of Zebedee: persons, whom he seemed to have regarded with peculiar attachment, as his most intimate friends among the twelve—a feeling belonging to human nature, even in the holiest and most liberal and expansive in their benevolence ;—persons, who before had been selected from the band by him to be witnesses in the room at the raising of Jairus' daughter ; and who were afterwards his companions in that scene of agony which he endured, on the night of his betrayal, in his last retirement for prayer before his crucifixion, in the garden of Gethsemane.

With these three chosen disciples he ascends the mount, probably towards the close of day, or in the evening ; for the glory, the cloud of light, the drowsiness of the disciples, and the declaration of Luke ix : 37, that they descended from the mount the next day, all show that, like the scene in Gethsemane, this also was a scene of the night. At an hour when all nature seems retiring to silence and rest on the care of its God, he. leaves the presence and habitations of men, and seeks the high mountain top, that he and his disciples may be apart by themselves, with nothing but the wakeful eye and heart of God turned toward them, that they may approach more nearly and intimately into his presence in prayer. There, with the broad heaven from which he came and whither he was to ascend, spread over his head, and with that world, which he came to save, wrapped in darkness and sleep far beneath his feet ; there, looking forward to that scene of agony soon to be encountered, which had occupied his thoughts and the thoughts of his disciples during the week that was past—agony, through which alone he was to reach again his exalted throne and raise up with him from the earth a redeemed people ; there, as a Mediator between heaven and earth, pressed with impending trial, he pours out his soul for strength and victory in breathings of fervent prayer unto his Father. He prayed with strong crying and tears unto God, who was able to deliver him, and he was heard in respect to that which he feared ; and, to encourage his heart, he was, for a few moments, invested by the Father with a shadow of the glory to which he was to be permanently exalted after enduring his agonies. " As he prayed, the fashion of his countenance," says Luke, " was altered "— " became another " : Matthew and Mark say that " he was transfigured "—" passed beyond the form or figure· he had to another "—" was transformed."  The change however was not to a form so essentially new in the mould and outlines as not to be still clearly recognized by the disciples as that of Jesus.  But the expression passed from the former lines of earthly care to the glow of godlike majesty and serenity : and, instead of the faint reflections cast upon it from the stars before, that made it barely visible, it has now become self-radiant with light as a sun.  The brief description given of his altered appearance is the following : " His *face* did shine as the sun " (Matthew).  " His *raiment* became shining, exceeding white as snow, so as no fuller on earth can white them " (Mark).  His face glowed with a *golden* radiance as of the sun, and his raiment was shining in a *pure white*, beyond the brilliancy of the sun-light reflected from the snow.  This visible form of light and majesty was the same as that in which, after his ascension, he was seen by John in his vision at Patmos—and was now a temporary representation, to himself and the disciples, of the splendor of his heavenly and eternal state.  As this glory passed upon his person, suddenly he was visited from the heavenly world by Elijah, who nine hundred years before was translated to that world, and by Moses, who more than fifteen hundred years before had been taken away from Israel on Nebo.  " Behold there talked with him two men, which were Moses and Elias, who appeared *in glory* "—themselves radiant in their glorified forms.  The subject of the conversation is mentioned by Luke.  They " spake of his decease which he should accomplish at Jerusalem."  The term which the evangelist uses, it is to be remarked, is not death, but departure out of the world —exodus.  The conversation therefore extended beyond the agony of the death he was to suffer, to the exodus he was to make, as the leader of his ransomed, beyond this world of trial to the world of eternal rest. The subject was the eternal glory he would obtain to himself through the sufferings of his departure and how in that hour also he would conquer sin, death and hell, the foes of his people, and ever after rejoice in witnessing their eternal escape and redemption. The great lawgiver who had conducted Israel from their earthly bondage to Canaan, and had bidden them expect on their land the coming of this Saviour, and an eminent one in the line of those prophets, who taught Israel for a succession of ages to look forward to him as their hope, seem deputed at this hour from the heavenly world, as appropriate messengers, to bear to Jesus an expression of the hopes which the Church of the first-born in heaven are all reposing on him as they wait for him to come among them after the hour of his sacrifice, a triumphant Saviour, establishing them in their justified and glorified state to eternity. They may also point to the long train of believers in the Christian Church whom they will yet see gathered to their company in heaven, as the fruit of his sufferings, in the coming ages of his reign. We have not been permitted indeed to hear the particulars of that deeply interesting conversation : but doubtless, at that hour of foretaste of his future glory among his redeemed people in heaven, fresh courage and strength was infused into his heart to go forward to endure that sharp conflict, out of which he was to pass into such exalted glory and joy forever, and by which, as at the triumphal exodus of Moses out of Egypt, he was to conduct the people of God in all ages to a permanent habitation in the heavenly Canaan.

But before this strange change had passed upon the person of the Saviour, and before the arrival of these heavenly visitants—while yet he was pouring out his soul in prayer, and was covered with the shades of night and distress—the disciples, it seems, fell asleep, as afterwards they did in Gethsemane. During this momentary sleep of the disciples, as Luke apprises us, the change took place : and, as they awake, this new scene is spread forth in its glory. "But Peter and they that were with him were heavy with sleep; and when they were awake, they saw his glory, and the two men that stood with him." They were waked probably by the sudden gleam of light that shone around them and illuminated the mountain top; and beheld with surprise their Lord, all shining in this glorious state, and at his side two heavenly attendants, resplendent in glory. They wait in breathless silence, as they hear these heavenly visitants converse with their Lord, and as they learn from the conversation their names and the stations they occupied while in the earthly Church. In this state of astonishment, as if in a species of ecstacy at the glory of his Lord, Peter ventures to exclaim to Jesus: "Master, it is good for us to be here; and let us make three tabernacles"—alluding to the booths or arbors constructed of the branches of thick foliaged trees, in which the Jews resided during the joyous feast of the tabernacles—"one for thee, and one for Moses, and one for Elias." For the moment, he felt that he never wished his Master to descend from this heavenly state to earthly cares and trials again, and would forever stay there himself in such heavenly society. But the historian represents him as "not knowing what he said." In making his strange proposal to Jesus, the same feeling was manifest that had received, a week before, the rebuke of his Master—the desire that it should be far from Jesus to undergo a violent death at Jerusalem, and leave his followers to encounter the hostility of the world.

But no sooner has Peter uttered these emotions, than a new appearance attracts the attention of the astonished disciples. The emblem of the presence of the Eternal Father—a dense cloud, whose whole surface is radiant with light, appears, enveloping Jesus and his attendants, and circling round the more distant disciples with its massy folds. "While he thus spake, there came a cloud and overshadowed them," says Luke; "a *bright* cloud," says Matthew, "overshadowed them : and behold a voice out of the cloud which said, This is my beloved Son, in whom

I am well pleased: hear ye him." This testimony from the Father enforced upon the disciples the instructive lesson they were to receive from the scene they now witnessed—that Jesus was the beloved Son of God, who, as sole Heir to his estate and kingdom, was to be exalted to the head of the whole creation : in whose conduct, as a Redeemer come on earth to make known the Father to men and to endure the sufferings of the cross to sustain his righteousness in the salvation of his people, he, the Father, was well pleased : and whose voice of instruction they were to regard as speaking forth his will, with a personal authority greater than that of Moses and the prophets, who were mere servants to him, the great Son and Heir. Thus,—in that glimpse of the heavenly state, in which Christ shone as head over Moses and Elias, and in this voice from the excellent glory, in which the Father placed him at his own right hand as his Son and Heir to his throne,—the disciples and Jesus were together assured, that he was conducting his people as their Head to an everlasting kingdom.

But as this cloud of glory invested all, and as this voice was uttered, the disciples for a while seem overpowered with their emotions. "They feared, as they entered into the cloud" (Luke). "And when the disciples heard it," —the voice—(Matthew)—"they fell on their face and were sore afraid." And as they were thus dismayed with the terror of the divine majesty, "Jesus came and touched them, and said, Arise, and be not afraid." This well known voice of their friend re-assured their hearts. "And when they had lifted up their eyes, they saw no man, save Jesus only." The glory and terror of the scene were past : and again they were alone with Jesus, and he, their familiar friend, clothed as before in the common garb of humanity. They were prepared now to descend again to the world they had left, and enter on the duties and trials that were to intervene before they reached the heavenly state. "And as they came down from the mountain, Jesus charged them, saying, Tell the vision to no man, until the Son of Man be risen again from the dead"

(Matthew). The reason for this injunction of silence till that period may have been, that their testimony would at that future time be more credible than now to the multitude, and be less apt to excite jealousy in the less favored disciples who were not present. In regard to the injunction Luke adds, " And they kept that saying with themselves, questioning one with another what the rising from the dead should mean": involved in this perplexity probably, because they as yet held to the idea of a temporal kingdom, and were unwilling to admit the thought of the death of their Lord. But after this injunction of silence was given, the disciples asked Jesus the following question: " Why then say the scribes that Elias must first come?" The connection of this question with the previous injunction of silence is of this kind. Elias has come from heaven, as we have just seen, upon the mount. The scribes constantly say, that Elias will re-appear on earth before Messiah comes, and that he will prepare the people for his kingdom ; and now they plead his non-appearance, as a reason for rejecting thee. Why do they say that Elias must first come? Is it not true? Why then may we not tell this vision, and assure them that Elias has come? Is he to come again in a more public and solemn manner? The answer of Christ is to this effect; that the scribes have erred, in concluding that the prophetic Elias that was to come is literally Elijah the Tishbite, whom these disciples have now seen on the mount: and that, involved in this error, they have rejected the true Elias, who has already come heralding the Messiah, and would in like manner also reject and condemn him, the heralded Messiah. " Jesus answered and said unto them : (Matt.) Elias truly shall first come and restore all things. But I say unto you, that Elias has come already, and they knew him not, but have done unto him whatsoever they listed : likewise also shall the Son of Man suffer of them. Then the disciples understood that he spake to them of John the Baptist." In this manner was the glorious scene of the mount ended, and Jesus and the three came down again, to unite with the whole band of the disciples.

From this scene of the mount of transfiguration, we may derive the following lessons of practical instruction.

1. It assures us of a heavenly glory obtained by Jesus for all the people of God, to which we should aspire as our final home. At that hour a brief foreshadowing of the heavenly world was brought down to the mount, and all that glory centered around and upon Jesus as its Author and Source. His altered visage wore the glory, that was to shine forth from him on the throne of God. Moses and Elias came down from heaven, showing that they had existed in a glorious state in heaven since they left the world, and that they and all believers, who looked forward in preceding ages to the coming of Christ as their Saviour, were resting on his decease at Jerusalem as the foundation of their acceptance with God. Three of the apostles were there to witness the glory of that Lord, whom they were following in faith, and whom they were to proclaim one day to the wide world, as the Author of eternal salvation. And soon around all and over all, the cloud of divine glory rested, and the voice of the Eternal Father pronounced over Jesus, and to the representatives of heaven and earth, ' This is my beloved Son, in whom I am well pleased : hear ye him.'

Who, on that mountain top, could doubt that there is a heavenly glory beyond this life for the people of God, and that Jesus, the Son of the Eternal Father, was appointed to procure it for them, as their immediate Head and Lord? But the glory of that hour, which strengthened Jesus on his own way to death and victory, and which set him forth to his attendants as the Hope of Israel, was sealed up in silence to the hour of his resurrection. The three favored apostles pondered the vision, and the words of Christ as to his death and resurrection ; but no man on earth, not any of their fellow apostles, heard of the scene till after it was fulfilled in the kingdom of God. But when apostles, having attended Jesus till after his death and exodus by a glorious ascension to the throne, went forth everywhere to preach him crucified, as the Author of eternal life, this scene was made known as among the evidences he left that he had gone into heaven, having obtained eternal redemption for his people. Peter, the apostle most prominent in that scene as a speaker, has left us this testimony concerning it ; when, at an advanced period of life, expecting shortly to put off this tabernacle, he thus exhorted those who had obtained·like precious faith through the righteousness of God our Saviour Jesus Christ. "Brethren, give diligence to make your calling and election sure : for so an entrance shall be ministered unto you abundantly into the everlasting kingdom of our Lord and Saviour Jesus Christ. For we have not followed cunningly devised fables, when we made known unto you the power and coming of our Lord Jesus Christ, but were eye-witnesses of his majesty. For he received from God the Father honor and glory, when there came such a voice to him from the excellent glory, This is my beloved Son, in whom I am well pleased. And this voice which came from heaven we heard, when we were with him on the holy mount."

What a glorious world beyond this life is thus opened to our faith and hope, where the Eternal Father and his Son Jesus Christ shine forth as its fadeless light, and where the ransomed of all ages are gathered together to dwell before the cloudless throne in joy and love forever! What a mercy to our world, that lay enwrapped in the shades of death and endless night, that the Son of God has visited it from on high ; that, by his decease at Jerusalem, he has parted the vail of eternity and opened for us sinners a way into the kingdom of heaven; that he has caused the radiance of that eternal world to fall on us to attract our hearts, and bidden us follow him on the way, that we may find our everlasting home and treasures there with him and his Father. Let us fix the eye of faith and hope intently on that state of glory. Let us seek earnestly to secure within it our final dwelling. Let us fear lest any of us seem even to come short of so glorious a kingdom !

From this scene in the life of Jesus, we learn,

2. That when the duties and trials which we are to encounter on the way to heaven press heavily on our minds,
we should seek relief and strength in prayer.

Jesus thus, when the suffering which the Father had
appointed him to endure at Jerusalem began to weigh
sorely on his mind and was broached by him to his disciples, betook himself to prayer. He retires apart from men,
in the shades of night, to the mountain top, to pour out his
soul to God for strength. That work which concerned
the glory of his Father above and the salvation of the
world below, and which rested upon him to achieve so
soon, was a burden he sought strength to bear. And
while he pleads with fervent desires for strength to accomplish his task and secure the glorious rewards of victory, the Father hears; and strengthens his heart with
foretastes of the personal glory he will win, and the joy
he will occasion the ransomed, by his decease at Jerusalem. The mount of prayer affords an antepast of heavenly joy,—a foretaste of his glory when, as the well-
beloved Son of the Father, he shall ascend with the
multitudes of his saints to heaven as the reward of his
toils and sufferings.

In this resort to prayer he has set us an example where
we are to find our strength, when pressed by the cares
and trials that we encounter on our path to heaven. Like
him, we are to betake ourselves to God for strength. Before him who appoints us our burdens, we may freely
pour out our fears and sorrows, and from him obtain the
help and grace we need. He has all the resources of our
strength at his command. He can, in answer to our
prayer, grant above what we ask or think. The elements
of this world and its population are all subject to his control. He can send heavenly messengers to us with their
refreshing ministry. He can cause the brightness of his
own infinite love and wisdom and power to pass before
us; he can enter our hearts with his own comforting
Spirit, and sweeten the toils and sufferings he appoints us
with foretastes of heavenly joy.

Brethren, let us learn of Jesus where to look for our strength. In his trials he retired into the presence of his Father.

> Cold mountains and the midnight air
> Witnessed the fervor of his prayer."

Ours is the same refuge, in duty, in trials and sufferings.

> When storms of sorrow round us sweep,
> And scenes of anguish make us weep;
> We'll look and see the Saviour there,
> And humbly bow, like him, in prayer.

I remark, again,

3. The foretastes of heavenly joy granted on earth are temporary, intended not to take the place of the duties of life, but to strengthen us in their performance.

Peter and his companions, when they awoke to behold the glory of their Lord and of his heavenly visitants, and saw the mountain top illuminated with the glory, felt that they were high above the dark world below and its cares; that they were on the mount of vision; that they were on the verge of heaven and its eternal glories. Emotions of strange wonder and exstatic joy fill their hearts. They are lost as in a pleasing revery, from which they desire never to be broken. "Master," exclaims Peter,—as if he had forgotten every care and duty of life, and the very errand of his Master in coming to the mount,—"Master, it is good for us to be here: and let us build three tabernacles." Here would he keep a perpetual feast with his Lord and his heavenly visitors. But the vision was intended only as a transient glimpse of the glories that lie beyond the vail of time. It was to strengthen for the duties and trials of life yet remaining: not to take their place. It could not last. Jesus and his disciples must leave the mount, go down to the world below, and set themselves to the duties and the conflicts which God had appointed them on their way to heaven.

So is it with believers on their course. Amid their duties and trials, it is their privilege to draw near to God and refresh their hearts with the joys of his presence.

And they may feel at times, when favored most with the divine presence, as if they would forever forsake all other cares and employments, to indulge only in these heavenly emotions and divine joys. They are on the mount of exstatic bliss. They would never go down again to the cares and sorrows of earth. But not such are the appointments of heaven. This is the world of their labors: that of their eternal rest is yet to come. The honor of God, the welfare of their race, their own progress in knowledge and holiness, call them to the discharge of active and laborious duties, and to the endurance of many and severe trials. Let believers learn then to prize their seasons of communion with God, as times in which to gather strength and refreshing to their hearts amid their duties and trials, not as substitutes to take their place, to prepare them for the discharge of their many active and passive duties of piety and benevolence, not to exalt them above these duties.

4. The voice of Jesus calms the hearts of his people when they are overwhelmed with the fearful glories of God.

The glories of the divine majesty are too bright for the endurance of mortal natures. We could not look on God and live. When his fearful majesty is revealed to us in the thunder, in the earthquake, in the utterance of his holy law, in the threatenings of his eternal curse, emotions of terror seize our hearts, and we are ready, like the apostles, as they entered the cloud and heard the voice of the divine presence, to fall prostrate in awe and terror before our God. But Jesus meets the fallen and trembling as the minister of grace, bearing upon him their nature, touched with the feeling of their infirmities, and bids them "arise, be not afraid." He lifts them up from their fears, to see in him, God reconciled, to hear in him, God as their teacher, to follow in him, God as their example, and to find in him, God their exceeding great and eternal portion. His voice allays the tempests of the mind—and calms the troubled waters of the hearts—uttering sweet promises from God, of forgiveness and eternal life in his kingdom. Wherever his voice is heard, there may his disciples follow without fear. The work, for which he came down to earth, was to conduct the humble and believing to heaven: and he, who is the well-beloved Son of the Father and is accepted by him, and strengthened by him in this work, will not fail to complete the work and to see all his obedient followers safe through all their fears and sorrows. Let them fear not then, when they hear his voice and follow it,—though he call them up into the awful presence of God, though he lead them down to fearful conflicts among their fellow men. Whenever and wherever he leadeth them forth, he goeth before them as their Guide and Protector, and so long as they hear his voice and follow it—in precept, in invitation, in encouragement, or in warning—they know that their Heavenly Shepherd is nigh. They trust in his care, and are not afraid. His presence quells their fears. Their hearts are established in quietness and peace on the everlasting rock of his love.

5. They who follow Christ are led by him from their errors into truth, while his enemies are left in their errors to oppose the plans of God and perish.

These different consequences, which arise from the different manner in which Christ is treated, are clearly exemplified in the case of the disciples as they descended with Jesus from the mount, and of the scribes as it was represented in the discourse of Jesus. The disciples, it seems, cherished the same opinion as the scribes concerning the coming of Elias: the opinion, that the prophetic passage in Malachi, IV: 5, which represents Elias to come to prepare the way of the Messiah, referred literally to the return of Elijah the Tishbite to the earth, and not, as a prophetic symbol, to a new prophet coming in the spirit and power of Elijah—the spirit and power by which he brought Israel back from Baal to Jehovah—the spirit of repentance and reformation. No doubt the disciples at this time saw evidence enough to convince them that Jesus was the Messiah, without this sign of Elias: yet they were expecting this sign also. And when on the mount Elijah appeared, they concluded, no doubt, that they had seen this prophetical signal, and were prepared to tell the unbelieving, even the scribes, of this evidence. And when Jesus enjoined upon them utter silence, as to the whole scene, to some future day, the wrong opinion they entertained was made obvious in their questions to Jesus. The opportunity was thus clearly presented to Jesus to make known to them their error, and that of the scribes in regard to this prophetic mark of the Messiah. He kindly instructs them, and corrects them of their error by making known to them the truth. Elias, indeed, must first come: but not the translated and heavenly Elijah. He will not leave the glories of his heavenly state, to encounter the trials of earth again in preaching repentance. The Elias of prophecy has already come, and these very scribes who pretend to demand his presence have rejected him and are ready to condemn me. The truth was now clear and obvious to their minds. They saw that John the Baptist had fulfilled the prophetic character of Elias. And this new signal, in harmony with the many others that had already convinced them, added new strength to their faith. They go forth from the glory of the mount, and with these new views of prophecy imparted to them on their descent by their teacher—to cleave to Jesus with increasing faith, and to follow him on the path to heaven with new courage and with livelier hopes. While the scribes in their enmity, refusing to hear and learn the truth from his lips, still cling to their error, and, emboldened by it, grow more hardened in their opposition to the Saviour; and, far from the way of life, fall beneath the curse of God, and perish in their sins.

Thus is it, that they who follow Jesus find, by his instruction and teaching, their knowledge, their faith, their hopes increased as they advance towards heaven, while they that reject him and refuse the light and aid of his instructions sink deeper into error, doubt, and darkness on their way to eternity; and must find on their entrance into that world, that they have opposed the plans adopted of God for salvation—that they have wandered forever from Jesus Christ, the only source of forgiveness and healing—and must perish forever beneath the weight of remediless guilt, remorse, despair, and anguish.

My friends, if you would enter into a heaven of glory beyond this mortal state ; if you would have a refuge amid the ills and burdens of the present life ; if you would cheer and strengthen yourselves on your way, with foretastes of the joy and glory to come ; if you would hear the voice of a Comforter and Almighty Friend, to quell your rising fears and apprehensions on the way ; if you would go on increasing in knowledge and love and hope and joy to the end ; look to Jesus, the beloved Son of God, who has come to make known to us the love and grace of our Heavenly Father.  Follow him, who by his death has opened the kingdom of heaven to believers, and who shines as their Mediator and Lord on its throne. Follow him, who guides his obedient people through this life by his counsel, and at life's close admits them with his own cheering voice into glory.

# MAN'S IGNORANCE RESPECTING HIS FUTURE IN THIS LIFE.

[A BACCALAUREATE SERMON.]

## ECCLESIASTES VI: 12.

WHO KNOWETH WHAT IS GOOD FOR MAN IN THIS LIFE, ALL THE DAYS OF HIS VAIN LIFE, WHICH HE SPENDETH AS A SHADOW?

WHAT is this life of man? How short and hurried from infancy to the grave! It passes like the shadow of the passing cloud that flits across the plain and disappears, leaving no trace behind. Vain as the airy bubble which, as its rainbow tints of glory attract the gaze, is gone. Brief days and few, comprehend it all: and these are often days of empty illusions, and hopes ending in vanity and vexation of spirit.

. What is good for man in this life? Who knoweth? Who can tell what schemes for happiness he will have length of life or power to accomplish? Who can tell what schemes, if successful, will most advance his temporal interests? Who, what degree of temporal prosperity will best comport with his spiritual and eternal interests? Who knoweth these things? or who that is ignorant on these points, can know what is in reality good for man?

The question of Solomon will have far different meanings attached to it, accordingly as we suppose it to come from the lips of a skeptic, who denies the existence of God and a future state, or of the believer, who admits both. From the skeptic, the question would imply that man passes his whole existence here in utter ignorance of any good that is worthy of his pursuit, dreaming amid shadows that terminate in endless night. From the believer, that man is ignorant, not of a good worthy of his pursuit, but of that temporal condition in life, and those temporal schemes which will be truly good to him, as the means of advancing his true welfare on the long line of his endless existence.

This is the thought, which will now occupy our attention—that man is ignorant as to what in temporal things is best for his welfare.

Let us look at this ignorance, in regard to its *nature*, its *extent*, and its *causes*.

I. It is not ignorance as to the *intrinsic nature* of good and evil. Good and evil, both natural and moral, are things clearly known to man. Indeed, the distinctions between right and wrong, and happiness and misery, are among the earliest lessons he acquires in life. His own nature is the deep seat of this knowledge. His own experience writes the lesson in plain and indelible characters. His observation of his fellow men ever confirms the truth of his own experiences.

Nor again, is he necessarily ignorant of the great object to which it is good to devote this life, or what are truly good and useful rules of living. The Creator has made known enough of his own self and the laws and plans of his righteous government, to point out to man the true and only path to a happy life and glorious immortality in his kingdom. In the works of creation he sets forth his eternal power and Godhead, so as to leave without the excuse of ignorance all who refuse to glorify him as God. In the riches of his forbearing and compassionate providence towards man, he calls upon him to return to him in repentance, and not waste these days of forbearance in hardening his heart and aggravating his final doom. Knowledge therefore of the true object of the present life is published abroad by the Creator through his works, even among the very heathen. Who then that has come to the knowledge of the Gospel, and hears God in Christ expressly calling upon him to pursue the path that leads to virtue and eternal glory, can claim ignorance of what object and rules of action are good for man?

But the ignorance justly attributable to man in regard to the good or evil of the present life, relates simply to the particulars of his temporal lot, as to what of good or evil will accrue to him from any merely temporal pursuit or condition. In managing his temporal affairs, and attempting to elevate his worldly estate, he cannot foresee what the precise and final result to himself will be—whether happy or disastrous. He is ignorant therefore of what, in the matters of the present life, is best for him. He knoweth not whether this or that course will prove prosperous, or whether both alike will not be adverse.

11. Let us now look over this field of his ignorance, and see its *extent*—how much there is here to affect the welfare of man, of the precise result of which he is yet in complete ignorance. This pall of ignorance covers this whole temporal scene—all the days of this vain life—this life, through whose mazes man passes not only with the rapidity, but in the darkness of "a shadow." From infancy to the grave, each step is taken by him in ignorance of precisely the onward and far stretching results.

But let us analyze, and look more distinctly at, the separate things in this great field of our temporal life, which are to affect our welfare,—and of the precise result of which, whether for good or evil, we are ignorant.

Man knoweth not, I observe, when he engages in any particular temporal scheme, whether he will meet with success in it or defeat. He may indeed bring to his aid the wisdom and experience of others, as well as his own, in devising his schemes; and there may appear to him that reasonable prospect of success, which is necessary to keep hope alive and stir up to industry. Yet for the actual result he must wait in suspense. He knows not whether he will be competent to cope with every obstacle that may rise up in his path. Defeat may overtake the wisest plans. The activity of others may foreclose the avenues to success. Unexpected dispensations of providence withdraw the means. The heart faint; the health decline ; life itself close, in the midst of the race.

Man knoweth not again, whether any particular instance of temporal success will promote or hinder his general prosperity in life. He knows indeed, that success in obtaining any valuable object is to be put down, on the balance sheet of life, as an item on the side of prosperity ; and that the sum total that is gained and kept during the progress of life, is to decide whether that life on the whole has been one of temporal prosperity or adversity. But whether prosperity in one thing, and at one particular period in life, will advance his prosperity in all the days of this life, how can he tell? That which he gains he may not be able to keep, and partial success at one time may hinder success in other things and at other periods of life. The friends you gain, the property you acquire, the reputation awarded you, in early life, may prove not the prospering gale and expanding sheet that is to bear your bark onward in safety to the port, but the syren song of the tempter, or the dead weights of care, or the fierce winds of passion, that set you on the backward current, and fill the voyage of life with disappointment and disaster.

Still again, man knoweth not whether any degree of temporal prosperity he may acquire will prove a good, in its results on his moral and spiritual interests. In both temporal *prosperity* and *adversity* the voice of *God* may be heard and heeded, or, on the contrary, the voice of *human passions*. Calls to duty may be heard in them, or solicitations to sin. Who then knoweth beforehand what in this life will prove good for him, whether prosperity or adversity will most favor him, in relation to a moral and religious life—and the endless life that is to come. Prosperity may speak of the kindness of God, of the duty of acting as his steward, and of the opportunities, fair and multiplied, of doing good : yet to weak and erring man, it may but bring pride and idleness and sin, fostering the animal passions in their growth, and deadening the religious sensibilities of the heart. How many, who walked humbly and carefully in their early days, when exalted by prosperity have fallen into profligacy and vice, and ruined their peace and their hopes for eternity ! Adversity too may remind man of his feebleness, his guilt and unworthiness, and show him the correcting hand of God that seeks to advance his holiness; and yet, to weak and selfish man, it may prove but the occasion of fostering rebellion and murmurings of heart against God, and of envy, malice, and fraud towards the prosperous among men. Who then knoweth what particular temporal lot is best—what will prove truly good to him on the long line of endless years which are before him, and to which this life is but the stepping-stone and entrance—what will best secure his love and moral obedience towards God, and fit and ripen his spirit for the glories of heaven?

III. Let us now trace this ignorance of man to its *causes.*

Man, however little he may think of it, while daily busied on the theater and in the pursuits of this life, is inseparably connected with the providence of God, and his very being interwoven into the deep plans of the Creator. The springs of his welfare lie beyond himself, beyond the created universe around him,—in the good pleasure and gracious working of the Almighty. His ignorance therefore of what is best for him in this scene of earthly providences, may be traced to three causes :—to the imperfection and weakness of his own nature ; to the complicate means and influences of divine providence surrounding him, that bear on his welfare; and to the ability of God, by the presence or withdrawal of his Spirit, to render at will all earthly conditions alike the means of good or evil, a blessing or a curse.

Man is a creature limited and weak. His views, feelings and purposes are continually exposed to change. He cannot therefore build on his present self the calculations of entire certainty. He cannot see, from what he now is, precisely what he will be in the future, or tell what may then be the effect of things upon him, from the manner in which they affect him now. That which pleases him to-day, may not on the morrow. That which benefits him to-day, may lose its influence upon him to-morrow. That which meets him harmless now, may tempt him to evil then. His own being, which is weaving along this woof of life, by its weakness, its fickleness, its changes, thus baffles his calculations of the future. His own being, that is subject to the plans of providence, does not remain that one fixed thing, that the same external things should forever have upon it one and the same effect. Here then is one source of his ignorance of good in this life. He is himself too variable a quantity to be always affected alike by the same things. He cannot therefore calculate the effect that the varying conditions of life will have upon him, even should he have power to foretell what those conditions shall be.

Again, the complicate nature of the means and influences that providence employs to bear on his welfare, is another source of this ignorance. In this vast earthly scene of human life, how many things, how various beyond all human computation, are influencing the feelings and working on the destiny of man. His animal constitution, with all its parts and propensities ; his mental, with all its powers and faculties ; his moral, with all its varied sensibilities, constitute a little world of causes and influences that bear mutually on one another and constantly on his welfare. The many objects and varying scenes of the natural world, and the varied influences that come up to him from the world of his fellow-creatures, all conspire to work upon him for good or evil. Here then are causes constantly affecting his well-being, too numerous and complicate for his limited mind to comprehend fully, and accurately compute. How then shall he arrive at the knowledge of precise results to himself in the future, from their causes ? What his earthly condition will be on the morrow, or how that condition will affect his welfare, are questions involved in such an intricate maze of causes and effects, that no reasoning on his part from cause to effect can solve the problem. They can be known beforehand only to that omniscient One, who guides the illimitable means of his providence at will. How then can man, involved in this complicate maze of providence, tell what particular earthly condition will come to him on the morrow, or know whether his lot to-day will work to him for *good* or *ill* in the future?

But still further, the mind and will of God as to final results are not known from the particular outward lot he assigns to man. He can employ at will the same earthly providences in kind, both for good or evil. His plan is to constitute this life a scene of discipline for the moral trial of men and their training for another life. He employs the temporal gifts and bounties of his providence, to support and comfort man on his way indeed, yet not as the end, but as a means in subordination to the higher end of carrying forward a plan of moral government and redemption, which is to issue in calling the obedient and faithful to eternal salvation and glory. No man knoweth then good or evil from God's distribution or withdrawal of merely earthly gifts. For, by means of the spiritual influences he employs through the revelation of Jesus Christ and a future state, and the power of his own Spirit, he can turn the same outward providences, which, through the perversion of man, become occasions of moral evil and ruin, into means of spiritual obedience and holiness. The good or evil accruing to man from earthly things can be truly estimated, only from the spiritual and eternal results which they are made to work within him—whether their effect is to bring his soul to the love, service and enjoyment of God, or to draw it away from God into the evils of sin, self-reproach and malice. God therefore is able to confound all human calculations, by turning any temporal condition of man into a good or an evil, a blessing or a curse. He can impart or he can withhold his Spirit, and in this way turn the issue. He can make all his providential dealings work together for good to them that love him, who are called according to his plan and purpose. He can make all work together for ill to them that hate him, and are rejected. How then shall man know good or evil from merely outward and temporal providences? He must seek his good from God himself, and not from his gifts. He must wait on God for the development of his hidden counsels of grace. He must solve the question of good or evil to himself in this life, by waiting on God for his decisions of grace or judgment, of eternal life or death.

If then we consider man as subject to the deep plans of infinite wisdom, how weak and changeable a being he is, how many and complicate causes and influences in the universe around him bear on his welfare, and how able God is to overrule every earthly state and condition for good or evil at his pleasure, is it any wonder that man should be ever ignorant, in his progress through life, of what earthly lot is best for his welfare?

We may derive from this subject some lessons of practical wisdom.

1. Let then your ignorance in regard to the things of this life, teach you moderation in your worldly schemes and pursuits. You are not your own lords and masters in the creation. There is an infinitely greater and wiser being over you, who has linked you to the plans of his own providence, and is watching over your interests. Be not rash and precipitate in your plans. Be not over confident in your ability to command success. Be not over eager in your expectations from the world. How often is the folly of this excessive confidence and eagerness in the pursuit of worldly good, reproved in the after revelations of providence. The men guilty of it, think the objects they seek are secure. As they rush forward in the chase, the treasures they covet float before them as realities: the way to them seems clear; the vision of their glory is bright: the heart expands with large hopes of coming joy. How does this over eagerness defeat the happiness and welfare of man. It unfits him for either disappointment or success. It gives to him, in disappointment, the heaviest pangs of wounded pride and blasted hopes. It renders success a curse, which ministers to that lust of the world and pride of life which separate him from the love of his Father in heaven.

2. Again, let this ignorance of what is best for you in this temporal life, teach you submission to the allotments of providence. Your Heavenly Father knoweth what

are your wants and necessities, and what is best for your welfare; and can and will make all things work together for good to those who in love entrust themselves to his care. Why then should you, in your blindness, vainly seek to assume the supreme disposal to your own hands, and refuse submission? To trust in his care, to rest in his love, to feel quiet in the thought that he seeks in every lot he appoints us our best good, is itself a spiritual treasure of peace and joy, richer far than any worldly inheritance can give. Why refuse submission? Do you allow yourself, in your blindness, to feel dissatisfied with his allotment, and to think that you can manage better than he? But that is to set yourself at known variance with God, which is a greater evil than any earthly privation. That is to fill your hearts with the spiritual evils of discontent, anxiety, covetousness, envy, hatred,—for which no earthly lot can compensate.

3. Again; let your ignorance of what is best for you in your earthly allotment, teach you to devote yourselves principally to the known duties of life. In pursuing the things of the world, we may justly feel doubtful whether we shall gain them, or whether, if gained, they will prove salutary or hurtful. But on the path of known duty to God and man, what is there to mislead or betray? or who shall harm us, while following that which we know to be good? For the path of known duty is ever the path of safety. Our chief business in this life then, is with our duties: not with our own pleasures, profits, or honors. These we may well leave to the disposal of God, while we seek, first of all, to serve him in his kingdom and follow him in his righteousness.

Our duties call us to the pursuit of noble and useful ends: to labor for the right, the good, the true, among men and before God. Whether we succeed or not to accomplish much in them for our God and our generation, we shall, at least, expand and cheer our own hearts with the sweet affections of charity, and carry along with us the approving testimony of God and our own conscience. On this course, if he cheer us with his earthly gifts and bounties, they will raise our hearts to him in thankfulness; if he withdraw our comforts, and smite us with earthly sorrows, we will take with patience the chastisement of his faithful love! On this course, we enter into sweet fellowship with God in his kingdom and righteousness, and our hearts are linked to his in the bonds of unity and love unfailing.

Finally, let your ignorance of good in this temporal life lead you while passing through it, to secure an eternal life with God in heaven. Amid the darkness and uncertainties of this temporal state, all is not dark. The way to secure an eternal life with God in heaven is made known and published. We have a sure word of prophecy from God himself, revealing to us the unfading glories of a heavenly state beyond this life. Jesus Christ has come, with signs of power before eye-witnesses of his majesty, and been accredited with a voice from heaven as the Beloved Son of the Father,—bringing with him the promise of grace and eternal life to believers.

Here then is a light shining upon us in our darkness; a light from the heavenly world; a light that marks out to us the way to reach its glories. The highway of life is the plain way of holiness. The wayfarer that travels it, however simple, need not err. The ransomed of the Lord, in every age, return upon it from all their wanderings, and come with joy to the heavenly Zion.

We do well therefore to look beyond the cares and anxieties of this uncertain life to an eternal life with God in heaven, and to seek for ourselves, in the forgiving and sanctifying grace which the Gospel offers, an inheritance in its pure and unfading happiness. Here, in the unfailing truth of God in the Gospel, we know our footing is sure. Here we build our happiness on the Rock of Ages. Here we enter into the knowledge and love of God and his Son Jesus Christ, whom to know and love is the very ingredient and principle of life eternal. The day of eternal joy already dawns within our hearts. The day-star of hope rises there, the harbinger of eternal rest. This is to make the true and proper use of the present life.

This is to render our passage through its vanities and flitting shadows, a cheering pilgrimage to a better land. This opens before us at our journey's end the portals of heaven, and gives us an entrance and a welcome into the eternal house of our Father above.

These lessons of practical wisdom I would set before you,—Beloved Pupils and Friends,—as my last and parting counsel. They are derived from that ignorance of good in your earthly lot which ever accompanies you in this life.

They have been inculcated upon you by your past experience. From infancy to this hour, as you have advanced along the pathway of life, you have been learning the incompetency of this world to form your satisfying portion of joy, and that, beyond the parents and kind friends around you, that have helped your progress, there is a God whose providence presides over this whole scene, and calls you to seek your happiness in his love and service. Have no mistakes, no sins, no sorrows, revealed to you your incompetence and danger? Have no deaths of once merry companions shown you your dependence?· The Gospel,—has it not been a treasure at your side, to tell you of the love of God in Christ, and win you to his heart and care?

These precepts of wisdom are strongly inculcated upon you at this hour, as you stand on the threshold of this brief home of your preparatory studies, about to separate from your instructors and each other, it may be forever. You now look out on the untrod and unknown paths before you. Shall your way through this busy life be prosperous or adverse? The darkness that lies over, and conceals from you your future lot, bids you be thoughtful and not rash ; to rely not on your own heart, but on the wisdom that cometh from above.

The secret of a happy life is easily told : a sound mind and body ; earthly passions subdued ; reconciliation to God ; useful employment among men ; and hope, stretching its cheering, animating vision onward to eternity.

This is the solution furnished by experience; embodied in precepts of wisdom.

Adopt them as your maxims of life. Go out from us, not to inflame your hearts with the ambition, the covetousness, the sensuality of the world. Go out, humbly and confidently entrusting the disposal of your lot to the decisions of an all-wise Creator. Go out, to serve God and your generation in some department of useful action. Go forth to seek, as pilgrims through this life, your richest treasures and joys with God and Christ in Heaven.

Make these the guiding principles of your lives, and you will be truly wise—wise unto salvation. Without them, this life will indeed be vain. All its most splendid visions of happiness will be but illusions to sicken with disappointment, to lead onward to stranding on the rocks of sin and vice and death. Its hurried progress will be the shadowy cloud gathering to its bosom the elements of an eternal night of tempest and storm beyond this horizon of hope.

With these words of counsel, I bid you, in my own behalf and that of my associates in office,—Farewell.

HEBREWS XIII: 14.

HERE HAVE WE NO CONTINUING CITY.

THE period was now approaching in which Jerusalem —the city of the Hebrews—the great metropolis built by their fathers, and ever their pride and joy, was, in accordance with the prediction of the Saviour, to be laid waste. They were to leave their possessions and homes, and flee, as the Saviour had directed them, into the mountains ; or, if they were inhabitants of other cities, were to sympathize with their brethren who should thus suffer. The apostle reminds them in these circumstances of trial, that they were not to consider any residence on earth as designed for permanence. They might grieve at the ruin of their beloved city ; but they ought not to be immoderately attached to the place that had served as a home to them and their fathers, because no residence on earth was intended to be the permanent dwelling of men. No city on earth could they call 'a continuing city' ; for they could dwell in none but a few years before they entered into eternity.

The instruction of the apostle is as applicable to us, as it was originally to the afflicted Hebrews ; and we need as much reminding as did they—if not for consolation especially under expected trials, yet for a spiritual improvement of our privileges—that we have upon earth no continuing city. This truth, at all times momentous, deserves peculiarly our consideration, at the season when we have just bidden adieu to another year of our lives, and are greeting a new one, with its uncertain prospects.

Let us, then, enter with seriousness into the contemplation of the fact, that *the world is not our permanent dwelling.* The certainty we feel respecting it is derived from the evidence we possess of our own approaching deaths, which will remove us out of the world, and the evidence we also have that our being will still continue after death for an eternity. From these sources we have been accustomed, from childhood, to consider the fact, whenever it has recurred to our minds, as certain beyond all question, that our dwelling on earth has no permanence compared with the eternity of our being. I shall say nothing, therefore, to establish a fact of which we all feel a perfect moral certainty; but shall take advantage of the mora. certainty we all feel about it, to speak—

I. Respecting some means that are calculated constantly to remind us of the fact;

II. Respecting some evidences of our great blindness to the fact; and,

III. Respecting some practical results we should derive from the fact, that ' here we have no continuing city.'

I. I am, first, to mention some means that are adapted constantly to remind us that we have no permanent abode on earth.

We have such a means, then, in the fact that *we have received our privileges from those who have already left the world.* Almost all our privileges are associated thus with the mortality of others, who have been instrumental in conveying them over to our possession. Other men have labored here before us : we have entered into their labors. In the city of our residence, we are always walking amidst the monuments of preceding generations—the works of immortal beings, who, as strangers here before us, tarried but for a day. The houses we inhabit, the streets we walk, the sanctuaries we frequent, the Scriptures of truth, all bespeak to us the agency of other beings who have been on earth before us ; who took up in it no settled abode ; who quickly passed through it to eternity. All our privileges are thus put into our hands, with the loud language of the dead to us for monition, that we do not take them into permanent possession. Everywhere, then, in the city of our residence on earth, are such mementos, to remind us constantly how short is to be our dwelling here.

We have such a memento, again, in the fact that *others, who have been sharing with us in our privileges, are constantly leaving the world.* They who dwell with us in the city of our residence on earth—beings of immortality—are constantly bidding us adieu, and entering into eternity. All our privileges thus become associated with the memory of former companions, who once had their abode below. They dwelt with us but a few days; they scarcely made themselves known to us, when they gave the farewell look, pressed the parting hand, bade adieu, and entered on an abode in eternity—the tolling bell, the mournful procession, the grave of their relics, the erected monument, signalized their departure;—and now all around the city of our abode are the traces of their former presence, reminding us of our having no continuing residence here. We look back at the days they passed with us before they entered into eternity, and they appear to us but an hand-breadth; and, from their dwelling in eternity, we seem to hear them say, as we miss them from the scenes in which they once mingled with us, that these are scenes where pilgrims to eternity tarry but a day. When in the habitations where they once dwelt, with us, or the streets where they walked with us, or the sanctuary to which they went with us in company, or at the mercy seat where they once bent with us the knee of devotion, or by the Scriptures before which they once listened with us to the words of Jesus Christ, we look for them; but they are gone;—the place they once occupied at our side is vacant; —they are far from us in their eternal dwelling; and the places where we once knew them are now so many mementos, that here we ourselves have no continuing city.

We have another constant memento of this fact, in *the advancement we are constantly making ourselves towards eternity.* Everything in the city of our residence on earth reminds us that we are never stationary in it, but are always advancing towards the period of our final departure. We have entered into a scene of divine wonders, but we cannot delay to spend our existence here in gazing upon them : we are constantly in motion, urging our way through them to an eternal dwelling. Each breaking morn, each radiant noon, each shadowy eve, as they pass by us, make no tarrying, but pass us never more to return. The jocund spring, summer with his swarms of life, autumn with her golden harvests, winter with his icy sceptre and his snowy robes, as each year they pass us, are in constant motion ; and while we greet them, take their leave of us forever. Each changing scene of life arrests our minds—enlists our feelings ; then takes its final leave of us, the sons of eternity. Creeping infancy, merry boyhood, aspiring youth, industrious manhood, decrepit age, we meet in swift succession ; just greet ; and bid adieu for eternity. In the midst of all the privileges of the city of our residence below, do our advancing steps towards the eternal world serve constantly to remind us that here we have no permanent dwelling. The aggregate of days that have passed by us, the yearly seasons, the scenes of life and periods of age, since we came into possession of our privileges—since we first knew our dwellings, and walked our streets, and visited our sanctuaries, and heard the words of God—are so many advances towards eternity ; and tell, as they thicken on the path we leave, how soon we reach the close of our pilgrimage and enter upon unknown worlds.

We have another constant memento of the fact, again, in our *inability of prolonging our continuance in the world.*

We have constant notices around us of our frailty, and inability to continue to ourselves our present privileges for the future. Ever, in the city of our privileges below, do we see ourselves hurried on by an unseen hand we cannot control ; the Almighty Guide who conducts us seems unwilling that we should stay ; the God of our spirits who goes with us designs we should have our settled dwelling in eternity ; and soon he will bring us to the gates of the city, and at the bidding we cannot resist must we take our leave of it for eternity. Around us, everything is betokening his design of our departure, and our inability to prolong our stay. The frail hold we take of every earthly possession tells us that our grasp on none is for eternity. We are hurried on from object to object, before we can call anything ours. We meet friends; but while we cling to them, the unseen hand of providence tears us away from their embrace. Beauty we would linger here to admire; but, while we look, the grace of the fashion of it perisheth. Power just takes us by the hand; and bids us adieu to greet a successor. Fame crowns us with her wreath; but, while we feel the rising flush of joy, she plucks it off to sport with others. Wealth comes to feast us and roll us in his car of pleasures; and while accepting his proposals, he dismisses us to tempt some other pilgrims on their way to eternity. The unseen hand of providence thus tears us away from object after object, to show that here is not our rest, and that our hold on earth is frail and giving way. Around the city of our habitation too, are the messengers he sends to warn us of our approaching departure. Decay stands, with tottering limbs and feeble breath; and lisps to us, with dying life, that we draw nigh the gate of our habitation, and soon will leave it for eternal worlds. Diseases—busy messengers—fly here and there to tell us of our frail abode, and whisper in our ears 'eternity.' Death, armed with resistless power, stands with his commissions and their unknown dates, to lead us out of our residence below, and bar on us its gates forever. Everywhere in the city of our abode are we reminded thus, that we have not the power to prolong our stay in it, and that soon we shall leave its privileges, its dwellings, its streets, its sanctuaries, its Scriptures, its busy throng, for eternity. 'Here have we no continuing city.'

There is another means reminding us constantly of this fact, *the voice of God the Saviour.* In the city of our habitation below, God has published his glories, his statutes, his offers of pardon and assistance, for our use as sojourners here who are passing to eternity. He, the infinite Being who is from everlasting to everlasting himself, has conferred on us an existence that is to continue and grow up by the side of his through everlasting ages. He has beheld us, in the first stages of our being here, engaged in unrighteous rebellion against his authority, and bent on neglect of its glories; and, moved with pity, has sent his everlasting Son to atone for our guilt and call us to repentance, and his Holy Spirit to indite his will and influence us to obedience. In our habitation, we have his word; here temples are erected for his service; a day is appointed by him for men to assemble; ministers are commissioned to teach; and they who love his name speak to one another and to their fellow-men of his designs. Wherever we go then, the voice of God the Saviour is reaching us, and re-echoing the truth that we are beings whose final dwelling is eternity, and who have here no continuing city. The Bible, whenever it meets our eye, reiterates the voice of God, that we must die and rise again in other worlds. In each reproof of conscience, his awful voice is heard to speak a reckoning day in eternity. In each act we do for God or for his kingdom here, his voice of love whispers of eternal joys. Each revolving Sabbath, with its pealing bells and open sanctuaries and solemn rites, bears on its hours his voice, that warns of an abode in heaven or hell. Each sermon is the call he makes to hear his voice to-day. In each season of prayer, we hear him say that we have not reached our home—that we are pilgrims here. From the throne of glory on which he will sit in judgment, and assign us our dwellings in eternity, God the Saviour now sends down the voice of monition; and, while it rolls around the world we dwell in, ten thousand messengers echo back the voice to our ears: that 'here we have no continuing city.'

II. But there are evidences that, in respect to a fact so momentous, and of which we are constantly reminded from so many quarters, there is in us *great blindness.*

One evidence of this is, that *we think so little* of our departure. There is a train of thoughts in which our minds are constantly busy, and over which we have a guiding control. When we look back on this past employment of our minds, and see the vast train of our secret thoughts, where are those we have had respecting the brevity of our continuance on earth, and our approaching departure into eternity? Do they rise up to our memories in that thick array, which testifies that we have lived sufficiently mindful of so important a reality? Do they not rather appear in such momentary glances of thought, and at such distant intervals from each other, as to evince our blindness? Do the secret thoughts of our departure occupy such prominence in the train, as do the thoughts of those worldly trifles that meet us in the city of our habitation? And has not this been great blindness in us; when the monuments of past generations, the departure of surrounding companions, our progress, our frailty, yonder throne of God the Saviour, have been constantly visible, to excite in us the thoughts of eternity?

Another evidence of our great blindness to the fact is, that *we speak so little* of our departure into eternity. We have been conversant with our fellow-men who have lived . with us in the city of our habitation. We have met them in our streets and in our dwellings, and many have been the words we have spoken with them that have been lodged in their memories. When we look back on the words we have spoken, where have been the allusions we have made to our and their departure into eternity, or where the direct mention? We have alluded to many subjects, we have directly mentioned many, in their hearing; and their memories can testify of us, whether, when walking or sitting with them, amidst the loud monitors of an eternity, we have given that prominence in our words, that we ought, to the hastening change in our habitation, or whether we have appeared blind to a change so momentous? Their memories may testify to our words of affection on many subjects—(oh! that they might not to words of deceit! to words of anger!)—but must they not, when they see the dearth of our allusions and mentions about an hereafter, testify, in their consciences and in eternity, that great was our blindness?

Another evidence of our great blindness to the fact is, that *we do so little* respecting our approaching departure into eternity. There is much to be done in the city of our habitation here, before we leave it for eternity. Duties to ourselves, duties to our fellow-men, and duties to our God, claim of us a discharge while passing through our abode below. Acts of penitence, acts of faith, acts of obedience, are to be done by us in our persons; acts of charity to the souls of our neighbors; acts of respect to God;—before we are prepared to enter with comfort on eternity. What, then, have we done for our departure into eternity? Does the remembrance of the acts we have done while dwelling in our habitation below—a habitation crowded with mementos of eternity—testify that we have done what we ought to prepare for our exchange of dwellings? Or that we have been exceedingly blind to a change so great? Alas, we can testify to many acts that unfit us for departing! Can we to any that prepare? Or, if we have turned our eye to a better abode, and done anything to prepare ourselves for it, have not our acts of preparation been feeble and sparse, and proved exceeding blindness in us to eternity?

Another evidence of the fact is, that we *feel so little* about departing from our present abode into eternity. We may have thought and spoken and acted, in the city of our habitation here, to some poor extent, with reference to an approaching eternity; but what has been the measure of feeling we have allowed ourselves to indulge on a subject so momentous? We have had intense feelings to expend on other subjects. The vanities, the pleasures, the vexations of our present abode, may have stirred all our souls within us to energy of feeling. Have we, while ten thousand voices have been proclaiming around us 'eternity!' allowed ourselves to feel as intensely as we ought on a reality so weighty? Or must not the past train of our feelings witness for us, that great has been our blindness? That while love has admitted the claims of other objects, it has here been cold ; that while zeal has been active for other purposes, it has here grown weary ; that while desire has been intense for other ends, it has here been wavering ?

When we look, then, at what we have thought, what we have spoken, what we have done, what we have felt, in the city of our habitation below, amidst the constant monitions of an hereafter, we may see evidence that we have been almost as blind to eternity, as though we were to have here our permanent dwelling. Impenitent sinners have closed their eyes, that they will not see ; and the followers of our Lord Jesus Christ have been either sleeping, or, in wakeful moments, but seeing through a glass darkly.

III. But the fact, of which we have so many monitions, and respecting which we have manifested such blindness, that 'here we have no continuing city,' nevertheless claims of us a *practical attention ;* and the *practical results we should derive from it*, I will endeavour to illustrate in my closing remarks.

The fact then should influence us to adopt a *settled rule of duty.*

What is the object of our existence here and in eternity ? What are the means of securing it ? Have we any rule of safety for our guidance ? Have we, in the gospel, the words of God ? Shall we take it as our guide and our hope in the house of our pilgrimage ? Or shall we reject it, and follow our own devices ?

This practical question the brevity of our abode below demands that we should firmly settle—and adopt, if worthy of it, the gospel as our settled rule, or prove it vain, and take some other rule. We have no time to waste in doubts. We must not squander time in hesitation ? We stand by the very gates of eternity. The gospel, that now tenders to us its guidance in the steps of this pilgrimage, we shall soon leave, with the city of our habitation, and have a whole eternity to employ in looking back upon our conduct here. If the Bible contain the words of God, we shall pass by his throne on our way to our eternal dwelling; and these words, which Jesus gave us, shall judge us in that day of meeting God.  If our Lord Jesus Christ has, 'by his divine power, given us' in this book, 'all things which pertain to life and godliness,' then they who take not this gospel to sway their opinions and conduct here will be found, in that day, 'without the faith that pleases God,' guilty of 'treading under foot the blood of the Son of God,' and will receive condemnation, and 'go away into everlasting punishments': and they who do make it their influential rule will, in that day, 'cleansed from sin through sprinkling of the blood of Jesus,' 'unblamable in love through sanctification of the Spirit,' receive the approving welcome of God, and 'enter into life eternal.'

Again; the fact should influence us to *moderation in the use we make of the present world.*  Our worldly enjoyments are designed only as accommodations for us on our way to eternity.  The city of our habitation is furnished with them by God the Saviour, to sustain and cheer us in his service, while distant from his habitation.  We are surrounded on every hand, even now while we are partaking of these joys, with the monitions of eternity; and soon shall we leave our abode below to part with them forever. How little ought *we* to make of its enjoyments, who are so soon to leave them for eternity!  Why attach ourselves immoderately to a habitation, erected to lodge us on our way to eternity?  Why draw away our hearts from our final dwelling?  Why labor to strengthen ties so soon to be burst asunder?  We are but increasing for ourselves the pangs of the parting struggle.  We shall but bid adieu to our habitation with greater regret.  While absorbed in time, we shall be but neglecting eternity.  Eternity! how should it swallow up the comparatively trifling concerns of time, and make them all as nothing!  "This I say, brethren, the *time is short:* it remaineth that both they that have wives be as though they had none; and they that weep, as though they wept not; and they that rejoice, as though they rejoiced not; and they that buy, as though they possessed not; and they that use this world as not abusing it: for the fashion of this world passeth away."

Again; the brevity of our abode below should influence us to *improve our passing privileges and opportunities.* In the city of our residence in this world are we favored by God the Saviour with many privileges in regard to his service, and many opportunities of doing good to fellow-citizens who are advancing with us to eternity. These seasons of doing service for God are rapidly rolling over us; and soon, in our hasty advance to eternity, shall we pass by them all, and leave the city of our privileges forever. Each season, as it meets us in our progress, invites us to the glorious work of God, then bids us farewell, and bears to eternity the report of what we do and how we serve our King. Soon, on the shores of eternity, shall we look back on these privileges that met us, when with fellow-pilgrims here we urged our onward way, and date, from these years below, the era of our eternal joys or our unending woes. There, through the progress of eternal years, shall the privileges we are passing now be seen attesting those works whose influence follows us, in songs we raise with fellow heirs of glory, or curses mingled by us with angry spirits of despair. Now is our time, as privileges are passing by us, to escape the woes of hell, and fill eternity with joys. Each opportunity we pass will tell of eternal losses, or eternal gains. While then we greet each passing season privileged with grace, how watchful should we be to seize and use it for our God! With what fear of misimprovement and its woes, pass every day of our sojourning here! How ardent in our love to God and man! How constant to urge our bright and burning way, and to spread the savor of our love around us on fellow pilgrims to eternity!

Again; the fact that 'here we have no continuing city,' should influence us to *maintain a constant readiness for our departure into eternity.*

Soon the period will come, when we shall exchange our abode; and bidding adieu to the beings, the scenes and the privileges of the city, where we spent the first years of our existence, pass through the gates of death, and enter the eternal abode assigned us by our God. We have before us this season of solemnities in exchanging worlds.

> That awful day will surely come;
> The appointed hour makes haste;
> When I must stand before my Judge,
> And pass the solemn test.

Oh! to be able, in the day of our departure, to know that we have believed in a Saviour who has prepared mansions for us above; to have our souls filled with love to his glories and joys in his kingdom; to look, with the even serenity of trust, alike on a retiring world and on an opening eternity; to leave a sweet savor of our godliness on friends below, as the joys of eternity break on our souls; to be able to pass the solemnities of exchanging worlds in such a state of preparation,—brethren, is it not worth maintaining a constant readiness during our abode below! What anguish will wring the hearts of those who come to these solemnities, without having confided with devotedness in a Saviour; when, torn from their portion below, they enter on endless wailings! What terrors will distract those who, having believed in a Saviour, are so surprised, in that state of worldliness and unwatchfulness, as to cling with desire to their present abode, and recoil with horror from the clouds of uncertainty that veil eternity! Think, fellow-strangers here, of this approaching season of solemnities! While loud monitions tell you of the scene, awake from your lethargy, and prepare! 'Take heed to yourselves lest at any time your hearts be overcharged with surfeiting and cares of this life, and so that day overtake you unawares.' 'Stand with your loins girded about, and your lights burning, like unto men that wait for their lord.' 'Be sober:' 'watch:' 'pray' 'always; that ye may be accounted worthy to escape all these things which shall come to pass, and to stand before the Son of Man.'

Fellow travellers to eternity! we have passed another year of our residence in the world below. As we have just bidden it adieu, and have closed up its concerns for the judgment and eternity, let us survey the paths in which we have been walking; and see whether we have been living for time or for eternity. Whither have been tending our thoughts, our words, our conduct, our hearts? At every step through the revolving year, God followed us with kind monitions of an hereafter. The ashes of the dead we trod, the monuments we saw of sleeping ancestors, these scenes where others lived, once busied here, now mouldered into dust, have whispered, as we passed along, 'eternity.' Companions too, flushed with health and life as we, when we stood together on the threshold of the year and hailed it with bright wishes, have passed beyond the vale and left their warnings. We saw them leave us; and as we looked around to scenes where once with us they mingled souls, the vacant place said for them 'eternity.' Our advancing life, and our frail tenements that scarcely held us here, have given us monitions. God the Saviour has passed us with his word, with his days of grace, with the triumphs of his redeeming love.

Have we lived for time? Or have we for eternity? Put the question home. The year is past. We cannot now recall its hours. Its records now are writ in heaven. When the archangel,

with his golden wing,
Sweeps stars and suns aside,

preparing the Son of God his way, the unrolled records of this year shall tell. When ages after ages roll away, high in the realms of bliss, or deep in the prison of despair, will you look back on years below, and date this year, celestial joys, or woes unending. Convert of Christ, who dost date this year the era of thy heavenly hopes, praise God that gave thee such a year of grace, and feel constraining love to yield him the willing sacrifice of life? Wavering follower of Christ, weep thy mis-spent hours, and pray the grace that blots such records out, and helps to spend remaining days for God! Christless sinner, see your path of death; awake, and live!

---

HEBREWS XIII: 14.

HERE WE HAVE NO CONTINUING CITY; BUT WE SEEK ONE TO COME.

THE Apostle, in the text, reminds his believing brethren of that better city,—the heavenly Jerusalem, in which they had laid up their hopes, and which, while on earth, they as pilgrims were seeking. Though their earthly city was not to continue,—though they were soon to see their hardened yet beloved Jerusalem laid waste, their kindred suffering, and themselves turned desolate upon the world, they were seeking a city to come, and soon would enter it, which would continue; where no hardening iniquity should ever defile, no curse of God descend, no enemy· lay waste, no sufferings enter: a city of unsullied love, immovable security, unending joys. Patient then might they well be in enduring the will of God awhile, who were expectants of so great and precious promises.

The apostle thus reminds all believers that, amid the instability of earthly things, they are to find their consolation in earnestly seeking that enduring city which God has prepared for the righteous in eternity.

Let us, then, for our spiritual benefit, direct our meditations to that continuing city to come; and inquire,

I. What are the sources of its joys?

II. Who are seeking it? and,

III. What are the evidences that they who do, will obtain admission?

1. What then are the sources of joy pertaining to this city of God in eternity? I answer,

First, *the inhabitants consist of countless numbers of intelligent beings, various in their orders and ages and origin.*

There is Jehovah, the greatest of intelligent beings, whose mysterious existence is forever exalted beyond the increasing researches of the highest creature, whose attri- butes know no limitation; whose age is from eternity; who has ever been present in all places of the universe; who reigns as the king, and shines as the light, of the celestial city forever more. And he describes himself as "dwelling among them," a fellow inhabitant! There also are the angels, whose number is "ten thousand times ten thousand and thousands of thousands." They are more in number than we are able to form an ade- quate idea of in the present state; being described by an apostle as "an innumerable company." From the des- cription given of them in the word of God, of their different orders and names and stations, it would seem probable that they are of different orders in their mental powers and attainments—some of them the most exalted in intelligence of created beings—and that they had their origin in different parts of the universe, and were trained up under different systems of providence, before they were collected "together in one in heavenly places." Their age goes far back, it is probable, of the date of the creation described by Moses; for Satan, once a com- panion of theirs, had already passed through his trial and fallen, when, in the early age of this world, he tempted our first parents; and Job, it has been supposed, describes angels, when speaking of the morning stars and sons of God as rejoicing over the creation of this system. There are also to be among the inhabitants of that celestial city —as it will ultimately be constituted—a multitude which no man can number of men from this world, collected from different ages and different parts of the world—from the east, the west, the north, the south—who constitute the redeemed of the Lord, rescued from sin, and trained up under a peculiar system of providence to prepare them for that city. Thus numerous and thus various in their orders, their ages, their origin, are the intelligent beings who reside in the city of God!

I remark again : all the inhabitants there are *actuated by holy love.* Jehovah, who has there fixed his everlasting throne, beams forth on the whole society the light of that intense love that awoke its various beings into existence, that followed them with his supporting hand and guiding care in the various places where they spent the first stages of their being. His is the love that collected them into one harmonious and happy society, to live under his smiles forever : the holy love, that adorns him with truth and justice and goodness and grace ; that preserved angels in holiness; that sent forth his Son and Spirit to the lost world to save the redeemed ; and that guides them, by his government in the celestial city, to waters of life and trees of life forever. All the innumerable hosts of created beings too in that city, are actuated by holy love. This is the character of angels that never fell, that were trained up in swift obedience to the will of God, that exercise their benevolence in deeds of ministry to heirs of salvation. This is the character of redeemed men, who turned from their rebellions to the service of God, and imitated their Saviour in doing good. to their fellow-men while on earth, and who were established unblamable in love on their admission to the city. These perfectly benevolent beings there spend, in one harmonious society, the days of their immortal existence.

Again ; *the deeds in which they are employed in that city are suited to gratify their benevolence.* In a society of intelligent beings who are completely perfect in love, there is nothing to hinder any one from engaging in conduct which he most loves. Though we know not all the peculiar employments of the inhabitants of the heavenly city, and probably could not know while surrounded with this clothing of flesh and blood, yet doubtless such a society gives scope to all the benevolent employment that is desirable to all the inhabitants. There Jehovah,—God and the Lamb,—is forever engaged in supporting, and reigning over, the society, guiding each and all in their employments and joys, leading them to fountains of living waters, and wiping away all tears forever : and he looks

with complacence on the everlasting fruits of his deeds of
kindness, pronouncing them very good ; and his deeds in
the society are suited to gratify his own heart of infinite
love.

There the innumerable company of angels and the
redeemed see, in each other, persons to whom they can
show forth kindness, and in whose holiness they can take
a complacent esteem, and in doing them good and par-
ticipating in their society can find employments suited to
gratify their benevolent hearts. Thus may a Paul find
his converts to be his crown and his joy above. There
too may they engage in various ways in doing the will
of God, in contemplating his perfections as they are
developing in his providence, and in studying the endless variety of his works. There too may they unite
in solemn acts of adoration and praise, as when the Seraphim vail their faces and cry, " Holy, holy, is the Lord
God of Sabbaoth "; or as when the elders " fall down
before the Lamb, having harps and golden vials full of
odors, and sing, Thou wast slain and hast redeemed us to
God by thy blood "; or as when the multitude of the
redeemed, " clothed with white robes and palms in their
hands, cry, with loud voice, Salvation to our God which
sitteth upon the throne and unto the Lamb "; or as
when the whole multitude of the numberless inhabitants
of the city throughout its remotest bounds swell with one
voice the chorus of praise, " Blessing and honor and glory
and power be unto him that sitteth upon the throne, and
unto the Lamb forever and ever." There in that everlasting city the innumerable inhabitants engage thus in un-
ceasing employments of benevolence and piety, employments that are suited to their high capacities of intelligence and their complete perfection in holiness.

Again ; the inhabitants are *secure in these joys for
eternity.* The city has immovable foundations, for its
builder and maker is God. He who liveth forever has
encircled it with walls of everlasting strength. He has
fixed his throne in it, to reign there forever and ever.
He has peopled it with perfectly holy inhabitants,

gathered from the whole universe, to set forth his eternal glories. Strong is his almighty arm to uphold and defend, to guide and bless; and he will employ it for the eternal welfare of his people. Unreached by death, unsullied by sin, undisturbed by enemies, unapproached by sufferings,—the countless multitude of its inhabitants, with increasing energies of mind and intensity of holy affection, continue the ceaseless round of their happy services forever and ever. No change awaits them more. They are now in their final home; in an everlasting dwelling; in a continuing city; an immovable kingdom.

II. But this city of endless habitation is to be sought during our present residence on earth, if we would obtain admission. Let us then inquire *who are seeking it as their final home.*

1. They who truly seek it are those who are *submitting themselves in faith to the word of God.* They are called to the new enterprise of seeking the kingdom and glory of God, by his word and Spirit. For it is God, by his word in Christ, who sets before us that eternal dwelling, and points to us the only way to reach its gates and have an entrance ministered to us into its everlasting joys. The vail that separates that world from us precludes vision: and they who are earnestly seeking it, confide themselves wholly to the word of God as the directory of their steps. They hear this, as it comes from the realms of eternity; and they start up at its call, to follow implicitly and unreservedly their guiding God. They are solicited indeed in their earthly pilgrimage by many guides, by many tempters, by many foes; but they hear the voice of God, and they confide all their happiness to that; and they say to every solicitation that would draw them aside from their purpose, 'Behind me; thou savorest not the things that be of God.' They yield to that word their opinions, and that is their faith; they yield to it their feelings, and that is their faith; they yield to it their lives, and that is their faith; they build on it their hopes, and that is their faith; and confiding solely in its guidance, as did Abra-

ham when leaving his kindred at its call, they are seeking that blest "city which hath foundations."

Again; they who seek that enduring city are *obedient to the will of God during their present life.* They continue to advance towards that heavenly abode, by holding on steadfastly to their confidence in the word of God, and following his will in the ways of obedience. In the strength of their confidence, they cheerfully engage in the services and patiently submit to the trials, which attend them on their way. The King of that heavenly city has filled it with holy inhabitants, who delight in exercising that benevolent love which is inculcated in his law. He designs to admit no being into it that will ever defile its society with sin—none but those who will adhere to obedience forever. He has therefore wisely appointed that men, coming as they do from a world of rebellion and rescued from a state of sin, should have time for the trial of their obedience—time for crucifying the flesh with its lusts, and strengthening their devoted-ness—time for washing their robes and making them white—before they enter that abode of perfect holiness. They therefore who are earnestly seeking it, follow the guidance of the Saviour in *doing his will* on earth. Here on their way they obey his statutes of benevolence; and, while actively employed in doing good to men and serv-ing God, and passing, with submission, through scenes of trial—while strewing their pathway with the fruits of benevolence and piety—are exterminating sin from their hearts, and strengthening that holy love which shall glow eternally in the city of God. Under the present trial of their obedience, they cast not away their confidence; they draw not back to perdition; but they confide through tribulation, patiently doing the will of God, intent on receiving the promise, earnest on attaining the end of their faith, the purity and eternal salvation of their souls.

Again; they who seek that endless city *subordinate to its attainment the present world.* They place dependence on the promise of God in his word, more than they do on the present world, for their happiness; and the world of his promise is far more desirable to them than the world of their trial. The city of their present habitation they regard with the feelings of strangers, who are going to reside for ever in a far better country. Like strangers, they abstain from those strongly ascendant attachments which would make them forget the abode they are seeking. They see in the scenery of this world, in its society, in its comforts, in its attainments, in its worship, in its partial manifestations of divine glory, much indeed that they love; but they hope, while trusting in the guidance of God, to reach a habitation that is not momentary, like the present, but endless; where exists a richer scenery, a better society, more solid joys, knowledge more elevated, employments and worship more satisfying and sublime— where the glory of God shines forth in the splendors of everlasting day. Confiding in the word of their guiding God, their desire after the world of promise is thus ascendant. They feel not here at home; not receiving here the promises they are seeking; but seeing them afar off, and being persuaded of them and embracing them, they confess that they are strangers and pilgrims upon the earth. Truly, if they were most mindful of their present abode, they have the opportunity of being wholly devoted to its joys; but, by subordinating the present world to their faith in Christ and their desire to attain the promises, it is manifest that they are seeking a better country. God is not ashamed to be called the God of such; for he hath prepared for them a city.

III. Let us in the third place inquire *into the evidences that they who thus seek the city of God will obtain admission.*

One such evidence exists in the direct *promises of God.* He has made plain *promises,* to accompany his calls of authority, to those who in obedience to his calls come out from the sins of this world, and are separate by devotion to his service? He has engaged to be a father and to adopt them as his sons and daughters, and admit them to dwell in his celestial family in heaven. A *single* promise of God cannot be broken; but he has *repeated* his promise.  A simple declaration is enough; but he has added to declarations the solemn formality of taking, on the throne of his heavenly habitation, "an oath for confirmation."  Now they who in this world are confiding in his guidance, obedient to his will, and desirous of a heavenly country, are the very persons to whom God has applied his promises, and how strong consolation have they! The word and oath of an omnipotent God!  When they enter eternity, therefore, the heirs of such promises, He will fulfill the word in which he has caused their souls to hope, his omniscient eye and almighty arm will see that none of them are lost, that all have admission through the gates into the city.

Again; such evidence is seen *in the mission to our world of the Lord Jesus. Christ and of the Holy Spirit*.  He has not merely caused his voice of authority and of promise to be heard in our world, but from the throne of his residence has he sent, to visit us in our condemnation, his beloved Son to make atonement for our sins, by dying and rising again for our justification.  He has beheld us in the strength of our rebellion and the temptations of our abode, and sent also his Holy Spirit to rescue sinners and help believers on their way to his heavenly habitation.  Now they who truly seek the glories of his kingdom, are the very persons to whom that cross on which Christ died becomes an effectual propitiation, in the application of his blood to wash them from their sins; and to whom his resurrection from the dead becomes a lively hope of immortality.  They are the very persons whom the Spirit is attending with his effectual influence; to keep in the way of holiness, and to preserve in it to the day of God, and to present before him unblamable in love.  When they enter eternity then, is there uncertainty respecting their final abode?  Will not he, who has given his Son to die for them and his Spirit to guide them, "freely give them all things?"  Will he, who has led them with the hand of infinite kindness up in all their way to the very border of his heavenly city, now bar on them its gates and refuse them entrance?

Again; another evidence God has given us, in the assurance *that he has already admitted the faithful from earth into that city.* He has not only given us his promise, and permitted us to see him using his agency in the present world for redemption, but has assured us of the fact that he has already admitted into his presence all those persons who have left the world in faith. The vail of the invisible world has he lifted up and permitted us to cast a glance on its holy inhabitants. There in that distant high abode we see, among the spotless multitudes before his throne, all those who, having followed with faith his guidance below till their last conflict with death, came out of their great tribulation with their robes washed and made white in the blood of the Lamb, having obtained the eternal victory. There now before his throne are all the spirits of those just men, who confided themselves to the guidance of his word when on earth, and who in the consummation of obedience and joy are made forever perfect ; all they who in faith passed the time of their sojourning here in preceding generations; and all our dear companions whom we once knew and loved, and with tears bade adieu, as in faith they closed their eyes on us and on these present scenes. And with all this cloud of witnesses already admitted into the heavenly city attestting the faithfulness of God, may we not believe undoubtingly that, by following our God with faith unto the gate of death, we shall not fail of entering into his holy habitation, but shall have " an entrance ministered to us abundantly " by willing angels, willing saints, and by willing companions, " into the everlasting kingdom of God our Saviour ? "

The view which we have now taken of *the city of God in eternity*, in regard to its constituent joys, the persons on earth who are truly seeking it, and the certainty of their admission, may serve to enforce on our minds some useful reflections.

We learn from our subject the value of the word of God. Blest volume from the Father of Mercies !—This light, that unfolds to view a celestial city, shines on our path, and shows the promises, the arm of power, the accomplished deeds of grace, that encourage guilty men to enter on the way to heaven, and persevere with hope till they receive the full fruition of their faith. Well may they who seek a heavenly country make these statutes of the Lord their song in the house of their pilgrimage. Here we behold his promises of life in Christ, sealed by miracles of the Holy Ghost and by the resurrection of Christ from the dead and ascension to immortality as the first fruits of them that sleep; and to that word which begot our hope we cling as the charter of our immortality.

Again, we may find in our subject a source of support under the *trials we are called to endure in this world.* Trials here will come. They are not joyous while they pass, but grievous. Yet they who trust in the guiding word of God, and follow his will in faith, see ground, in their final and better home, to endure with patience all these sorrows of the way. The storms that blow upon the city of their residence below are momentary, and give exercise to that faith that will be found unto honor and glory and praise in the day of Jesus Christ. 'The night soon flies; and day eternal shines.'

Again; we may learn from this subject to be reconciled to the *brevity of our residence on the earth.* The life of man in this world, what is it but a busy dream, an empty vapor, a flying shadow? nothing compared with immortality. While we are in this world admiring its beauties, tasting its provisions, conversing with its inhabitants, engaged in its employments, it may at times seem undesirable that we should be hurried through it with such rapidity, as that all our opportunities of acquaintance with it should leave us still comparatively strangers to it; that when we have but just entered into its scenes, and been introduced to its inhabitants, and become interested in them, we should be torn away from them forever. But the city of God to come, may reconcile us to the fact of our having no continuing city on the earth. If we are seeking in earnest that habitation while passing through this, we shall forever feel satisfied in the end that we spent no more days than we did of our existence here. For as no joys of this abode are worth an immortality, but such as are connected with the love and service of God, so these joys will be continued and greatly heightened in the heavenly city. There will all they enter who loved the Saviour and his people here; and they will find all the ages of eternity spent in services so much more exalted and satisfying than any in which they engaged below, as to make the exchange of dwellings their endless gain. If the city of your abode here is to be dissolved, the nobler city of God above hath foundations that shall not be shaken through eternity: and if you are a willing stranger here, seeking by the word and Spirit of God admission there, you may well acquiesce in that appointment that allots you so few days below; and see, without concern, days and seasons rolling away, that bring you nearer a better and more ending home.

> " They'll waft us sooner o'er
> This life's tempestuous sea :
> Soon we shall reach the peaceful shore
> Of blest eternity."

Again; we may learn from this subject to be reconciled to our *departure out of the world* in the painful manner of death.

The manner in which man leaves his present habitation by death, invests that future unknown period of his being with terrors from which we all instinctively shrink. The pangs of dissolution, and the silence of the dead, from whom no voice of information reaches us—the terrors of what is seen, and the uncertainties respecting what is unseen,—render the event one of gloom, which cannot be penetrated except by the light of revelation. We look at the event as exhibiting in God the frowns of his displeasure; and our terror of the conflict is allayed, only by the faith that sees beyond the shades of death a Redeemer ready to admit us to the enduring city of God. If we are so happy as to enter that blessed place, we shall, when from its heights of salvation we look back on the dark passage of death, feel forever satisfied that God the Saviour was leading us in the right way to a city of habitation. The pangs of dissolution were only giving exercise to that submissive love that glows eternally in the heavens ; a body unfit for immortality was laid aside, to be resumed again incorruptible and glorious ; the dying groan scarcely ceased, before the songs of victory arose ; and rising, though with the desert of hell, out of all conflicts to a habitation among the myriads of the holy, was almost an annihilation of death, a swallowing of it up in victory and immortality.

If your residence here below, then, must be left with struggles, the joys of entrance into that above will obliterate the pain ; and if you are seeking entrance there by following the word and Spirit of Christ, you may learn to acquiesce in the thought of your departure ; and not to fear the lapse of time, which, while it brings you nearer the last conflict, brings you nearer also to the final and endless victory.

Amid the trials of the present time, the brevity and uncertain continuance of life, and the daily progress of all towards the grave, they who are seeking a heavenly country then need not fear. Omnipotence speaks the word of promise from heaven, and reaches forth to them the arm of assistance, and points to companions above. " Hold fast then, brethren, your confidence, which hath great recompense of reward." " Hope to the end, for the grace that is to be brought unto you at the revelation of Jesus Christ."

> " Cease, ye pilgrims, cease to mourn ;
>     *Press onward* to the prize.
>   Soon our Saviour will return,
>     Triumphant in the skies.
>   Yet a season, and you know
>     Happy entrance will be given :
>   All our sorrows left below,
>     And earth exchanged for heaven."

And will that day of glory come?  Shall they who follow their Saviour here have entrance given them into the everlasting joys of their Lord? . What hopes then are theirs! What joys will be theirs when they shall be introduced as happy members into that heavenly Jerusalem, which is filled with such countless multitudes of beings of glorious orders, actuated by perfect love, engaged in the sweetest employments, and secure in their joys through eternity! To spend the days of eternity in that central residence of God, where his glories eclipse all these starry worlds, the mere suburbs of his celestial city. To glow with mental energies and love and adoration increasing through eternal years! How glorious a termination of our cares and tears and faith below!

And what must the loss be to him who exhausts his heart on this abode; who obeys not the gospel of our Lord Jesus Christ, and seeks not to partake of his heavenly calling! His doom is already written. Banishment, with everlasting destruction, from the presence of the Lord and the glory of his power! What loss! when, torn from the joys of this abode—a fleeting dream—all happiness below for ever past—he gazes on that glorious residence where millions of celestial spirits dwell in love and adoration; and finds its gates forever barred upon him, and his eternity to be passed with a few apostate angels and the lost of Adam's race, in the mere prison house of this universe.

My friends, travelling to eternity, in prospect of the approaching year I can but wish you all a year of life, health, and spiritual and temporal happiness. But you begin it in a world of uncertainties. Its record will doubtless place some name among us on the roll of death. Where is he? Who is he? Whose fate is sealed the present year? Is he seeking now a city which hath foundations? Is he clinging to this world? Oh could I now unroll the record of divine decrees, and shew him to himself so soon to die, might it not stir him up to preparation for eternity? In these uncertainties, blessed be the Saviour, he calls you all to hear his word of grace. Rise up then at his command. Obey his call. Forsake the world, and seek a better country far,—the city of his presence and eternal love. On the way he calls you, go; and the year will be a year of happiness, whether you spend it here, in these scenes of time, or in the city of your God above. But ah, if clinging to this world you die, it will be 'a year—an age—a whole eternity—of woe! So soon? So nigh? So thoughtless? Yet I tell thee, sinner, *now*, that when I meet thee at the gates of death, and on the passway to eternity, I may not need to tell thee *then*, PREPARE!

------

### I. PETER II: 7.

UNTO YOU THEREFORE WHICH BELIEVE, HE IS PRECIOUS.

THE coming of Jesus Christ in the flesh was an event of great joy to our world.  An act of astonishing mercy on his part, fulfilling the hopes inspired for ages in Israel, the pledge of a treaty of peace both honorable to God and consoling to man,—it was meet to be heralded forth by heavenly attendants as glad tidings of great joy to all people.

Yet when we see his humiliations in the flesh, and trace him on his way of poverty and reproach and suffering for our sins, and witness the agonies of Gethsemane and Calvary—when we see how his offers of mercy are rejected by a thoughtless world, who only take license from his long-suffering to be more bold in sin, it becomes us to see that our joy in his coming be placed on the right grounds.

The joy, though offered to all, is truly participated in only by those, who in their need and guilt resort to him as their Saviour, who yield themselves to his instruction and care, and depend on his grace for perfect restoration to the favor and service and kingdom of God.  They see in their own experience how precious he is, and join with the heavenly hosts in desiring all nations to hear the glad tidings of his grace, and earnestly pray that their depraved and guilty fellow-men may be partakers with them in like precious faith.

Such was the joy of Peter, when he addressed his fellow Christians in the text, " Unto you therefore which believe, he is precious."  At that time he felt that he owed to the Lord Jesus Christ the obligations of a rebel humbled and forgiven, of a backslider reclaimed and restored, and of a believer confirmed in his faith and devotedness and joyful in the assured hope of future glory. By his own experience he had learned that Christ, who visited our world from the throne of heaven on the embassy of redemption, was in all respects suited and adequate to his spiritual wants.

His fellow Christians too, he knew could unite, with his, their testimony to the preciousness of Christ. He could confidently address them: " Unto you which believe, he is precious."

The value of Christ to himself and his fellow Christians, he places in this one comprehensive consideration: that CHRIST IS A SAVIOUR ADEQUATE TO ALL THE WANTS OF BELIEVERS. Peter learns his preciousness from this one extensive promise: " He that believeth on him shall not be confounded." Shall not be disappointed in his hopes. Therefore is it, he adds, that to believers he is precious.

I shall manage the subject then in its true light, if I exhibit to you the believer, and the adequacy of Christ to his wants.

I. Who then *is* the believer?

Peter describes believers in a passage immediately preceding the text, and to that description we will now look for an answer to our question. According to his description, believers are those who have " tasted that the Lord is gracious." They are those, who by their belief bring the great object of faith home to their own experience; who not only believe that Christ the Lord offers grace to their acceptance, but who come to him personally and in faith, to accept and to *taste* his grace. They make real in their own feelings the truth of his gracious words in the gospel. They give reality to divine truth and yield their hearts to its deep and sacred impressions. They believe with the heart. Such is the mode in which they believe.

The great object on which their faith terminates, according to this description of Peter, is Christ in his character of a Saviour. They taste that the Lord is gracious; the Lord

Christ, who is said, in the immediate connection, to be disallowed of men but chosen of God and precious. The Lord Jesus Christ has undertaken the work of a Saviour, to turn his believing people from sin and Satan unto God. He is the Captain of Salvation ; the Head of the Church ; the exalted Prince of Israel, to whom the penitent in all ages have looked for redemption.

The believer then places his reliance on Christ ; and on Christ as gracious : a Saviour bestowing an unmerited and a free salvation. With him the Bible is the word of grace from Christ ; the whole family of the redeemed, the kingdom of his grace. To believe on Christ, then, is to believe the *doctrines* which Christ teaches in his word ; or, which is the same thing, those principles of grace on which Christ proceeds in relation to our world and in the establishment of his kingdom of redemption.

Among the truths of his word which are illustrated in that kingdom, or which enter into the belief and experience of the believer, the following seem to be fundamental.

1. That men are *immortal.* Christ has brought this truth into clear light by his coming. He has not merely *asserted* it, with a plainness not to be misapprehended ; but confirmed his assertions, by miracles, by the resurrection of others, and by his own resurrection as the first fruits of the sleeping dead. I say that this is a fundamental truth in the kingdom of Christ; because that kingdom is eternal. This truth the believer admits, and commits his immortal soul to the keeping of Christ as the true Shepherd and Bishop of souls.

Another essential truth, included in believing on Christ, is,—

2. That men are *under the power and guilt of sin.* They are not merely immortal ; but in consequence of the fall, their immortal existence, unless redemption is found, is involved in sin and misery.

This is a truth which Christ maintains in his word ; and it is an important principle on which he conducts, in establishing a kingdom of grace. On this principle he acted, when he assumed our humble nature, and died on the cross in order to conduct his followers to glory. Were we, as prospectively seen by him, innocent beings, or were our guilt trifling, what need was there of his appearing on earth and pouring out his precious blood a sacrifice? A race of innocent beings could receive sufficient *instruction* from his *messengers.* Unless we are sinners and justly exposed to endless miseries, why does the Gospel proclaim the glad news of a Saviour? A Saviour from what? Not from annihilation surely; for we were already immortal. Why else, too, is the erection of a kingdom of endless holiness and happiness among men, an act of grace? There is no grace, surely, in sustaining and blessing forever a race of holy beings. On what other principle than our depravity, too, does Christ make the universal call on men to repent, that iniquity be not their everlasting ruin?

Now the believer admits this truth, and brings it home to his feelings. He has read it in his own experience. He sees in some measure the infinite amiableness of the divine character, and the astonishing hardness of his own depraved heart. He sees and feels his depravity to be an immense evil. With shame and sorrow over it, and with heartfelt renunciation of it, he turns to God in Christ for redemption.

Another truth, essentially connected with believing on Christ, is—

3. That his death is the *only ground of pardon.* The believer relies on the atonement of Jesus for justification.

That his death is the only sufficient atonement for sin, is proclaimed by the very fact, that in instituting a kingdom of grace he chose this method of pardon. "He died for our sins." For our rebellion against the righteous government of Jehovah, he laid down his life. Now Christ acted, in making this sacrifice, on the principle, that his death only could make amends to the honor of the violated law: that, without it, there could be no remission of our offenses. The believer, then, admits this truth and brings it home to his feelings. He despairs of his own righteousness, or of any other pardon, than that which is freely received at a throne of grace through the blood of Jesus. An immortal being, perishing in sin,—he feels his need of pardon from his God; and he receives peace of conscience, only by humbly approaching God for it, in reliance on the blood of Christ.

Another truth included in believing on Christ, is,

4. That *his power must sanctify.* The believer seeks, for his spiritual recovery, the influence of his Spirit.

The whole work of salvation is in his hands. He is a Saviour, not only on the ground of his merits, but by means of his power. When, after his crucifixion, he arose from death and ascended on high, he was exalted to the throne to give repentance unto Israel. By his Spirit he draws men unto him. He has declared his kingdom to be a kingdom of holiness, established by his Spirit. They who belong to his kingdom, are born of the Spirit; they are led by the word and influence of the Spirit; they walk in the precepts and power of the Spirit. The Spirit of life in Christ Jesus makes them free from the dominion of sin and death. Now the believer admits this truth, and brings it home to his feelings. He goes with supplication to Christ, to receive grace to help in time of need. Without the power of Christ, he can do nothing to overcome his spiritual foes. Would he succeed in the Christian warfare? He must be clothed with the armor of God. Would he be strong? He must be so in the Lord and the power of his might. Would he have hope? He looks to the God of hope to fill him with joy and peace in believing, that he may abound in hope. Would he have eternal life? It must be the gift of God through Jesus Christ. Deeply impressed with this truth, he goes, a needy and humble supplicant, and seeks from Christ his sanctification and eternal redemption.

II. From this brief contemplation of the believer, we turn now to inquire *why* he esteems Christ to be precious.

The comprehensive reason is stated by Peter in the context, in which he quotes from Isaiah xxviii: 16, this extensive promise: "Behold I lay in Zion a chief corner-stone, elect, precious; and he that believeth on him shall not be confounded." He who looks in true faith to this Saviour will never be disappointed in his hopes. He will find in him all suitable and adequate supply for his spiritual and immortal wants. "Therefore," adds the apostle, "unto you that believe, is he precious." On this account is he precious.

The believer then esteems Christ to be precious, because he finds in him a Saviour in all respects suited and adequate to his wants.

The believer is constantly experiencing wants; around him are temptations; within him, remaining depravity. Who then can uphold him in the path of duty but a *present* Saviour? He is exposed to a burdened conscience; to wander in darkness and be distressed with apprehension of the frowns of heaven. Who can speak peace to his troubled spirit but a present Saviour? Believers are exposed to trials from an ungodly world; to have their name cast out as evil; to suffer bodily pains and infirmities; or to experience the loss of estate or of friends. Who can administer comfort to them in their trials but a present Saviour? And such a Saviour is Christ. He has left his promise on record, that he will come and make his abode with believers. His declaration is, "My sheep hear my voice, and I know them." I know who they are and what is their situation. Not a contrite sigh for sin arises from any soul, but he is present to hear. Not a secret emotion of love to his cause springs up in any heart, but he perceives its rising. Not one cry of faith for deliverance is raised to heaven, but it reaches his ears. When passing through the fires or the waters of tribulation, his children may plead the promise, "I will be with thee." Is not Christ, then, precious to the believer, who is so very present a help in trouble?

Again; believers need not only a present, but a *powerful* Saviour.

What matters it that Christ is present to witness their wants, if he has not power to relieve?

The believer needs a Saviour powerful enough to manage his heart; one who is able to subdue the obstinacy of his depraved will and corrupt affections; who can melt a heart which threatenings and promises do not touch. Such a powerful Saviour is Christ; exalted as King on the hill of Zion, bestowing the heart of flesh on Israel, bringing into captivity the wills of his people.

The believer needs a Saviour who can manage all the concerns of the universe. His welfare depends on the minutest things as well as the great. He needs a Saviour who can manage, at least consistently with his good, all beings and worlds and events; who will not suffer one thing to befall him contrary to his own wise and gracious pleasure. Such a powerful Saviour does the believer find in Jesus. For he assures his disciples that all power in heaven and on earth is in his hands. He promises that *all* things shall work together for good to those who love him and are called according to his purpose.

The believer needs a Saviour powerful enough, too, to manage his cause with an infinitely holy God. He has offended the Sovereign of the universe, whose laws are most holy and just and good. The penalty he has incurred is just, and it is everlasting. Who, then, is powerful enough to manage his cause before the Infinitely Holy and Righteous One? Who shall stay the execution of the dreadful sentence of his King? The believer sees in Christ his Saviour, the Son of God; in whom the Father is always well pleased; whom he always hears. Such a powerful advocate is managing his cause; one who has laid down his life to ransom his followers, and pleads the infinite sacrifice above. Shall not then the blood of him who through the Eternal Spirit offered himself without spot to God, purge the consciences of believers from works of death? They may now draw near the throne, sprinkled from a guilty conscience, and behold with joy the face of a forgiving God, and hold joyful communion with him as a Father reconciled in Christ.

Thirdly; believers need not only a present and powerful, but a *compassionate* Saviour.

Not one who shall wink at their sins and leave them to perish ; but one who shall be mercifully faithful to rebuke, reclaim, and forgive.

The believer who knows the least of his own heart, cannot but see that he needs constant compassion to be shown him from God. He has long abused divine grace ; and, since the time when he was brought to confide in God and experience the sweet pledges of pardoning mercy, he has not found his heart perfect with God. He sins still ; and he sins now against greater love and mercy ; and he knows that nothing will answer his wants but boundless compassion. Point him to a Saviour whose compassions fail, to a God whose mercies consume,—and you drive him to despair. No such Saviour can bear with his hard, ungrateful, rebellious heart. He must be rendered contrite and made ashamed of his guilt by a God, whose mercy is as high above our ways as the heavens are above the earth. The sinner, who has not seen the glory of the divine character and government, and the vileness of his own heart, may not feel the need of compassion in God, and may, like the infidel Rosseau, rely on the justice of his Maker. But O ! the returning backslider, the broken-hearted penitent, can never find relief for his burdened soul till he meets a God of abounding grace.

What had become of Peter had not his Saviour been compassionate ? Called freely by Christ to his service ; admitted, next to John, as his bosom companion ; one of the favored three who witnessed the resurrection of Jairus' daughter, and beheld his glory on the mount of transfiguration : and yet, when his Master is apprehended and led to the house of the high priest—in that time of his greatest sufferings,—he openly denies having had any connexion with Christ, and adds to the crimson guilt of denial the dreadful impiety of curses and oaths. Oh, what horrid iniquity ! Is there a God that can forgive ? He had a Saviour who could compassionate him, who could be " merciful to his unrighteousness ; " an advocate, who could even anticipate his wants ; who, in full view of this hardness of heart, could pray for him that his faith should not utterly fail.

The compassion of Christ undertook the work of salvation, in full view of all its difficulties,—all the reproaches which he must suffer from an ungodly world, all the perversities with which he must bear in the hearts of his own followers. Nothing unexpected then can occur to turn him aside from his resolution of mercy. It is a motto in his kingdom which, however much abused by the licentious, is precious to the humble-hearted; 'once forgiven, always forgiven.' Whom he once receives to his love, this faithful Shepherd loves and keeps to the end. He shows in the work of redemption, that he has infinite patience; and that, when he pardons, he pardons like a God. "How shall I give thee up, Ephraim; how shall I deliver thee, Israel? How shall I make thee as Admah? How shall I set thee as Zeboim? My heart is turned within me; my repentings are kindled together. I will not execute the fierceness of my anger; for I am *God*, and not man."

Lastly; the believer needs not only a present, powerful and compassionate, but an *everlasting* Saviour.

He perceives a boundless eternity before him, and he seeks some firm rock on which to rest his everlasting hopes. Where then shall he go for consolation?

Will you direct him to heathen sages or modern infidels? His soul starts at the thought of annihilation. He cannot bear the idea that, when called to close his eyes on the world and this pleasant creation, his faculties should be crushed and his perceptions and enjoyments be forever lost. Cold consolation this to the heart that beats and lives for immortality, and that is made to receive its happiness only from the Fount of Infinite Love and Being!

Will you tell him to banish the thought of futurity? Will you advise him, with the Epicure, to consult his present pleasures and dismiss the idea of the future? 'Let us eat and drink; for to-morrow we die.' He knows that these gratifications are unsatisfying to a rational soul. He knows too, that time is bearing him rapidly on its current to eternity, and that no struggles of his can delay his progress.

Where then, as he surveys the prospect of an endless existence, shall he turn for light and comfort? His faith, like that of Peter's, can find no support but in Jesus. Turning from all other objects in the universe, and looking to Christ, he exclaims; "to whom, Lord, shall I go but unto thee; thou hast the words of *eternal* life!" From the throne of Christ, light breaks in upon his prospects. United in faith and love to his risen and glorified Saviour, he feels the joys of immortality already springing up in his soul.

But is there *no* failure? May there not a period in eternity arrive when this refuge shall fail me? The possibility of such an event would shake the very basis of the Rock of ages. I shall not find a Saviour adequate to my wants, unless I find one who will watch over my existence forever, and render it holy and happy. And such is Jesus Christ. He is the *eternal* Life. They which are called by him, receive the promise of an *eternal* inheritance. He has become to those who obey him, the author of *eternal* salvation. They who have fled to him for a refuge, have found a shelter which shall endure through all the convulsions and all the agitations of the moral universe,—so long as God is on the throne, and the holy enjoy the tranquility of his reign. On this ground do we find the apostles speaking with such ardor of the love of Christ: it passeth knowledge; its riches are unsearchable: it constrains them, like an overwhelming torrent, to pass through trials and hardships in extending his kingdom. They seem burdened for words to express its height and depth. They pray that their converts may be enlightened, in order that they "may understand what is the hope of his calling, and the riches of the glory of his inheritance in the saints."

Is not a Saviour then, thus *present, powerful, compassionate* and *eternal,* justly esteemed precious by all his fol-

lowers, who are expecting from him their eternal union
to the kingdom of glory?

My Friends, permit me to inquire, or rather inquire of
yourselves as in the presence of God, is he *your* Saviour?
Do you believe? Do you as immortal beings and as
perishing sinners, feel your need of his atoning blood and
renewing grace? Have you ever experienced their vital
efficacy? Do you supremely aim at obedience to his
will? Do you habitually approach his throne of mercy
for the pardon of sin and the joy of reconciliation? Do
you depend daily on his gracious aid for guidance in
duty, and for strength to conquer your enemies and give
you the victory?

If so, then may you have seen and felt something of
the preciousness of Christ in this faint description. You
may have perceived more of it in your own experience.
But our powers have not yet fathomed the extent of that
love which passeth knowledge. Be faithful to Christ and
to your souls, live near to him, and you shall know more
of his excellence as you advance in the journey of this
life. More of his preciousness will be manifest to you,
when you pass the valley of death. More of it will be
unfolded to you, when you rise to meet him in the clouds
of the air. More of his preciousness will beam on your
souls, while permitted to pass in his presence the ages of an
eternity to come. The sweet experience of his loving-
kindness, the near view of his surpassing glory, will draw
from your tongues the everlasting song; "thou art worthy. Thou wast slain, and hast redeemed us to God by
thy blood?"

But, to those who, like the Jewish builders, disallow
the precious corner-stone which God hath laid in Zion,
he is a stone of stumbling and rock of offense. Precious
as he is to believers, he is so to none else. Indeed, the
very qualities which render him precious to his people,
render him terrible to all his enemies. Is he present?
He is registering their deeds of guilt in the book of his
remembrance. Is he powerful? That power, which man-
ages this mighty universe, will crush his obstinate foes.

Is he merciful? That mercy, which crowns Zion with eternal glories, will not spare her persevering adversaries. Is he everlasting? He will live forever to execute the penalties of his righteousness.

Turn then to this Saviour, while you are prisoners of hope and he offers you life. Come now, while he freely invites you to enter his kingdom of grace and of glory. He that believeth on him, shall never be confounded. He that believeth on him, will find him precious both now and forever. Can you not, will you not, trust your soul on his promises? O, come to his cross in penitence and taste that he is precious!

JOB X: 21, 22.

I GO WHENCE I SHALL NOT RETURN, EVEN TO THE LAND OF DARKNESS AND THE SHADOW OF DEATH. A LAND OF DARKNESS, AS DARKNESS ITSELF, AND OF THE SHADOW OF DEATH, WITHOUT ANY ORDER.

IN this manner Job spake of his death and descent to the grave. He looked on the grave as a land whither he was going, and from which he should never come back to mingle again in the scenes and duties of this life. He regarded it, not indeed with the skeptic, as the final land of annihilation, but as the middle land of passage, from which he was to go forward to an eternal state. For though he was to lie down till the scenes of this world are past and the heavens be no more, yet, said he, " I know that my Redeemer liveth, and that he shall stand at the latter day upon the earth, and, though after my skin worms destroy this body, yet in my flesh shall I see God." He characterized the grave—this middle land—as a land ' darkened with the shadows of death,' where the body lies in the darkness of insensibility, unconscious of the pleasant light of day; and also, as a land in which is no " order," to which mankind descend irregularly, without respect to any precise and established arrangement, or rule of succession.

It is the latter thought, more especially, to which I now design to call your attention—that there is no order, apparent to men, in the demands of the grave.

To present the subject more fully and clearly, I will attempt,

I. To define the sense in which the grave is without order ;

II. To specify some things in which this want of order is most manifest ; and,

III. To show the wisdom of God in so conducting his providence that the grave should be thus without order.

I. In what sense, then, is the grave said to be " without order?"

The expression does not mean, that mankind become the subjects of death and the grave without the operation of adequate *causes.* For, there are causes in operation among men sufficient to extinguish animal life, and which operate, according to established laws, in producing every instance of temporal death ; as truly, as there are causes in the natural world to produce the regular vicissitudes of day and night and of the seasons.

Nor, again, does the expression mean, that these causes operate by *chance,* without the supervision and control of the Creator. For he holds all the secondary causes which operate in his kingdom in his hands, directing and turning them according to his own will. Nor are the causes of temporal death, any more than others, excepted from his control. Sickness, disease, violence, and even what we call the accidents of life, come and go, at his bidding or by his permission ; and, when it is his pleasure, come with sufficient force to extinguish temporal life.

But the expression means, that the causes which operate to produce temporal death are so controlled by the Lord, as that the result is destitute of any regularity, or *without any order apparent and visible to man :* breaking in upon, and disturbing, more or less, every plan and system of arrangement adopted among the living. The irregularity in this case, though not the same, may be illustrated by that of the drawing of the lot ; the result of which is not without the operation of precise and sufficient causes, nor causes removed beyond the supervision and control of God : but yet it depends on no known principle of order, on which man can fix the calculation of certainty. Just so in the selection of the subjects of death from among the living, there is no one principle followed, apparent to man, by which he can fix the certainty, as he can in those parts of nature where order is established on known and precise laws.

But I proceed,

II. To specify some things in which this want of order is most manifest.

In the selection made from the living, there is no order in respect to *age*. If death were fixed for all the individuals of our race at one precise period of life, never occurring before or deferred beyond its arrival, there would then be manifest, in regard to the event, the order of time—the particular order of age. But such an order is broken up and wholly destroyed by the process of the grave. Alike from its dark halls are the summons issued, to take from the living the infant, the little child, the maturing youth, the full-grown man, the man of hoary age; and down to its chambers they descend together in promiscuous ranks, and take their station side by side, totally regardless of age.

Again: there is no order apparent, in respect to the *character* of those who are selected. We can see no plan adopted which proceeds at all on the principle of character, either in respect to its usefulness or perniciousness to the living, or to its fitness or unfitness for happiness in another life. The good and useful are not all spared to old age. The evil and injurious are not all cut down in earlier life. The youthful Christian, and the venerable disciple who has spent his days in the service of his Lord, the youthful trangressor just entered on the stage of life, and the hardened offender grown old in his crimes, yielding to the summons of death, march, side by side, to the dark and shadowy land of the grave.

Again: there is no order in the grave, in respect to the *station* of those who are taken. Every principle of order, in relation to station in the family, in the church, or in the state, is broken in upon by the demands of the grave. The parent is not spared for his importance to the household, or the pastor on account of his flock, or the ruler on account of his subjects; but alike parents and children, pastors and their people, rulers and their subjects, go down together to the land of silence, and dwell, side by side, in their narrow mansions.

Again : there is no order in the grave, in respect to the previous *health* of its subjects. The weak and feeble are not selected in preference to the strong and vigorous. The debility of one does not necessarily subject him to the immediate call of disease and death ; nor the vigor of another certainly exempt him from its sudden approach. Both alike and indiscriminately are spared, or fall the victims of fatal disease, accident or violence ; and pass together to the land of silence.

Once more : there is no order in the grave, in respect to the *manner* in which its subjects are *summoned out* of *life*. We might suppose one invariable *mode* adopted in respect to the departure of all to the grave. But no such principle of regularity is at all followed. The diseases and causes which take men out of life differ exceedingly, in regard to the certainty with which they operate, the pain which they occasion, the time in which they continue. One disease is no sooner fastened on the system than it is known that death must follow, and all hope of recovery is forever extinguished. Another disease goes forward , insidiously to its work, not destroying the hope of recovery, it may be, till death itself suddenly announces its presence. One person lies the subject of a long and lingering consumption, while another, by the bursting of a blood-vessel, the stoppage of the heart, or by apoplexy, falls suddenly and without warning from the vigor of health into the arms of death. There is no regularity, no settled plan, according to which the grave summons its subjects away from life : but alike the long-forewarned and the suddenly-called, pass together into its dark domains.

In these various respects, there is a total disregard of all appearance of regularity and plan in the demands which come up to the living from the shadowy realms of death. Let us now consider, as was proposed,

III. The wisdom of God in so conducting his providence that there should be no manifest order in the grave.

In the midst of all this apparent irregularity, there is indeed a general plan pursued in one respect : that all mankind in their respective generations are removed from this world in the one way of temporal death. Respecting the wisdom of God in this general plan of procedure, I shall not now speak. But taking it for granted that this way of removing our race from the world is wise, I am to speak more particularly of the wisdom of accomplishing the removal without any obvious and fixed rules of order.

Now, though we may not be able to discover all the positive reasons of wisdom which exist for this irregularity, or to trace those which we can discern out to their full extent, we shall at least see evidence of wisdom, if we find that any ends, important to God and his kingdom, are dependent on it, which could not be obtained by the opposite course of adhering to rules of known and strict order.

Now, the present irregularity arises from the plan of varying the *time* and *manner* of removing individuals from the world by temporal death : and the only alternative which exists in the case, is between a plan confined to one invariable time and manner in all cases, and a plan open to variation of time and manner : between perfect regularity of time and manner in these respects, and irregularity : and between these plans the choice lies.

With this general view of the ground on which we proceed in the inquiry, I remark that the following ends of wisdom are clearly dependent on the present course of providence, which could not be obtained without it.

1. The care of human life itself is made to enter as an element into our present state of probation.

The use of all lawful means for the preservation of our own lives and the lives of others around us, is in this way devolved on us as an imperious duty : and this particular duty is thus made to enter, as a part, into that system of duties which constitutes our trial, and is to form and manifest our character. That this is a consequence of the present plan of providence, is at once obvious. For the means by which life is supported, by which it is defended from violence, or subjected to it, by which it is guarded

from the attacks or the fatal progress of disease, or
exposed to them, are now, to a limited extent, entrusted
to our hands.  And by these means, to the extent they
are entrusted to us, are we tried in respect to our voluntary care of life.  The precious deposit is left with us by
the Creator, under the solemn injunction of his authority,
" Thou shalt not kill."  And, in their treatment of this
deposit, mankind will be proved and tried as the faithful
servants of God, the negligent and the careless, or the
violent and murderous.  I say, this care of life in ourselves and others is devolved on us as a duty, under the
present procedure of providence only.  For, if the opposite course were adopted by the Creator, to remove men
from life invariably at a regular time and in a uniform and
regular manner, the present laws of animal life must be
altered or suspended in their operation, and he would take
the care of life wholly out of the hands of man into his
own hands.  The continuance of life and its termination,
would have no more connection with the care and conduct of men, than have now the movements of planetary
worlds, the revolution of the seasons, the rise of the tides,
the succession of day and night : so that it is only under
the present system of irregularity, in which the causes of
death are to a certain extent entrusted to man, that the
care of life is entrusted to his hands, and comprised
among the duties which constitute his probation for eternity.  Nor does it need labored argument to show that,
while this life is constituted a scene of probation for the
formation of character in reference to a coming eternity,
it is wise to devolve on man the care of so precious an
interest as that of the continuance of life in himself and
others, and to constitute it one of the means of his trial.
For this interest is thus put on a harmonious footing with
all his other interests, each of which is made so far dependent on his agency, as to appeal to his feelings, to impose
on him a duty ; to constitute a trial, in which his character
is formed and tested : and it favors more strongly the cultivation of respect to the will of God, and benevolent
affection towards our fellow-creatures, to have so precious

an interest of humanity devolved in some measure upon our care. Just as in entrusting the Gospel to the hands of men, as the means on which the spiritual and eternal life of the race depends, the care of that high and ever-lasting interest is devolved on us who receive the Gospel as a means of trial, and a most powerful call addressed to our hearts to enter into fellowship with Christ in his love to God and compassion to the guilty, by publishing the Gospel of his grace abroad in all lands to every creature.

Again,

2. The present course of providence renders the call on man, to attend to the duties of his passing probation, more pungent.

For now the probabilities of continued life, gathered from the general course of providence, are sufficiently strong, to remove from man an absorbing and overwhelming fear of immediate death. He has a sufficient prospect of continued life, to allow him to give his earnest attention and interested feelings continually to his present duties, by means of which alone he can avail himself of the true privileges of his probation, and form a character of diligent devotion to God and to the interests of his fellow-creatures—the true preparation for eternal blessedness. But while, on this hand, the probability of continued life is sufficiently strong, to free his mind from that distracting and overwhelming fear of death, which would prevent hearty attention to his spiritual duties,—while the probability is sufficiently strong, to allow him to give his supreme attention to them,—there is, on the other hand, that possibility of his being called away at any moment, which constitutes a most loud and imperious call upon him, not to loiter away in worldliness and sin the passing moments of his day of grace. The irregularity of the very *manner* of death too, as well as of the *time*, not only rebukes the presumption of delaying attention to his duties to future years and times, but of waiting even for the monitions of disease. For it is possible that disease may be short and hasty in its work, leaving him no time for preparation; it may be too violent and forcible to permit the exercise of his rational faculties, or, hidden, internal and unfelt in its subtle approaches, it may strike him down instantly while in the full career of life. The possibility of instant death, and a death of which he is unwarned, therefore, calls imperiously upon him to address himself immediately to the great duties of this life: to be instant in season and out of season in the great work, which alone will fit him for happiness in another world. To this voice of providence the Saviour appealed, when calling on man to make the preparation. " Be ye ready: for in such an hour as ye think not, the Son of Man cometh."

But if, on the other hand, a system of regularity were adhered to, all this influence to favor the calls to preparation for another life would be lost. The entire certainty which would occupy every mind in respect to the precise age and manner of removal would, in the earlier periods of human life, too strongly facilitate the presumption in man of neglecting the *duties* of this state, and giving himself to the *pleasures* of the *world*, and with the increased worldliness and hardness of heart nourished within him in this presumptuous career, his unwillingness be increased to address himself to the duties of religion and preparation for eternity, until, finding himself on the brink of removal, he should wake up, at the last hour, like the criminal condemned to execution, only to be absorbed with the fears of death and the terrors of despair. Such at least we can see to be the tendency of such a system on such a being as man—a being who is inclined to such a course even now, amid all the present powerful monitions of providence to the contrary.

Is it not wise, then, on the part of God, to proceed, in the removal of man from the world, in a way which ever renders the grave so powerful a preacher; calling alike on the young, the mature, the aged—on man at every point and station in this life—to address himself to his present duties, and thus prepare himself for a blessed immortality? not throwing on man such a despair of continued life as to palsy all hope and exertion, nor giving him such a warrant of long-continued exemption from the call of death, as to embolden him to neglect the present and vainly presume on the future.

Again,

3. A superior moral discipline is exerted over mankind by means of the present course, of providence in the infliction of death.

If death were brought on each individual of the race at a precise age and in a precise manner, unvarying in all, there could be in the event no opportunity for the Creator to make any special manifestation of his feelings, to address any special admonitions to mankind, or specially to adapt the trial and chastening to the state of survivors. There would be only the one, general and unvarying expression of divine feeling, exhibited in the general plan of removing man from the world in the way of temporal death. But now, those ends of superior moral discipline are gained. There is now opportunity for God to manifest his feelings towards men in this part of his providence. He has not cut himself off from the opportunity, as he would have done by the adoption of one invariable time and manner of removal. And if we look to the actual course of his providence, we shall see that he has availed himself of the opportunity to testify to men the feelings of his heart, and bring them near to him for moral discipline. The patience of his heart he now proves to us, in permitting the transgressor to live on to old age amid the abused privileges of this state. For while it is in his hands to kill or keep alive each moment as he pleases, what patience must be in his heart to be willing to endure the hardened transgressor with such long-suffering! Compassion too he now manifests, in restoring men to life from the borders of death. For, as men now sink under the withering power of disease, they ask it as a mercy, that he spare them a little longer before they go hence, and if he hear their cries and raise them up, they see and feel the pity and compassion of his heart. This exercise of his compassion, in healing sickness and saving from death, is referred to by the inspired writers,

in their appeals to the feelings of men : it is thus described
by David. "They draw near unto the gates of death.
Then they cry unto the Lord in their trouble, and he
saveth them out of their distresses. He sent his word
and healed them, and delivered them from their destruc-
tions. O that men would praise the Lord for his goodness, and for his wonderful works unto the children of
men !" The feeling of displeasure or vengeance towards
sin is also at times specially manifested. It is often supposed, that because one event—that of temporal death—
happeneth to all, neither the love or hatred of God can
be shown in the event. That it is not the usual method
of God so to administer temporal death, as by that event
alone to publish his hatred or approbation of the conduct
of its subjects to the world, must be acknowledged. Yet
that he does not occasionally make special manifestations
of his displeasure, cannot be affirmed with truth. The
way is open for him to administer death, whenever he
shall see occasion, in that signal and fearful manner which
shall publish aloud his judgments. And he has done it.
The memorable instances of a deluged world, and the
consumption by fire of Sodom and Gomorrha, are recorded as eternal monuments of his vengeance. And the
revelation made of his future providence show us death
on his pale charger, riding forth to execute vengeance on
the guilty nations. And not only in the method of public
judgments, when war, pestilence, famine, go forth as
executioners of men, does he manifest vengeance. But
also in suffering individuals, in many instances, to be
executioners of themselves, by means of their own sins.
They are left to reap temporal death, as the direct and
obvious wages of their own folly. They cut themselves
off from life by their iniquities. Their sin itself has upon
it the brand of death and divine displeasure. This is seen,
not merely in the direct and wilful suicide, who, fretting
against God and providence, is left to be devoured in the
fire of his own rage and by the blows of his own wrath :
it is seen written also on that slower progress of awful
forms of disease and premature death, which spring from

the particular sins and vices of men.  They flow as direct retributions for infringements on the laws of God.  "Fools," says the Psalmist, "because of their transgressions, and because of their iniquities, are afflicted.  Their soul abhorreth all manner of meat, and they draw near to the gates of death."  If their diseases are not arrested in mercy, but are allowed to go on unto death, is not the displeasure of God against their sin at least—whether their souls are penitent and pardoned or not—proclaimed in the manner of their death?

There is now opportunity also for God to address special instruction and warning to mankind.  Indeed every special manifestation of his feelings, which he now lets in upon the world, is an appeal to the feelings of men; he sets before them the feelings of his own heart, in order to affect theirs and bring them into sympathy and harmony with him.  His patience towards us is manifest, to put down our impatience and fretfulness towards him and towards our fellow-men.  His compassion,—to enkindle compassion in our breasts for the needy, the suffering, the guilty, who surround us.  His displeasure,—to awaken displeasure in our hearts against sin, that we may crucify it in ourselves and labor to exterminate it in others.

But beside the admonitions arising to men from these manifestations of divine feeling, there is more especial warning still addressed to men from death : in its coming near us and removing the friends and associates, who are at our side, into eternity.  A removal would indeed take place on the plan of regularity in death.  But in far different circumstances, with no special appeals addressed to any ; all of whom are assured of the same fixed length of life.  Now it is the removal of our associates and friends, our co-equals in age ; their removal at every stage of our journey ; their departure from us in childhood, in youth, in manhood : bursting from the closest sympathies of life, and leaving us here, who might have been called away in their stead, to go onward still in our probation, from the stage and point where theirs is closed for eternity.  What an appeal is thus brought up to us on all our way in life, from the death of companions falling at our side; to remind us of our duty, to affect us with the providence that permits us to linger amid the privileges from which they have been withdrawn, and bids us be ready to follow them at any time into eternity?

There is now opportunity also for God to adapt the chastening, which he administers through death, more wisely to the spiritual welfare of survivors. Death is to invade every family circle. But when shall it come, how shall it approach, whom shall it invade? All is now open and free for the Lord to do as seemeth good in his sight. And does it make no difference how he proceeds? Though we may not see what particular course wisdom might dictate, yet is it not obvious that to infinite wisdom one course must appear preferable to another? He must see who most need correction, what extent of correction will be most profitable, and we are assured from his possession of infinite wisdom, that in the present procedure of his providence he adapts the chastening and correction he administers through death, in a manner the most profitable to afflicted friends, consistently with the other ends he is seeking at the same time in his kingdom. We are assured from his own mouth that he doth it for our profit, that we might be partakers of his holiness—that we may be brought into subjection to him, the Father of our spirits and live.

Such are the modes of superior moral discipline, which the present manner of inflicting death enables the Lord to administer to mankind.

I remark, once more only,

4. By means of the present providence of God in respect to death, the exercise of superior wisdom is admitted in the removal of men from their stations on earth into those they are to occupy in eternity. This consideration opens before us a field too boundless in extent to be traversed by our feeble faculties. The eternal world is wholly beyond our sight, and we know not what change is affected there by the introduction of a new inhabitant, or who of the millions of this world it is best should

arrive there on the morrow. In the present world too, we can trace the results to arise from the removal of a single person but a little way, as these results circle forth from the vacancy on the surrounding mass. How little then can we know of the relation the removal may have on the plans of wisdom for this world, in all its ages, and in all the relations it bears to the future world! We stand on the verge of an illimitable field of beings and results, extending far beyond our ken into the regions of immensity and eternity. Yet we know that there is One, whose piercing vision takes in the whole; and we have confidence in his wisdom, that at whatever time he takes any being from this scene of life and transfers him to eternity, he sees it best for the interests of his whole kingdom, that the removal should then be made. We know that, on the present plan of providence, there is free opportunity for the Creator to remove whomsoever he pleases, at whatsoever time, and in whatsoever manner: that consequently there is a range for the exercise of his wisdom in best adapting the removal to the interests of his whole kingdom, that would be entirely excluded on the plan of removing all from the world at one and the same period of life. Now we have this confidence, that when the good and useful man is cut off from the earth in early age, the world will not suffer on the whole, or that if it should at all, there will be gain more than enough to counterbalance it in the kingdom of God above:—or that, when the guilty tyrant and oppressor is continued long on earth, the world will not suffer more on the whole than were he more early removed, or at least that results will be gained in the whole kingdom of eternity, more than enough to counterbalance the difference that remains. The problem is simply this: all other things remaining as they are; that is, in a world of sin where grace is carrying forward its conquests, and from which all its generations are to be removed to their endless retributions, is it best adapted to advance the objects of infinite wisdom and goodness in both worlds taken together, to remove all men at a precise age of life, or to vary the time and manner with the individuals? Every one who admits the connection of means and ends in the kingdom of God, must have confidence that the present plan of removal is the true solution of the problem—that it is best adapted to gain the ends of wisdom—that it lets in the exercise of superior wisdom in the providential management of this world—that it gains more to the kingdom of God on the whole.

Such then I conceive to be some of the important ends gained by the present providence of the Creator, which breaks in upon every apparent principle of regularity and order in the infliction of temporal death—ends, which must totally be excluded from attainment under a system of uniform regularity and order, and which consequently evince the wisdom of God in pursuing the present system.

To recapitulate them in the order we have considered them, they are the following :—the care of human life is made to enter as an element of duty into our present state of probation ; the call to attend to the duties of our probationary state, and prepare for another life, is rendered more powerful; a superior moral discipline is exerted over mankind by means of the infliction of death ; and the exercise of superior wisdom admitted, in the removal of men from their stations on earth into those which they are to occupy in eternity.

And now what are the practical conclusions we are to derive from the whole?

We find ourselves here in a world of probation, going soon through the shadowy realm of death to a state of eternal retribution. When we once go, we shall never return : and with no return to the privileges of this day of grace, our eternal condition is irreversibly fixed. If lost, we are lost forever: if redeemed, redeemed beyond danger and thrall. We have seen that, in this situation of deep interest in which we are placed, there is no visible order in the demands which come up to us from the grave ; and we find that, in this very departure from any fixed law of order in the time and manner of death, the

Creator is favoring our spiritual interests in this state of probation,—increasing the motives to that devotion and holiness which constitute the only true preparation for future blessedness; and consulting, at the same, the highest good of his entire kingdom.

Does not the subject then obviously call upon us, not only as sinners to be reconciled to God—without which all our interests are wrecked to eternity—but more especially, to submit as reconciled children to his Fatherly wisdom, and occupy ourselves diligently in his service?

To submit as reconciled children to his Fatherly wisdom. Any evidence which he gives us of his wisdom and goodness, should indeed lead us with a filial confidence to commit ourselves and our friends and fellow-creatures to the disposal of his will. But it may assist us to submit, more peacefully and calmly, to a trying part of his providence, if we can see, amid the darkness that surrounds it, some clear traces of wisdom and goodness—that the light of his love shines forth, even from the gloom and darkness. When we look on the apparently indiscriminate and irregular path of his providence, there is much that looks dark and mysterious. We fix our eye perhaps on some affecting instance of death; and we instinctively ask, why should not death have longer delayed? Why should it not have come in some other form? But why shall we doubt or complain? If we cannot trace the ways of Jehovah through all their intricacies, does he not let us see that he is ordering this branch of his providence in a way to conduce to the spiritual welfare of mankind and the best good of his kingdom? We can see at least, that the general plan on which he is proceeding, out of which these cases of trial arise, is the best, and therefore adopted by fatherly wisdom and goodness. Let us then without a murmur or complaint, without a wish to take the disposal of ourselves or others out of his hands, calmly leave all with him; rejoicing that, in this part of his providence, he doeth all things well—that, as a faithful and compassionate Creator, he is consulting the well-being of his kingdom and the true welfare of all who commit their ways and their souls to his care. This is true submission : unlike the stoic apathy which submits, as to a blind fate, with a hard-hearted indifference towards God and his creatures. This is the submission of filial love, which honors God and cherishes the best affections in the heart of man.

The subject calls upon us also to occupy ourselves diligently as his servants. For the Lord is ever near us, calling upon us to value that life on which hangs our destiny, and to occupy its hastening hours in preparation for future glory. He is near us continually, appealing to our hearts from affecting scenes of death. He is ever near, taking his servants from this world into eternity. While the Lord is constantly so near, showing his footsteps in the darkest storms of his providence, opening a path of light for all his devoted and faithful servants, be assured that your wisdom, your safety, your happiness lies in being fervently and diligently occupied, as obedient servants, in the great work he has given you to do in this life. This course calls down the light of his countenance upon you, and brings you into communion with his Spirit, as you pass along your way to the grave. It lets you, with peaceful hope of heaven, leave calmly, at his disposal, the hour and manner of your departure ; and prepares you to meet the event, when it comes, with joy, as the time and way your Lord appoints you of resting from your earthly labors and trials, and entering upon immortal blessedness in heaven. Be ye then servants of God in this world of your probation. Be ye followers of Jesus in these scenes of his trial. Be diligent, unmovable, always abounding in the work of the Lord, while here on your way to his immovable kingdom above. For Christ, our Master, will soon dismiss us from these scenes. ‘ Blessed are those servants whom, when he cometh, he shall find so doing ! ’

How, when, it shall be<br>
We cannot foresee ;<br>
But Lord, let us live, let us die, unto thee !

---

MATTHEW XIV: 3—11.  MARK VI: 17—29.

THIS distinguished preacher of righteousness was sent as a prophet to Israel, to announce the Messiah and introduce him into his public ministry.  He had been engaged in this office somewhat more than a year and a half, when his faithfulness gave such an offense to the family of Herod Antipas, king of the Tetrarchy of Galilee, as was never forgiven; which led to his immediate imprisonment, and subsequently to his death.

The offense was given by a speech which John made in the presence of Herod Antipas, in regard to his marriage. That speech excited the displeasure of the king; but the venom of anger rankled deepest in the breast of his proud, ambitious and pleasure-loving consort,—the beautiful, yet faithless Herodias.  This aspiring matron, as we learn from the Jewish historian Josephus, the grand-daughter of Herod the Great, had first married her uncle Herod Philip; and becoming disgusted with him, as a man who had fallen into disgrace in the family, and was left without place and without fortune in the world, she intrigued with another uncle, already married, this Herod Antipas, the king of Galilee, with whom for a husband she would secure herself a palace and a crown.  The plot succeeded: the enamored Herod Antipas divorced his wife, without cause, and sent her to her father, king Aretas: the faithless Herodias, taking with her her daughter Salome, forsook her first husband; and these parties, in full violation of their existing marriage vows, united their fortunes in an incestuous marriage in the palace at Tiberias in Galilee.  They were

living in this strange union, and she with her daughter
were reveling in the splendors and luxuries of a Roman
court, when John the Baptist, that stern preacher of the
laws of righteousness, that zealous promoter of the cause
of repentance and reformation, came into Galilee exercising his ministry among the people. His increasing
fame and reputation as a prophet, brought him into notice
in high places. Herod, on the throne of Galilee, could
not be indifferent to the influence which he was acquiring
among the people, and which might be, if not rightly
managed, wielded against him for purposes of sedition
among his subjects. He watches the prophet. He seeks
occasion and opportunity to hear him. He regards, in his
outward practice before the people, many of his precepts.
He appears for a while pleased with his discourses. But
the occasion soon arrives for the prophet to be more
direct in dealing with the conscience of the king, than he
could do with propriety and without appearance of scan-
dal in the promiscuous assemblies of the multitude. In
consequence of the popularity of the preacher, it is
probable that he was invited to attend at the palace
and preach before the court, where the king and queen
would stand prominent before him ; and faithfulness to
the highest interests of his host and hostess, would seem
to demand an utterance of the truth and an application of it in favor of personal repentance and reformation.
On such an occasion, probably, was it (if it were not a
still more private interview taken with the king alone)
that the speech was uttered, which proved the source of
his persecution even unto death. The speech is short, as
it is reported ; but it unfolded the whole enormity of their
sin, and sent an arrow to their hearts, that gave a wound
never to be healed except by repentance : " It is not lawful for *thee* to have *her*, thy brother's wife." On that
annunciation, Herodias, more than Herod, trembles.
' Will the prophet prevail over the conscience of my husband to put me away ? and shall I, with my daughter, be
thrust out of the palace in disgrace ?' She turns with
rage against the prophet. She forthwith sets her pliant

husband to the work of silencing this reprover. She
would have him executed' instantly : but her husband,
troubled a little in conscience, and fearing more the indignation that might be excited against him in the populace,
though desirous to gratify her will, forbears to slay the
prophet : but withdraws him from the people, and closes
his opportunities of giving farther reproof, by shutting
him up and enchaining him, within the prison of the castle.
This account of the imprisonment of John is briefly
stated by Matthew and Mark, but in the plus-perfect time,
because in their history the narrative of the imprisonment,
being omitted in its proper place, is introduced as a past
and prior transaction, to preface the account of his death.
" Herod had laid hold on John and bound him and put
him in prison for Herodias' sake, his brother Philip's wife.
For John said unto him, it is not lawful for thee to have
her." The two historians present different motives that
induced Herod to forbear the execution and content himself with the bare imprisonment of John. Mark says,
" Therefore Herodias had a quarrel against him [John]
and would have killed him ; but she could not : for Herod
feared John, knowing that he was a just man and a holy,
and observed him, and when he heard him he did many
things and heard him gladly." His respect and reverence
for the prophet, notwithstanding the offense which made
him wish his death, checked him from proceeding farther
than imprisonment. Matthew says, " And when he
would have put him to death, he feared the multitude,
because they counted him as a prophet." His own displeasure and his wife's entreaties, both made him wish for
the death of John, but he was held back and restrained
from such extreme violence, partly by his reverence for
the prophet and partly by his fear of the people.

A year had elapsed and more. Herod, with Herodias
and Salome, lived on amid the pleasures of royal wealth
and extravagance. John is effectually silenced in the
prison ; and though his friends and disciples, through the
leave of the king, may occasionally have access into his
presence, his discourses before the multitude have ceased,

and they become less and less interested in his fate and fortune.

The day arrives at length, on which the incensed Herodias has opportunity to indulge the malice of her heart. "When a convenient day was come," says Mark, in introducing the narrative. That was the birthday of Herod,— to be celebrated with great pomp and with riotous feasting in the palace. "Herod, on his birthday, made a supper," says Mark, "to his lords, high captains and chief estates of Galilee." The guests invited were the men of the Tetrarchy who ranked highest in military and civil offices, and who, being nearest him in command, were the most familiar friends of the king. The tables were ornamented with the rich and splendid furniture of royalty; the dishes were filled with savory viands to regale the appetite; the cups and goblets were sparkling with wine. The company recline on their couches around the extended tables. The halls glare, at this evening hour, with a flood of light from the many burning lamps. And as the feast advances, and the king and his courtiers become excited with wine and yield themselves to unrestrained hilarity, at this fitting opportunity to gain promises and presents, the young Salome, the daughter of Herodias, decorated and sent in no doubt by her artful mother, appears before the company in the dress and with the graceful movements of the dancing girl, to perform a part which was often enacted in those days, for the entertainment of a feasting party—the graceful, giddy, and voluptuous dance. As she enters the hall of feasting, and stations herself opposite the king,—her brilliant features radiant with smiles, her decorated form illuminated with light, and waving to and fro in the dance, her gestures of beauty and love, attract all eyes and give a crowning joy to the feast. The step-father on his royal couch is pleased most of all. The excitements of the wine-cup have driven away all prudence from his heart and all discretion from his tongue. Before the whole company so filled with pleasure, he gives way to the pride and pleasure awakened in his own heart at receiving such an entertainment from his daughter, and utters the rash promise "Ask of me whatsoever thou wilt, and I will give it thee." He was not content with the bare utterance of such an unguarded promise. Like a fool overcome with wine and pleasure, who, regardless of the future, lets the feeling of the moment rule his words and actions, he repeats the promise, and binds himself to it with a loud oath before the whole company. " He sware unto her, whatsoever thou shalt ask of me, I will give it thee, unto the half of my kingdom."

Upon securing that promise, Salome leaves the room. The promise of half the kingdom—half its revenues of wealth and luxury—she now holds in her hand. She goes straightway to her mother. Is she a dutiful child that seeks advice of her nearest earthly friend, or a successful complotter, who has gone to tell the triumph of the scheme and give her malignant mother the joy of presenting an order through her that shall compel the obedience of the king? The sequel determines. " And she went forth and said unto her mother, what shall I ask? and she said, the head of John the Baptist." Behold, the value put on revenge! The wealth of half a kingdom is thrown away to gratify this one malignant passion! If the daughter was not an accomplice with her mother before, she is now. All the wealth she might appropriate to herself is neglected, that she may gain her mother's will. Perhaps she and her mother both felt, that if John the Baptist lived, he might yet turn them both away from sharing the kingdom with Herod, and that, to enjoy securely their estate in his good graces, this preacher of righteousness must be effectually silenced. So she returned quickly with her mother's message. " She came in straightway with haste unto the king." The king was to be taken, while yet in the excitement of his cups; while his promise and oath were still resounding in the ears of his guests. And quickly, too, must the boon be given her by the king. For time, delay, reflection, were dangerous things to be allowed to come in before the execution of such a request as she was to make. The first thing was to obtain her request: to have it accomplished; to get the head of the Baptist taken off while the king was in the humor to fulfill his promise: and then,—let thought and reflection come on the morrow,—they can not defeat her purpose of revenge.

Again before the feasting company Salome stands. There is now a cloud on her brow; a smile of malicious triumph on her cheek. She appears more thoughtful than before. To the astonishment of the whole company, to the grief of the king, she asks the horrid gift. "I will that thou give me—by and by," or as the Greek word is more appropriately rendered, *forthwith*—"in a charger—the head of John the Baptist." See how artful has been the malice of the mother, so to frame the request as to make all things sure. *Forthwith*—that there may be no opportunity, between an order given to an executioner and the time of its fulfillment, to allow of arresting the process by the intervention of any counter-order. The *head upon a plate* or dish—that there may be no deception practiced as to the person or his execution. "Give me forthwith, in a charger, the head of John the Baptist." O what a miserable entertainment was this to be to that feasting company! Instead of the fascinating dancing girl, entertaining them with joy, she stands before them as a murderess seeking revenge through death, and waits in their presence till she shall receive, and hold, reeking in its blood before them, the head of the hated prophet. "And the king was exceeding sorry: yet for his oath's sake, and for their sakes which sat with him," lest perhaps they should reproach him for his fickleness and inconstancy, or on account, perhaps, of the desire of many of them to court the favor of the queen—"he would not reject her. And immediately the king sent an executioner, and commanded his head to be brought."

Let us leave now awhile this hall of splendor, in which the king and his guests are still feasting, though with misgiving hearts, and where the damsel is in waiting to receive her dowry, dreadful as it is, yet more valued than half the kingdom of Galilee; let us leave the palace and visit that dark apartment in the castle, in which the prisoner John resides, confined in chains. He has passed now within these walls more than a year and a half: for he was confined not long after the first passover after Jesus was inducted into office, and now the third passover is at hand. During this period he has at times seen his followers: and, soon after the second passover, he sent, in great trial, an embassy to Jesus to learn what he might expect from him in regard to setting up his kingdom. Jesus returned an answer which probably satisfied this righteous prophet, that his kingdom would be set up in his own time and way, and led him to submit without offense to the providence of Jesus, as ordered in wisdom, and wait with patience for blessedness in his kingdom. Yet his ministry, though suddenly and early closed, had produced its effect: and his life, though now to be cut off . from the earth, was to be exalted to a more peaceful state than befel him in his fastings, his preaching of repentance, and his cruel persecutions on earth. He has passed his last day in the castle. He is there because he has faithfully told a fellow-creature to leave off his sins and turn to God in repentance, so that he may have joy in the kingdom of God. Nothing of enmity was in his heart. He loved the pure and righteous laws of his God. He sought the reformation and salvation of a sinning brother. And here in his prison, suffering the enmity of those whom he warned to flee from the wrath to come, he has no heart to wish them any evil in return. He may pray, if any faith yet remains in their behalf, for the spiritual welfare of the king and his consort, that they may yet see their sin, and forsake it, and turn to God and so find a place in his kingdom. And now as his evening prayers have risen to God, and, committing his soul to his care for the night, he is about to rest in his slumbers, there come sounds of joy and revelry from the halls of the palace into his cell. He sees in imagination the festive halls of the king, and weeps at the thoughtless folly of sinners who take all their feasting and joy in this life— who substitute the pleasures of sense and appetite, in

their momentary and intoxicating excitements, for the
deep and pure river of those spiritual joys that flow
through the heart of the pious forever, from the love and
friendship of God.  Perhaps his thoughts turn towards
the grave and eternity : for God is wont to draw nigh to
his friends on their near approach to death.  Perhaps
these sounds of feasting carry forward his own mind to
that happy paradise into which no sin shall ever enter, and
where he shall feast, with Abraham and all the prophets
and friends of God, upon the riches of divine knowledge
and love forever.  'Thanks be to my God,' may he say,
'that he has employed me in his service on the earth.
Give me all my temporal fastings and present trials with
God for my friend, rather than all these feastings of sinners to end in the wrath to come.'

The hour of his eternal release is come.  The executioner, commissioned from the king, arrives.  He turns
the key.  He opens the massive door, and stands before
John, the herald of wrath from the queen, the herald of
mercy from God.  The prophet bows to the will of
Providence.  He bends his neck to the block.  His head
is severed from the body.  And that night his soul is in
Paradise !

The executioner "beheaded him in the prison and
brought his head in a charger, and," in presence of the king
and his guests, "gave it to the damsel."  The promise of
the king was now fulfilled, and this treasure, which she valued more than half the kingdom, she took with her from
the room and " brought it to her mother."  That head,
what will she do with it?  Will she insult those lips and
that tongue that once stung her with reproof?  But the
soul is now far away in triumphant joys.  That head—
what will she do with it?  Methinks it will stare upon
her now a frown deeper than tongue and lips ever uttered.  Methinks it will stare upon her in all her pleasures
and in all her sufferings in this life—stare upon her at
death—stare upon her in eternity.  That head she never
can dispose of.  She may bury it; but it will come up
again to her waking and sleeping moments.  She may

burn it; but it will have a resurrection again to her mind. That reproving head, and she, the guilty sinner, have now met, beyond the power of prison walls or bars ever to separate. The stain of blood has been affixed upon her memory and her conscience that ages will not wash away.

But the body of John received kind testimonies of affection. "His disciples," having obtained permission, doubtless, of Herod, "came and took up the body and buried it." Their leader was now gone to heaven, and they could not wait on him any more for instruction. "And when they had buried the body, they went and told Jesus." They sought sympathy and instruction thenceforth from Jesus, the friend of their master. In this mysterious manner, the ministry of John was closed, and his true and faithful disciples transferred forever to the care and kingdom of Jesus.

In respect to this scene recorded in the sacred history, I would remark,

1. That above all the sad workings of human passion in the scene, the wisdom of an overruling providence is manifest in giving this extraordinary termination to the ministry of John the Baptist.

The office of John was a peculiar one, as he was not merely to call the people to repentance, as the prophets before him had done, but to do it with distinct reference to their preparation for receiving the Messiah and inheriting the blessings of his kingdom. He stood at the close of an old economy, to introduce the long foretold Messiah : as an intermediate link to bind it to the new. He was to labor as a zealous reformer to prepare the way of the Lord, to point him out to the people and introduce him into his ministry. From the very nature of his office, therefore, it was necessary that it should soon terminate; that, as Jesus began his ministry and gathered around him disciples, this ministry of preparation should cease; that John should not be gathering around him his disciples longer, as it would make a diversion of the people from their Great Deliverer, and set up an opposing sect in the land.  He was but the morning star to harbinger the coming of the Messiah : and when Jesus arose to gather the people to his standard—when he arose to give light as a perpetual Sun of Righteousness, the star that was bright at the early dawn must fade away.

How appropriate, then, was the close of his office.  It was appropriate that, as a zealous reformer come in the spirit and power of Elijah, he should be willing to face another Ahab and provoke another Jezebel, that he should reprove wickedness on the throne as well as among the multitude : and it was appropriate that, as a reformer come to prepare the way of Jesus the Christ, he should in some way be withdrawn from his office soon after Jesus began by his teachings to draw around him his disciples. Mark now the course taken by an overruling providence. He is not, while moving forward in his ministry as a burning and shining light, giving joy and hope to many hearts, suddenly silenced by a command from heaven : for that would leave him lingering on earth among his waiting disciples, as one who had withdrawn his testimony and abated his zeal ; and might defeat, rather than consummate, the object of preparing them for the school of Christ.  He is not allowed to die a natural death in the bosom of his family of disciples : for that would prevent him from receiving, as a zealous reformer, the appropriate and. glorious reward of martyrdom ; from riding, like another Elijah, on the fiery wheels of persecution to a distinguished seat in glory.  Neither is he struck down by the hand of violence and persecution at once, while in the full career of his ministry and reputation among his disciples and the multitude.  Providence has marked out another course, whereby gradually to diminish the interest of the people in his teachings ; to prepare him and his disciples, both the better to bow to the will and authority of Jesus ; and yet, to reward his just and holy life with the high honors and exalted crown of martyrdom.

The hand of divine providence leads him up to the court of Herod.  Faithful to his high office, fearing not the consequences that may arise to his own person, he reproves the king: warns him by repentance to flee from the wrath to come. How wonderful the result! Brought thus into contact with the family of Herod, the instruments of providence are ready to execute its wise will concerning John. The queen resolves on his death, with an inappeasable hatred, which will never fail to be ready, when opportunity shall be given, to execute her purpose. The king is himself incensed, yet restrained by his conscience and by the tide of popular favor that surrounds his reprover: he refuses the entreaties of the queen for his instant death, and merely confines him in prison. John is thus withdrawn from his ministry: the field is left open to the ministry of Jesus, and, as his fame increases and that of John diminishes, the prisoner, in an hour of dejection, sends an embassy to seek, for himself and the followers that still cleave to him, and gain instruction from Jesus that comforts him and the more prepares them to transfer themselves to the care and instruction of that Great Teacher. The hour comes around when the queen, seeing an opportunity to circumvent the king in the moments of intoxication, plots her nefarious scheme; employs the beauty and boldness of her daughter to aid her plans; obtains from the king, amid his cups, a rashly unlimited promise and vow for her daughter; and thus secures the accomplishment of her long harbored purpose of revenge. In this mysterious way, a wise and superintending providence awards to John at the close of his fastings and self-denial and preachings of repentance, the honor of ascending, before Jesus, to the kingdom of heaven to wear the bright crown of martyrdom: and his few true and faithful disciples yet remaining, that providence hands over to the care of his successor, but superior in office. From the scene of bloodshed and the death of their leader, they go, with aching hearts, to pour their sorrows into the sympathizing bosom of Jesus. To him and his school of spiritual instructions they thenceforth cleave: and thus, without schism and rent, from the co-existence of separate religious schools of disciples in the land, all is peacefully transferred to the care and instruction of the Heavenly Teacher, Christ Jesus. Thus providence ever interweaves its own plans into the endlessly intricate maze of human interests and passions; and succeeds, even amid the darkest conflicts of human malice, to fulfill its counsels of wisdom and love.

2. The portion of history before us well illustrates the nature and foundation of decision of character.

Decision as a trait of character includes the formation of distinct purposes in the life, and a steady and unbending adherence to their execution. It is founded, either on strict integrity in purpose or in utter recklessness; on virtuous regard to justice towards God and man, or the selfishness that is regardless of both. But he who aims at the middle path between these is the double-minded man, who is unstable in all his ways.

This subject is very clearly illustrated in the principal characters that figure in this scene. John the Baptist is decisive on virtuous principle. He maintains in his heart integrity of purpose towards God and man. He has but one errand on the earth ; to publish and maintain the law and honor of God, and prepare his fellow-men by repentance for happiness in the kingdom of God. And all the steps of his pilgrimage he directs to accomplish that one great errand. He denies himself the luxuries of life : he fasts in the desert : he proclaims, alike fearlessly before all, the great duty of repentance. The common people in their fickleness; the scribes and Pharisees in their pride of sanctity and learning; Herod and Herodias on their throne of guilt and power; move him not one moment aside from his high purpose of calling men to respect the laws of heaven and to prepare for the blessings to be brought by the Messiah. He has one holy aim and purpose : and he cannot be turned about by the winds of human passions. He leans back on an upright conscience and a God of righteousness ; and the foundations of his strength are immovable.

Herodias, on the other hand, the proud and revengeful, is decisive through utter recklessness of justice to others.

Her purpose was to exalt herself to power and pleasure, and for this one end she formed her plans, regardless of the laws of God or opinions of mankind. She sought the pleasure and pomp of a throne at Tiberias. Nor was she moved from the purpose by any moral obstacles in her way. To gain that place, she scruples not to abandon her first betrothed husband and the father of her child. She hesitates not to make the king of Galilee put away from him his faithful wife. She shrinks not from encountering the guilt and odium of a life of mutual crime. And when she has gained that place, it is her fixed purpose to keep it and enjoy it, whatever obstacles may arise. And when John, by his stern inculcation of moral duty, begins to work on the conscience of her husband to put her away, instead of yielding for one moment to this troubler of her prospects, she adopts at once the fell purpose to silence him forever, by taking away his life: and, unmoved through the delay of a year's waiting, embraces the first opportunity to accomplish her purpose, and succeeds to bring before her in a supposed triumph his trunkless head. This is the decision of utter recklessness: the only decision that remains for those, who will not with simplicity and integrity of purpose yield themselves to the service of God—a decision, that must sooner or later dash the subject of it on the rocks and barriers of eternal righteousness.

Herod, again, stands forth on the scene as the indecisive man, whose regard to justice on the one hand, and regard to his private and selfish pleasures on the other, are ever brought into conflict, because neither of them is allowed to take the supreme rule : and, thus in perpetual conflict, they prevent him from having a definite will to which he immovably adheres. At the time he imprisons John, he would gratify his anger and that of his wife. He loves his pleasure too much, to have it marred by this faithful preacher. Yet he cannot go forward to take the life of the prophet, for he still reverences him too much as a just man and a holy, and fears the people too much to have his own way. And again, when, by the arts of his wife and daughter, he has bound himself before his court to execute John, he would save him, but dare not. He cannot take the unshaken purpose to save the prophet's life at all hazards, regardless of his rash promise and oath ; regardless of the opinions of the court and his queen : for his mind is not made up to fear God above all and follow the prophet's warnings. So he is compelled, against his will as it were, to slay the prophet. At one time he would slay John, through his love of his own pleasures ; but fears John and the people too much. At another, he would save John, through regard to him and the people ; but fears the queen and her daughter and the nobles too much.

Into one of these three classes mankind ever divide themselves : the decisive on virtuous principle, who are lifted up by regard to the right above all momentary and changing considerations: the decisive on utter recklessness of right, in pursuit of selfish pleasure: and the vacillating, who can never make up their minds decisively to either course.

3. The history sets before us the deceitfulness of unlawful pleasures.

Pleasures that are unlawful, however smiling and insinuating their appearance and promises, infringe on some fixed laws of heaven ordained for the welfare of individuals or of society, and necessarily bring back a recompense of guilt and woe. To seek for pleasure by violating either the physical, mental or moral laws ordained for our welfare, is a course that can end only in disappointment : for these laws are walls of everlasting strength, and if we dash against them, we ourselves must break down,—not they.

The beautiful Salome, moving before the king on the night of the feast in the dance, stands forth as it were the personification of the treachery that lurks behind the promises of sinful pleasure. Could the king have thought, as he looked upon her fascinating smiles, that she meditated anything but to gratify the guests of her father, and give him pleasure in the feast? All is fair and winning to the eye. Yet that beauteous form conceals a treacherous heart, that seeks not to please the father so much as to win from him a dreadful favor. She takes advantage of his hour of weakness, that she may fulfill a fell purpose of her mother's, and draw the king into the commission of a horrid crime. Her happy smiles of pleasure but deceived him, and led him onward, in vile subservience to plots of murder.

I say, she personifies the deceit and treachery of the promises that attend on sinful pleasures.

Thus treacherous are the promises of the wine cup— they were so to the king. He took the exhilarating draught, that he might obtain pleasure. He thought he saw nothing in the cup but innocent hilarity. But there lurked the demon of intoxication. There lurked the poison that was to work on his physical, intellectual and moral nature, to turn him into the brute, without reason or reflection. His brain is maddened : his wisdom and prudence forsake him; and he becomes an accomplice with murderers. Such is the brief, sad history of many a life of intemperance, wretchedness and crime.

Such treachery too was there in that first dream of unhallowed pleasure which united the fates and fortune of the guilty pair. Herodias seeks to find the pleasure of luxury, of lust and of pride, in living with Herod in his palace. Doubtless, as she forsook her first husband, all the future appeared to her proud and ambitious mind as the dream of enchantment. Uninterrupted joy and honor is to be her happy lot. But, while indulging in this dream of pleasure, she is warring with the laws of heaven : and up to her palace, on his mission of righteousness and mercy, comes John the Baptist to utter those laws. Now is she agitated, as she still clings to her place at the side of Herod. The venom of revenge poisons her peace. She makes her daughter and the king accomplices in the murder of the prophet. And never after does she prosper. Thus did those fair dreams of pleasure deceive her, and lead her on to many crimes and cruelties in warring against the laws of heaven : to hate the holy prophet of the Lord; to compromise the modesty and honesty of her daughter; to abuse the weakness and confidence of her husband; to indulge her own heart in deadly revenge: and thus fill her soul, in all its future remembrances, with the elements of remorse and wretchedness.

So it is ever with all the promises of sin. Satan, wicked men around us, our own hearts, may trust in them awhile; but they are promises set up against the laws and engagements of God. He will fulfill his own promises and threatenings, and scatter forever all who trust in lies.

4. Finally: We may learn the folly of employing force and violence against those who seek the repentance and reformation of their fellow-men.

Reformers who set up to reclaim men from their sins, and call them to walk in the laws of heaven, have a task that is not welcome to our weak and perverse nature. They are generally, like John the Baptist, true men and honest, just men and holy. Otherwise they would not apply themselves with earnestness to their severe task. Men love quiet and ease in their pleasures. Whether their pleasures before God are lawful or unlawful, they would pursue them without any moral disturbances or hindances. Agitation is their dread. But this world is not intended, chiefly, for pleasure; but as a world of probation, in which men are to be reclaimed from sin and trained to holiness, that so they may escape the wrath to come, and inherit pure and fadeless happiness in the holy and heavenly kingdom of God. Reformers therefore, the hearty and true, who set up the law of God as their rule, are engaged in the work of God; and, whether they are judicious in the world's estimation or not, it is wiser surely to repent of our sins than to blame the zeal of our reprovers: wiser to reason with them, if we deem them wrong, than violently to assault their persons. This moral lesson is taught us in the history of the Baptist.

This zealous reformer was a just man and holy, as even Herod acknowledged. He approved of the wise and holy laws of God. He sought the honor of God and the welfare of man, in his zealous advocacy of repentance. But his agitating reproof administered at the palace was unwelcome. Instead of yielding up their sin, the royal pair assail the prophet; exclude him from the field of his labors by force of imprisonment; and with murderous revenge take away his life. But have they gained by their violence? The prophet is calm, in the flow of pious and virtuous affections in his heart; in the conscious sense of having pursued the highest welfare of his fellow-creatures in his labors; and in the hope of inheriting the favor of the eternal God in his kingdom—a joy beyond the reach of any violence from men or devils.

But how is it with the guilty trio in the palace? Can their hatred of John, their imprisonment of him, their murder of him, alter the laws of heaven; annihilate their own crimes; or prepare the way for future peace and joy?

Who would not sooner take the place of John in his prison on the night of his execution, than that of either of the guilty inmates of the palace during the feasting? He went up that night from his cell to take a crown nobler far than that of Herod—the martyr's crown of everlasting glory.

Salome and the queen are taking their feast of revenge over the platter that holds the lifeless head of John. Poor triumph of an hour, that embitters the peace of the king; that stains their consciences with guilt; and that sends an accuser up to the Heavenly Altar to cry, "How long, O Lord, dost thou not avenge our blood on them that dwell on the earth?" If we may believe the report of profane history, vengeance did not long wait. The fair Salome, while walking across a frozen river, it is reported, broke through, and fell in such a way as that, on the return of the parted fragments of ice, as she rose, her head was severed from the body. And Herod and Herodias were called, by imperial authority at Rome, away from their palace, and sent in exile to Lyons, to end their days in want and disgrace: and all went at death to meet their victim at the bar of eternal righteousness, and receive the just award of their deeds.

Such is the folly of persecuting the just, who labor to give efficacy to the laws of God.  Inspiration has declared, " He that justifieth the wicked, and he that condemneth the just, even they both are an abomination to the Lord." Doubly hateful in his sight, therefore, must that man be, who combines both crimes in one: who upholds the wicked in their sins, by smiting down with violence their just and faithful reprovers.

## THE RIGHTEOUS TO LIVE HEREAFTER WITHIN THE SCENES OF A MATERIAL UNIVERSE.

II. PETER III: 13.

NEVERTHELESS, WE, ACCORDING TO HIS PROMISE, LOOK FOR NEW HEAVENS AND A NEW EARTH, WHEREIN DWELLETH RIGHTEOUSNESS.

THE apostle had just spoken of the destruction of the present world by fire at the close of the probation of our race, when all shall be summoned from their graves for judgment. In that day, "the elements shall melt with fervent heat, the earth also and the works that are therein shall be burned up." But shall the saints of God have no dwelling? Are the material worlds and suns of the creation literally to be annihilated, and are their souls to wander forth homeless, shelterless, on the void expanse of infinite space and duration? The apostle did not thus present the last conflagration, as the total annihilation of matter and material worlds. He set before his fellow Christians a more glorious edifice to arise from the ruins, new heavens and a new earth, fitted to be the immortal abode of righteous beings. The promise of the Lord assured him that the object of the last conflagration was not destruction, but the process of purgation, repairing and reconstruction; in order that, the wicked being gathered out of his kingdom, the righteous might have a pure and joyous residence for their immortality.

My design now is to set before you the evidence, that, after the final judgment, the righteous are to have for eternity their dwelling still within the bounds of a material universe. There can be but two positions taken on the general subject, either that the material worlds are to be annihilated, or are to continue forever; that the visible universe is to cease utterly, or is perpetually to remain; that the righteous are to float forever through utterly empty space, or are to live still within the anchorage ground of a physical creation. It is no part of my present design to enter into any particular theory of a future physical creation, among the many that have been or that might be broached on the subject: but simply to advocate the future existence of at least some physical creation, as the abode of the righteous.

I would first call your attention then to the fact that we have no positive evidence to show that the universe of matter is ever to be annihilated. There is no evidence of such annihilation furnished us, either by reason or revelation. Reason furnishes none from secondary causes or from analogy. In all the researches of man into the chemical and astronomical structure of the universe, no causes have been found which are adequate to the work of annihilation. The utmost which can be predicted from known secondary causes, is that there may possibly occur some great changes in the world or the solar system: but there is nothing which indicates, in the least, the effect of annihilation. Indeed, all the researches of reason lead us up to the conclusion, that the annihilation of matter, if it ever occurs, can be the result only of that immediate and direct omnipotence of the Creator, which first called it into existence. Is it then the will of the Creator, to annihilate by his omnipotent power the worlds he has made? If we reason from the analogy of a past providence, it would seem, from the facts as evinced in the geological history of the world, that great convulsions and changes have passed over it, which have been only preparatory to its improvement and better subservience to the accommodation of its inhabitants, increasing in the scale from the lowest animals to the race of man; and, so far as reason can argue from the past, it would seem probable that the world, if carried through any great convulsions in the future, would be still spared in its existence and improved for the accommodation of beings more exalted still, or for man himself in a more exalted state of being than now.

But from reason, we pass to the book in which this great Being has given us a revelation of his designs. Has he told us in this book, that he is to annihilate the worlds? Here again I assert, that revelation furnishes us no evidence of such a catastrophe. There are many passages which speak of a great event to take place in the physical universe, at the close of the probation of our race—the time of the general judgment—represented as destruction by conflagration. Yet if we examine these passages carefully, inquiring what that destruction is and how far it extends, we shall see that they do not touch the question of the utter annihilation of the worlds. The most explicit of all, is that which immediately precedes our text. There is no doubt in the case, that the material world is spoken of, and a description given of the destruction which it is to undergo at the period of the judgment. The destruction is here ascribed to the agency of fire. But fire, whatever destruction it might accomplish in the present forms of the matter of the globe, is not an agent to destroy its substance, or to destroy that centripetal force which binds it together in a world. But, if we pass from the nature of the agent employed to the effects which are specified by Peter as resulting, we do not come to annihilation. There are three results which he specifies: the heavens being on fire are dissolved—the elements are melted with fervent heart,—the earth, and the structures of divine and human skill that are in it, are consumed. We have seen substances dissolved in gases or smoke, and passing off from their former place ; we have seen the solid materials of the globe melted down into flowing and liquid masses; we have seen the forms of nature or art consumed, in the fires:—yet in none of these things have we witnessed the annihilation of matter. All the results therefore which Peter ascribes to the last conflagration, involve not the annihilation of matter. The matter still subsists, notwithstanding the conflagration, to be moulded into new combinations and forms, and for new purposes, if such shall be the will of the Creator. There is one result of the conflagration mentioned by Peter, which, however, deserves more attentive consideration. "The heavens," he says in one place, "being on fire shall be dissolved," and in another place, "shall pass away with a great noise." Now if this were spoken of the whole starry heavens, that they are to pass away, it might seem that the description referred to the total annihilation of the present universe. But the starry heavens, it is clear from the context, are not intended. For Peter had introduced the whole description, by referring to a former heavens and earth standing in the water and out of the water, destroyed by the deluge: and the heavens and the earth, which are now, being reserved unto fire. The heavens here spoken of consequently must be those which immediately surround our globe, the aerial, not the sidereal. The translation given by Rosenmüller to the phrase, 'the heavens and the earth' in this chapter, accords with this, viz: "the earth with its atmostphere." The truth is, the eye of the apostle was fixed on this world as the great scene of conflagration, this world which is reserved unto fire, against the day of judgment and perdition of ungodly men. His description therefore is optical—the scene is presented, as it would appear to the eye of a spectator on the globe; these skies are filled with the crackling flames and smoke, before which all the fowls of heaven and the living swarms of the insect tribes that move in it are destroyed, and for the time, day and night, the sun and stars, disappear,—this solid globe is melted down to one liquid mass; and, in the burning cauldron, sinks consumed every vestige of the works of God and man that once adorned it. But if the description were literally extended to all the starry worlds of this immense universe, our globe would constitute, in so vast a conflagration, but a small and trifling flame, and it would be against all the proportions of harmony and truth, to present it as the principal and grand scene of dissolution. I see therefore, in this description of Peter, no other destruction than that which is occasioned by fire, and that scene of destruction, too, confined to this one globe and the contents of its atmosphere. No evidence is furnished in this description of the annihilation, even of this globe, much less of this solar system or the immense starry heavens. Again, John in his first epistle, chap. ii : 17, asserts, "the world passeth away, and the lust thereof." The world here I understand in the moral sense, to denote "worldly men:" these pass away, and with them the objects of their lusts. In which sense nothing more is asserted, than that death puts an end to the gratification of their worldly lusts, or that, to them, all the objects of their happiness are transitory. Again, the apostle Paul, in his first epistle to the Corinthians, chap. vii : 31, asserts: "the *fashion* of this world passeth away." The "scheme," the plan, of this world is here asserted to be transient. This declaration again may be interpreted in the moral sense—that the state of man on the earth is ever unstable and changing. If on the other hand it is interpreted in the physical sense, then it supports the conclusion of a certain writer, that not the "matter and substance of the world, but the mode and form of it, pass away; for, after this world is burnt up, a new one as to form and fashion will arise, in much more beauty and glory." There is a passage again in the book of Job, which asserts of the dead, that they will not arise "till the heavens be no more." This phrase may refer to the destruction of the world at the last day, in which case what we have already said of the last conflagration, in its relation to the heavens, is to be taken into consideration—that the heavens in such descriptions are taken, not literally for the whole starry universe, but optically for the atmosphere and surrounding appendages of the globe. But there is reason to suppose that the phrase is here used in the rhetorical sense, as we shall presently find it used in other instances, to express a thing that the writer is confident will never take place. We have an instance of this rhetorical and tropical sense in Matthew, chap. v : 18, "till heaven and earth pass away, one jot and one tittle shall not pass from the law," meaning that the law never will be impaired. If this is the use of the phrase in Job, then the declaration refers not at all to the future resurrection to another life, which is to take place at the end of the present plan of the world, but simply to a return to this present life itself; that the dead are never to come back again to this present scene of trial; they are forever removed from it by death. That is, the heavens will as soon vanish as the dead come back again to the scenes and occupations of the present life. This interpretation accords with the whole drift of what in the immediate context precedes and follows. Another instance of the tropical use of such phraseology, is to be found in Jeremiah, xxxi: 35, &c. "Thus saith the Lord, which giveth the sun for a light by day and the ordinances of the moon and the stars for a light by night—if those ordinances depart from before me, saith the Lord, then the seed of Israel also shall cease from being a nation before me forever." This tropical use of phraseology relating to the destruction of the heavens and earth, it is obvious, proceeds on the strong impression we have of the permanency of heaven and earth, and all its force and appropriateness are lost, if we suppose there is the least reference made to their actual destruction as ever to take place. The following passages may be classed, either under the tropical use of phraseology or under the literal; and without deciding which, it is enough to show that neither interpretation establishes the conclusion of utter annihilation. Isaiah li: 6, "Lift up your eyes to the heavens, and look upon the earth beneath; for the heavens shall vanish away like smoke, and the earth shall wax old like a garment: but my salvation shall be forever, and my righteousness shall not be abolished." Vitringa remarks, the prophet does not here declare absolutely that the heavens and earth are to perish, but comparatively, in hyperbolical speech, that the heavens and earth, if either, will sooner fail than the salvation promised to his people. God will sooner destroy all the physical laws he has instituted, and break down all the worlds of his creation than violate his promise. Ps. cii: 26, 27, quoted Heb. i: 11, 12. "They," the heavens and the earth "shall perish, but thou remainest, and they all shall wax old as doth a garment, and as a vesture shalt thou fold them up and they shall be changed, but thou art the same, &c." Rosenmüller gives this interpretation : 'should all these things perish, thou wilt still remain.' But if we interpret these passages in the literal sense, and not the tropical, that the time is to come when these great changes shall pass upon the heavens and earth, that these things will change their present forms : they can refer to no other events than those which are so directly and explicitly described by Peter : and according to this full and explicit description, they are changes by the agency of fire, changes in the form and arrangement of matter, not the utter annihilation of its substance.

There is one more use still of phraseology relating to the destruction of the heavens and the earth, which is to be found in the Scriptures—that of prophetic imagery. According to Lowth "the prophets derived the materials of this imagery from the chaos and creation, which compose the first pages of the sacred history. As the sun, moon and stars are there represented as ruling the day, so they are made in prophecies relating to the fate of empires, to represent the destruction of the reigning powers. If the subject be the destruction of the Jewish empire by the Chaldeans, or a strong denunciation of ruin against the enemies of Israel, it is depicted in exactly the same colors, as if universal nature were about to relapse into the primeval chaos." Isaiah thus speaks of the ruin of the enemies of Israel, "All the host of heaven shall be dissolved, and the heavens shall be rolled together as a scroll, and all their hosts shall fall down." Joel thus foretells the destruction of the enemies of Israel. " The sun and the moon shall be darkened, and the stars shall withdraw their shining, the heavens and the earth shall shake." Similar is the language of Christ, in predicting the destruction of Jerusalem : " The sun shall be darkened, and the moon shall not give her light, and the stars shall fall from heaven, and the powers of the heavens shall be shaken." All this prophetic imagery which is intended to describe merely things in the political or ecclesiastical world, it is clear, can furnish us no evidence of what is to be the fate of the material universe.

The conclusion, to which this examination of the Scriptures brings us, is the following: that in all the phraseology relating to the destruction of the heavens and the earth, contained in the Scriptures,—for our examination has exhausted those uses,—there is no evidence that it is the design of God to annihilate the material creation: that the passages may be arranged under the heads of prophetic imagery, rhetorical figure, or literal description, either moral or physical; that of these, only the latter class afford any testimony as to the fate of the material creation; and that from these, no more can be learned than the destruction of this globe and its surrounding ether by fire—a destruction of form, arrangement, organic structures, human edifices—that which marks the present mode and scheme of the world—but not the destruction of its substance.

If, then, reason discerns no adequate cause in the material universe to effect its annihilation, and must refer the subject to the decision of the divine will, of which, independently of revelation, it can know nothing; and if, in the revelation which this great Being has given us of his designs, he has nowhere taught us that it is his design to annihilate the material universe, it is clear that we have no positive evidence whatever to show that the material universe will ever be annihilated.

Let us see now how far this consideration carries us. We have at least cut off all positive evidence of the annihilation of the material universe. But, so far, the conclusion is negative only. We have no authority positively to believe in its annihilation. But we are not, on the other hand, authorized in the positive belief of its perpetuity. Yet we have shown at least that, if there is any positive evidence of its perpetuity from other sources, that evidence is unembarrassed and free, and is to be allowed all its force. More than this even. The presumption, at this stage of the argument, is in favor of the perpetuity of the material universe. The material universe now exists. All the destruction which revelation *attests* is to come upon it, does not amount to its annihilation. It is therefore to exist, notwithstanding such destruction. It is possible, indeed, that God intends ultimately its annihilation, without giving us any *intimation* of his purpose. But is this probable? Is it not probable that, if it is continued after the judgment at all, it is to be continued forever? But I now verge on another consideration, which I allege, in connection with the first, as positive evidence of the perpetuity of the material universe.

2. That the state of redeemed men after the judgment is to be a permanent one for immortality. The descriptions of the Scriptures are full, that the future inheritance of the saints is permanent, incorruptible, and unfading in its glory. Now if the righteous in their immortal state are to be totally severed from a material universe, they must be severed from it, either by its annihilation or by their removal beyond its bounds.

If they are totally severed from the material universe by its annihilation, then this annihilation must take place, either at the period of their entrance upon immortality or at some period afterwards. But at the time of their entrance on immortality, they cannot be separated from the material universe by means of its annihilation : for it is not then annihilated, as we have already seen. The destruction, which immediately precedes their admission into their immortal state, is simply that of this world, and that, not the annihilation of its substance. If they are ever severed from the material universe, therefore, by its annihilation, they must thus be severed from it at some period afterwards. But how can this comport with all the many declarations of Scripture, which represent their state to be permanent, to be incorruptible, never to fade away—to be undiminished and undiminishing in its ingredients of glory? If, on their entrance upon an immortal inheritance, their dwelling should be assigned them within the bounds, amid the beauties and glories of a material creation, there would be doubtless many sources of joy and praise, arising out of these relations of their being: and could it comport with the permanent and unfading nature of the inheritance, which had always been held out to their expectations in the promises, ever afterwards to eject them from these habitations of joy; to strip them of these sources of blessing; and throw them forth as wanderers on mere empty space?

From the immutable permanence of the inheritance to be given to the righteous therefore, we infer that they are not to be severed in their immortal state from a material universe by means of its annihilation; if the severance therefore is to take place, it must be not by its annihilation, but by means of their own removal beyond its bounds.

But if they are severed from it by removal beyond its bounds, this severance must take place, if at all, at their first entrance on immortality, while as yet the material creation exists: otherwise, if it takes place after their entrance into its bounds and within its glories, whether the material creation be continued forever afterwards or not, they must experience the same change in their subsequent removal and exile, which we have already considered as incompatible with the unfading glories of their inheritance.  Are they then removed beyond the bounds of the material universe, on their first entrance upon immortality?  This is the only question that remains.  The consideration of the unchanging state of the righteous in their immortality, does not alone enable us to answer this question: yet, if it can be shown that the full glories of their immortality have any dependence on their connection with the material universe, the question will be met; and the proper evidence furnished, that they will not be removed from the bounds of the material universe on their entrance upon their full immortality.  The present argument has gone no farther than to show that, if they are connected with a material universe on their first entrance into eternity, then it is not consistent with the testimony to the permanency of their immortal state, that the connection should afterwards cease.  But to render the argument complete, I now advance another consideration.

3. That the preparation of the righteous for immortality, made within the bounds of the material creation, and the fact of the resurrection of their bodies at the period of entering on their immortality, show that the full and complete glory of their immortal state depends, in part at least, on their connection with a material universe. They are fitted for, and enter on, their immortal state, not as disembodied spirits, but as spirits clothed with a bodily organism to connect them with a material universe.

There are many and vague declamations often made about matter and spirit, as if the one were essentially vile and the other essentially pure; and as if the great effort of man should be to extricate himself from the one and absorb his being in the other. But this is not consistent with the order of creation, which assigns to man these diverse parts of his complex being; nor with the order of providence, which assigns him the duties of preparation for immortality in this complex nature; or with the awards of the future, which place him, with this complex nature still, on the retributions of eternity. The truth is, that this organic life of ours, which is the necessary medium of our connection with the material universe, though the inlet to us of many temptations, (as are also the constituent elements of our minds,) is not the source of temptation alone: it ministers to us many pleasures which are pure; it subserves the purposes of our mental and moral education; it opens to us many beautiful, sublime, instructive lessons in the works of our Creator. And whatever fine spun theories any may propound, of literal abstraction from matter and literal absorption in God, our grand duty and grand preparation for immortality is, to consecrate both body and spirit to God—to render this organic life and our connection with the material world subservient to our discipline for a higher life. And though this present structure of flesh and blood is not sufficiently refined for an immortal life, yet utterly to divest us of any, and to send us forth mere disembodied spirits upon empty space, would be to create a chasm between our present and future life too great and devastating to minister to our perfection and highest joy. It would be like the devastation, though not so great, of annihilating the souls which we have here consecrated to Christ, and sending us forth upon the theater of eternity with only the animal senses of an organic life. Man is not complete here without both; nor his education for eternity complete, without the consecration of both to Christ; nor will his joy in eternity be complete, without the continuance, the refinement, and perfection of both in that higher state. For this reason, the intermediate state of the soul between death and the resurrection is unfitted to the full perfection of redeemed man; and revelation teaches us, that he is not to enter on the full glories of immortality till, by resurrection, he is invested with a body strong, incorruptible and glorious.

Can it be then that man, educated for an immortal state in the body and within the material creation, and raised again after death, with a pure ethereal body, for entrance on that state, shall be utterly removed, on his entrance into it, from the material universe? Does not the preparation of this life and the resurrection of the body furnish evidence, that God designs the continuance of a material system still, and the residence of man during his immortality somewhere within its bounds? The doctrine of the resurrection of the body teaches us, at least, that redeemed man will have an organic structure to add in some way to the joys of his immortality—that some medium of connection with a material universe will still be attached to his being. But of what use will be this structure, if not to constitute relations between him and such a universe—if not to give him, within the bounds of such a universe, those materials of joy and praise which arise from the Creator's works of wisdom and love, and for which he has been educated in the scenes of this life?

To this course of argument in favor of the conclusion, that after the judgment the righteous are to have their dwelling within the bounds of the material universe, I will only add the positive testimony of revelation.

I observe therefore 4, That revelation affords us positive testimony in favor of the conclusion. "Nevertheless," says Peter—notwithstanding the conflagration of the world at the last day—"according to his promise, we look for new heavens and a new earth wherein dwelleth righteousness." There can be no doubt here that the apostle speaks literally of a material creation. He had spoken of the heavens and earth that were, which were once desolated by the waters. He had spoken of the heavens and earth that now are, reserved unto fire. And after describing their destruction by fire, he immediately adds: " Nevertheless we, according to his promise, look for new heavens and a new earth wherein dwelleth right- . eousness." Can there be a doubt here that the description is literal?—so far, at least, as to imply a local and material habitation—that the world, once purgated of the wicked by water, and then purgated and renewed by fire, is thenceforth to be the delightful habitation of the righteous? Or, if we consider, as some have done, the catastrophe of the last conflagration as still more extensive, yet the reconstruction of a world with its heavens is clearly asserted as literal,—to be the dwelling-place of the righteous—so that the residence of the redeemed, still within the bounds of a physical universe, is obviously intended by the apostle; who would not send . forth the purified and redeemed inhabitants of this world from their burning dwelling, homeless and shelterless, as wanderers through infinite space; but plant them in a purer and more glorious world, under serener skies, without disturbance or convulsion more, to be happily employed . with their vigorous and immortal powers in studying the works and ways—the wisdom and goodness of God; in assisting each other in growing up into his likeness for ever; and in forever uniting in acts of high devotion and praise before the manifestations of his heavenly majesty.

This expectation of which Peter speaks, he asserts, is founded on divine promise. " We, according to *his* promisc." Now Isaiah, in prophetic imagery, had spoken of the change of the Jewish economy and the introduction of the kingdom of Christ on the earth, at his first coming, in such language,—" Behold I create new heavens and a new earth : and the former shall not be remembered nor come into mind. But be ye glad and rejoice forever in that which I create, for behold I create Jerusalem a rejoicing and her people a joy." Yet even here, while looking forward to the first coming of Christ, and the blessings diffused by his gospel on this earth, the prophet might have dimly discerned, in still remoter distance, his second coming to dwell with his redeemed, and have seen the distant realities of the last conflagration, and the reconstruction of a new world and heavens for the ever-lasting dwelling of his purified and triumphant people.

Jesus Christ, while on earth, frequently spoke of his coming to judge the world, to gather from among the redeemed all the wicked, that he might cast them out into punishment, and to dwell with all the redeemed in their immortal life. And he told his disciples, that at the time of the renovation of all things, when he should come in his glory, they should sit on twelve thrones. And no doubt, in the promise of the resurrection of his followers, and their union to him in the heavenly state, there was conveyed to the minds of his apostles the idea of some abode, not perishable, fitted to their new organization and life, where they should dwell in the immediate pres-ence of God, amid the bright and full manifestations of his majesty. The idea which the apostles received from their Saviour, however, is gathered distinctly from the writings of two of them, Peter and John. Peter says to the Christians to whom he wrote, as if he had often told them so in his preaching about Jesus Christ, " We, according to his promise, look for new heavens and a new earth." But John, in the Revelations, has more fully completed the sketch of those glorious scenes, which Isaiah dimly saw and which Christ foretold. Chapter xxi : 1–4. " And I saw a new heaven and a new earth : for the first heaven and the first earth were passed away ;

and there was no more sea. And I John saw the holy city, new Jerusalem, coming down from God out of heaven, prepared as a bride adorned for her husband. And I heard a great voice out of heaven, saying, Behold the tabernacle of God is with men, and he will dwell with them, and they shall be his people, and God himself shall be with them and be their God. And God shall wipe away all tears from their eyes; and there shall be no more death, neither sorrow nor crying, neither shall there be any more pain; for the former things are passed away. And he that sat upon the throne said, Behold I make all things new." This was the last vision of John, which presented to him the happy state of the righteous after the close of the last judgment, and after the casting of the wicked into the lake of fire, which is the second death; and the remainder of the chapter, with the chapter that follows it, and closes the book, is occupied, principally, in setting forth more minutely the glories of the New Jerusalem,—the great citadel of the renovated earth,— the city of the immediate presence of God and the Lamb, whose presence constitutes its only temple of worship, whose glories pour over it the beams of eternal noon, from whose throne wells forth the river of the water of life—the holy city of joy and worship, to which all the nations of the holy and saved have free access forever.

This vision of the new heaven and the new earth, it is manifest, refers to the *final* state of the righteous, and not to the *millennial.* For the millennium, which John foresaw in a previous vision, precedes the day of final judgment, but the new heavens and earth follow it; the millenium is for a limited season, but this is forever and ever; under the millennium, Satan is bound till near the close, when he is loosed again; but in the new heaven and earth there is no more approach of the enemy—Satan and all his accomplices having been cast into the lake of fire and brimstone, to be tormented forever and ever.

Whatever interpretation therefore is given to the vision of the millennium; whether, as the most judicious expositors have judged, it is a period of the universal triumph of the cause and friends of Christ in putting down every system of opposition before upheld on earth, and of his taking spiritual possession of all the nations; or whether, as the literalists will have it, who warn us to expect very speedily the personal coming of Christ, it is a period in which Christ, surrounded by the raised martyrs, will be bodily present on earth to set up a universal monarchy— to carry on the work of converting and sanctifying men by sight instead of by faith : I say, whatever interpretation be adopted respecting the vision of the millennium, it is clear that the vision of the new heaven and earth presents a state of things altogether distinct from it, and not to take place till after the millennium and after the universal judgment.

We are clear therefore in the conclusion that this final vision of the apostle sets forth the final and immortal state of the righteous, and depicts that day of eternal glory at the end of these present days of trial, when Daniel shall again stand in his lot, and Job shall see his Redeemer standing upon the earth ; when the Redeemer shall come to bring up his people from their graves, and to transform those who are still living ; that, with ethereal bodies like his own, they may live with him forever amid the multiplied and perfected glories of immortality.  And though, in the particulars given of the new Jerusalem, it may not be the intention of revelation to sketch precisely the scenes of that state in their minute outlines, but to present the ingredients of it in emblems ; yet it were to depart too far from the vision to deny, that any material creation with its glories can be included or intended.

I will close, with presenting to you the conclusion of Dr. Andrew Fuller respecting this vision, as given in his Lectures on the Revelation.  " The whole of what is said, instead of describing the heaven of heavens, represents the glory of that state as coming down upon the earth.  It is a representation of heavenly glory, in so far as that glory relates to the state of this earth on which we dwell.  The earth will not be annihilated by fire any more than it was by water.  It will be purified from sin and all its effects. The generations of a corrupt race of creatures having terminated, it will become the perfect and perpetual abode of the righteous."

In the argument which I have now completed, it has been my design, not to dwell on the more important part of the immortal life of the saints, in their purely spiritual joys, as righteous beings communing in spirit with one another and with God, but to complete the picture of that immortal life, by presenting a scene of subordinate and concurring joy, in their converse still with the glories of a more finished physical creation, and that—without attempting to establish more than the general outline :— that the saints, re-clothed with a pure and ethereal organization, which is strong and imperishable for immortality, may yet move among the visible works of God ; and mingle, as they do here on earth, yet in sublimer and more exalted ways, in those beauties and works of creation, which instruct the mind, which charm the taste, and afford the heart fresh matter of rejoicing and praise before the eternal throne.

And now, as we close our meditations, let us attend to the practical conclusion of the apostle: " Seeing that ye look for such things, be diligent, that ye may be found of him in peace, without spot and blameless."

We have been contemplating the opening scenes of eternity. We behold the righteous, who have followed the Redeemer on earth, rescued from the powerful flames that are to consume the world, and replaced in a new heaven and a new earth, beyond sorrow, decay and death ; blest forever with the purity and love of perfect beings ; growing in the love and friendship of God, and gathering fresh incense to offer upon his altar from the glories of his surrounding works.

O ! is not this an object worthy to enlist the aspiration of our hearts, and encourage us in the diligent use of those means of grace which our Lord now grants us ; and should it not call off our thoughts and hearts from those sins and deceptive pleasures which pollute our souls, and which, persisted in, must render us unfit for so glorious an inheritance, and cut us off forever from its joys?

We are advancing to this day of God, when Christ shall come in the heavens in great glory, and, refining the world by the flames of universal desolation, shall put his redeemed in the new heavens and the new earth, constructed upon the ruins of the old, and shall cast off the wicked into the lake of devouring fire.  O! how much will be involved—in respect to each one of us—in the one question whether we then meet our Lord in peace, without spot and blameless, or meet him in wrath, defiled still with reigning iniquities!

If we then are found among the reconciled and sanctified, what will be our joy to enter on the new earth of purity! God and the Lamb ever with us, with the shining light of their friendship!  Friends with us, who drink sweetly their joys from the same fountain of purity! And everything around us to instruct our minds and cheer our hearts: the beauties of color and form, the concord of sweet sounds, the bright waters of the river of life, the ambrosial fragrance of the trees of life; our powers of motion strong as archangel's, and all the glories with us that an Almighty Architect can minister to his delighted children in his material works!  O, thus escaped from the pollutions and miseries of sin, and triumphant over death, the first and the second, how shall we adore God, and praise him for all the grace we sought and received from him in this world; by which we met him in peace, and entered, for eternity, pure and blameless, into our high places of rest!  Every joy there is innocent.  Every varying joy goes to swell the sum that is welling up in every heart, and to bind all in closer bonds of love, praise and devotedness to God and the Lamb forever.

But if, through present negligence and sin, we continue estranged from God, and meet him at last unreconciled and enemies, what must be our wretchedness to be cast off from his presence and from the society of his love, and to take up our residence in the flames of devouring wrath. If in that world, perchance, you lift up your eyes, and descry afar off the world and mansions of the blest ; if, in your utter destitution and torment, you behold them in their shining and immortal robes, quaffing joy from the pure water of the river of life, with all the resources of infinite love pouring forth to charm the intellect, the taste, the heart, O! how must you reproach yourselves that, in your present life, you suffered all these glories to pass before you, presented to you and pressed upon your acceptance by heavenly mercy, in vain; and, in neglect of God and his service, seized upon the momentary objects, included in the present plan of the world—which were to be burned in the fire—as your only portion of joy for eternity !

O! then now, before your Lord has come, now, while on his throne of mercy he asks you to procure of him reconciliation and purity, now, while the fate of eternity is pending and turning, be diligent in attending to the great duties of religion. Be diligent in consecrating both your bodies and spirits to the pure and holy service of God through Jesus Christ. Be diligent, that ye may be found of the Saviour at his coming, in peace, without spot and blameless: that so an entrance may be ministered unto you into his everlasting kingdom, and that, with all the millions of his redeemed, gathered in all ages and from all nations, you may participate, in body and spirit, in all the varied glories of that kingdom forever.

# THE PURCHASE OF THE TRUTH.

[A BACCALAUREATE SERMON.]

---

PROVERBS XXIII: 23.

BUY THE TRUTH.

A VERY short precept; easily remembered; difficult to practise always; yet ever indispensable to our well-being.

To all classes of men, truth is the only safe basis of their estimate of things and of their practical decisions.

At all periods of life and in all situations, there arise practical questions which we must decide. And if our welfare demands that a decision be made, still more essential to our well-being is it, that our decision be made in accordance with the truth.

To the life of the scholar, the precept applies with special force: for that he should utter fallacies or act upon them, is less excusable in himself and more dangerous to his fellow-men. He, of all men, can best afford to pay the price of truth: and, if he refuses to procure it, he can most easily impose his false articles and wares upon the community for the true.

But *what* is the *truth?*

*Where* is it to be had?

What *price* must we pay for it?

*Why* must we make the purchase?

These are questions which will lead us into the fuller appreciation of this precept of wisdom. The answer to them will show us the *nature;* the *source;* the *price;* and the *value* of the *Truth.*

I. *What* is the Truth? Solomon, who gave us the precept, has not defined this term, considering it obvious, no doubt, to the common apprehension of mankind. The very question was once put in the judgment-hall at Jerusalem to a greater. than Solomon, perhaps sneeringly, perhaps sincerely ; but no answer was deemed necessary on that occasion. We need go no further than our own consciousness and experience for an answer. We have all had occasion to see that a judgment may be formed on a certain subject, or an affirmation be made, which, when tested, differs from the reality, as well as one which agrees with it. Now, the object of all truth is to represent to the mind the reality of things ; and truth is either that judgment of the mind, or that affirmation of a judgment in language, which corresponds to the reality of things. The agreement of the judgments of the mind, or of affirmations, with the reality of things, then, constitutes truth ; while their disagreement is the essence of error. Conformity to the reality of things, is then the most general and comprehensive idea we can form of truth : and this quality may belong, either to verbal propositions which affirm a judgment of the mind, or to the mental judgments themselves. The precept of Solomon, no doubt, respects our mental judgments and decisions ; that, as these may be true or false, we should procure, at whatever price it may cost us, (at least on all questions that concern our interests and our duties,) such judgments as are true and correspondent to the nature and reality of things. For one may procure a set of verbal propositions which are true, without procuring the truth. He may buy books of truth, and yet in his mind be ignorant and destitute of the truths they contain. Your own experience tells you the difference between owning a copy of Euclid, and being masters of geometrical truth ; between furnishing your library well, and well informing your own spirit. To possess the truth, one must see that his views and judgments correspond to the reality of things, and that they do not differ from the reality. He must see that his judgments rest on such evidences and proofs, as give either certainty or necessity to his conclusions. He must settle them on these deep and firm foundations. He must have the moral demonstration of certainty, or the scientific demonstration of necessity.

The nature of Truth in the mind, then, is to conceive of things as they are, and to found our conceptions on reasons which give certainty to them, or necessity.

II. But *whence are we to procure the truth?* To what source must we look to inform ourselves?

To conform our views and judgments to the reality of things, it is clear that we must study things themselves in their reality. The universe of existent things is before us : and in order to ascertain the nature, properties and relations of existent things, in which the whole field of truth is comprehended, we must, in each specific case, see that the particular property or relation which we affirm or judge to belong to a thing, does belong to it with certainty or by necessity. The deep sources of truth then lie in universal nature, and in God, the author of nature : for these comprehend all existent things.

Universal nature teaches us her own truths, and truths respecting God. For in this field of study, what is true in the natural, the intellectual and the moral world, becomes obvious, either as facts of which our consciousness or our observation takes cognizance, or as general principles obvious to intuition or experience, or as truths deduced as the necessary consequences and conclusions of the reason. That which is true here is seen to be so in its own nature, independently of the judgments or affirmations of mankind. It is therefore to nature that we look, and not to the works of men, for the deep source of truth. Men may assist us, by their testimony to the knowledge of facts beyond our personal observation. They may, in their published works, set before us their deductions of truth from nature. But we are to be judges of the process and results, whether they are true to the nature of things or not. We are to see that their conclusions are founded on evidence and proofs, which show certainty or necessity, if we would obtain a personal possession of the truth.

But the field of nature is itself the product of the Creator, and, from the consequences of his agency seen in his works, we may make some deductions respecting him, their author, as certain and necessary. From the visible effects, we may reason to the unseen cause: and thus nature teaches us truths beyond her own domains; truths respecting God; his nature, perfections, thoughts, designs.

But a source of truth, higher than nature, is the infinite God himself. In respect to his own being, perfections, purposes and works, his knowledge is perfect; his testimony infallible. A revelation from the Author of nature expresses his infallible judgment, and gives the certainty of truth to his creatures. Jesus, when he was in that world which was made by him, declared; " for this cause came I into the world that I should bear witness to the truth." "*I* am the truth :" as God, comprising in himself the sum of all truth; and as a Revealer, in the perceptions of his understanding and in all his utterances, conformed to the reality of things. Here in revelation is truth expressed: and here is a deep and infallible source of truth. In our inquiries therefore into the truth, we are to come to the affirmations of his word: and our inquiries terminate on the true or the false interpretation of the language. We are to distinguish true interpretation and inference from false: and our reliance is not on the interpretations of our fellow-men or their judgments, but on those proofs and reasonings which render a given interpretation certain and necessary.

III. But *what is the price we must pay* in order to *procure the truth ?* What! methinks I hear some exclaim, is a *price* demanded for obtaining the truth? Are not the books of nature and revelation open and free for our perusal and study? Are we not invited to come and receive the benefits of divine instruction without money and without price ?

True: the field of truth is open and free for us to enter and occupy. There are no costs imposed other than those which arise of necessity out of our nature, character and condition. The means which our fellow-men impart to us, to aid us in the pursuit of truth, by the communication of their knowledge in teaching or by books, justly demand a literal price: and, were I speaking to that point, I might give some advice as to selection, rather than the price: that you furnish your libraries with the Bible, the great fountain of truth, and with such books, as lead you to a knowledge of God and his works, and qualify you for the duties of your station.

Yet with all the means of knowledge in our possession, in order to procure to ourselves the advantages of the truth on our course of life, we must needs pay the price of

*Mental labor*, to undergo the necessary processes of study ;

*Temperance*, to subordinate our sensual enjoyments and passions to the reason ;

*Moral courage*, to venture on the ill-will of the false and licentious ; and

*Humility*, to remain contented with ignorance in matters beyond our present opportunities of knowledge.

Severe mental *labor* is a part of the price you must pay in order to procure the truth. You have learned, in the course of mental discipline to which you have already been subjected, that close, methodical, protracted effort, is necessary to render yourselves masters of the truth in any branch of knowledge. But, in your researches after truth, you have but just begun that course to which your whole after life should be devoted. There are many fields of knowledge to invite your attention through life; and if you would make proficiency in them, so as to have the truth clearly and fully in your possession, there must be passed many and many an hour of close attention and study. And the questions of conduct and duty, that will ever be rising up to demand of you the estimate of truth, cannot lie neglected with safety. They must be taken up, they must be analyzed, they must be brought to the standards of evidence and duty, and your judgment must ascertain those conclusions which are certain and founded on good and sufficient reasons, if you would stand firm in the truth.   A life then of *severe* study, that will examine matters fully and thoroughly to their foundations; of *methodical* study, that will take up one thing at a time, and proceed with it in that true and logical order which alone leads to a clear and satisfactory conclusion; of *constant* study, that will take up and thoroughly solve the new questions of interest or duty that are continually arising in this world;—such a life is the price exacted of you, if you would be sure to have the truth with you on your way.

Another necessary condition of having the truth with you on your course, is that of *temperance*, to subordinate your sensual enjoyments and passions to the decisions of the reason.   To say nothing of the time consumed by those supremely devoted to sensual enjoyments, which is subtracted from the opportunities of intellectual effort, or of that clog which is put upon the mental operations themselves by too great indulgence of bodily appetites and passions, both which must detract from the progress of the student in all the fields of knowledge, I now speak of the influence of false tastes and appetites, to pervert the judgments of the mind on the great topics of our moral and spiritual interests and duties.   The estimate of good and evil, of right and wrong, must, if made in truth, rest on the basis of reason and not of the passions.   The passions are limited and local, and not universal and perpetual in their dictates, as is the reason.   They exaggerate the good or diminish the evil of their own estimates beyond truth and reason: they are ready to prejudice the cause of truth and set up that of error.   There is a necessity therefore of subordinating the passions of our sensual and earthly nature to the dictates of the pure reason or the clear revelation, which are our only safe guides, if we would procure the truth.   This is a part of the price we must pay, in order to secure ourselves in the truth: and to most,—so earthly and sensual are our natures,—the price is great: demanding no little sum of self-denial and self-government.

Still another item of cost to us in securing and maintaining the truth with us in life, is that of moral courage, to bear, when necessary, the ill-will of the false or the malicious. The history of our world abounds in examples of those, who, for putting faith in the word of God and the dictates of reason,—who, for adhering to the truth, have suffered from the ill-will of the ignorant, the prejudiced, the licentious and malicious. There have been martyrs to the truth of God, to the truths of nature, to moral truths, and to political. So ignorant are men, so prejudiced by their passions, so corrupt often in their lives, that to stand up among them as the holder and defender of truth, must sometimes cost the courage of facing, if not a physical, yet a moral martyrdom. To have the name cast out as evil, to be defamed and mocked and threatened, is the punishment visited upon them, even in the best regulated communities, from the ill-will of opposers. One must make up his mind then to pay this cost whenever it is necessary, if he would be a holder and friend of the truth : The moral courage to decide according to truth and the nature and reality of things, however much it may cause us to differ from the judgments, the customs, or practices of the age : To hold on to the truth, as that which will support us and will survive the prejudices and ill-will of a present generation.

I have named also, as a part of the price at which truth is secured, the *humility* that remains contented in ignorance on matters beyond our present opportunities of knowledge. There is a pride, which is much in the way of all real progress in knowledge, and we must sacrifice it if we would advance in the truth. The pride that claims knowledge without having it in possession, and the pride, that grasps at what is beyond its power. The pride, that claims to know what it has not yet attained, surely stands in the way of ever making the attainment; and, until one is willing to sacrifice such a pride, and confess, to himself at least, and feel, his ignorance, he cannot truly and earnestly set himself to procure the truth: he must remain destitute of it. But there is a pride in the way of truth, and that must be sacrificed to its attainment:—a pride of another kind,—a pride which grasps at what is beyond its power. There are some, who think themselves equal to cope at once with all the branches of knowledge; and thus defeat their own end and aim, by grasping at too much and at what is beyond their power. They would fain think themselves sufficient to master all the branches of science and all the departments of truth and knowledge, and this disposition, by preventing their thorough attention to the study of any, renders them miserable dabblers in all. It is a price we are to pay for acquiring truth, that we have the humility to remain confessedly ignorant in some things, while we are faithfully studying others. We may thus reach a larger circle of thoroughly investigated and established truth in the end. This humility is necessary, too, to keep us to the attainments which are within our power. For the time and attention bestowed on subjects which are not within our power and means of attaining, is so much lost from our progress in those which are attainable.

These considerations set before you the necessary cost at which you are to procure the truth, and keep it with you at all times as your guide in life.

IV. But *why should we make the purchase?* There is something in the precept of Solomon that exalts greatly the value of truth. The precept is absolute: it sets no limit on the price: it enjoins the purchase, whatever be the cost. *Buy* the truth. Make the purchase *at any rate*. Pay the price *whatever it be.* The truth will be of far greater worth to you than the cost. You cannot afford to do without it, in the management of any of your interests or duties.

But wherein consists its value? What is that value, compared with the price? What, compared with the necessary losses to arise from ignorance and error?

The value of truth may be estimated in part from its positive advantages, as a treasure of joy to the mind, a qualification for doing good among men, a means of serving God acceptably, and a means of preparation for an immortal life with God in his kingdom.

The truth is itself a treasure of great joy to our minds. Truth satisfies the understanding : administering to that immortal faculty its own pure, solid, and durable aliment of knowledge. Who can tell the satisfaction of the mind, when turning to some field of knowledge, and pursuing its eager search after the truth, its perceptions become clear and definite, and the truth is first seen looming up beyond doubt in the certainty of its proofs and evidences. How is the labor of the process at once turned to joy, as the discoverer exclaims : "I have it, I have it now!" Yes, he has it now for an everlasting possession among the treasures of his knowledge. Not only does truth give satisfaction to the understanding, but each item of truth obtained enlarges the comprehension of the understanding. A new treasure is added to its stores, a new domain from the field of knowledge is added to its territories. The mind thus, by acquiring truth, comprehends more and more within its possessions; and, while itself becomes constantly enlarged, it feeds at an everlasting fountain. For truth, the aliment on which the understanding feeds with expansive joy, ranges on forever beyond the world and time and all created things into the depths of the infinite spirit of Jehovah. But there is more in the treasures of truth than the joy of knowledge. For truth supplies the pure and lovely materials, on which the imagination and the heart may dwell with safety and delight. The fields of beauty and loveliness opened to us in nature, in the various creations of God, in the means and ends of his providence, in the history of his dealings, in the teachings of his word, and in his own infinite loveliness of perfection and character,—so far as they are surveyed and ascertained by our understandings,—give a free scope to our meditations. Here, in this field of truth, the imagination, in picturing to itself, in the full and glowing features and coloring of life, the limits and outlines of truth, can feed itself with pictures of loveliness ever new and varying, yet ever true and ever awakening the affections of the heart to purity and love. It is thus that, with the truths of nature and God for our guide, our thoughts may ever rove through fields of beauty and loveliness with fresh and immortal joy. The truth also settles the aims and purposes of our wills on a firm and satisfactory foundation. For the estimates of wisdom, in propounding the end to be pursued in this life and the particular means to be adopted in pursuing that end, are founded surely on the truth. The truth ascertained and clearly seen, shows us the ends which God propounds to himself in his works and to his intelligent creatures in his kingdom, and the rules and methods by which that end is secured: and when our estimates conform to his,—when our purposes and plans, as to the end and means of our pursuit, are seen by the truth to conform to his, those purposes and plans are strong and satisfactory to our own minds. They are seen to be founded on the everlasting wisdom and strength of God; approved of him; and consequently immovably satisfying to ourselves, and matters of our own approbation at the time and ever after, whatever the particular issues.

Thus the truth set before us in the field of nature and the word of revelation, the truth to be acquired as our possession, is a treasure of immense joy and satisfaction to our natures.

> 'Tis a broad land of wealth unknown,
>   Where springs of life arise ;
> Seeds of immortal bliss are sown,
>   And hidden glory lies.

But truth not only ministers thus to our natures from its immortal fountain, it accompanies us into our relations to the society of our fellow-men, and fits us to fill our stations to the honor of God and the benefit of our race. The value of a mind well informed and settled in the truth, and acting as the minister of God for the welfare of others, is seen in many a bright example on the page of history, in the effects that have been left on the living age, or that have passed over to succeeding generations.

Through the truth have they gained their victories for God and the race. Into whatever station you enter in society, at that post, no qualification is so valuable as a mind and heart well informed and grounded in the truth, and able to employ its treasures wisely to advance the ends of your station. For all the great interests of humanity, in every department, depend on conformity to the laws which a God of truth has stamped on the nature of things in his kingdom, and by which he sets forth to his intelligent creatures the ends and means, on which their happiness necessarily depends. Who then is fit to guide men in conformity to the laws of nature and God, and thus to further their welfare, but he who has acquired the truth ; who sees distinctly, on topics of public interest, what are the right and true conclusions, and rests their certainty on clear and indisputable evidences and proofs? He is prepared to dispel the mists of ignorance before him ; to silence the pleas of error, and bear along with him, sooner or later, in his own generation, or in generations to follow, the convictions of mankind.

In society at large, then, would you serve God and your generation? What speaker, what writer, can so command attention, so fix the views of his hearers or readers to clear and definite apprehensions, so settle and establish their minds in his own positions and judgments, as he who thinks clearly, definitely and truly himself, and has at his command all the materials for illustration and proof, by which to settle others in the truth? To say nothing of the earnest pleading and sincerity, which underly all outward means and appliances used, in the heart devoted to God and to the benefit of the race, who else can so fitly manage the outward means and appliances themselves? In the Church, would you serve God and your generation? If you minister at the altars of religion, if you serve at the desk of religious instruction, what more necessary or more valuable qualification than to have acquired the truth of God for a personal possession? To have the understanding, the imagination, and the heart, largely and deeply conversant in the things of

God; and to be able, out of such treasures, to feed the hungry with understanding, to guide the weak and the straying into the right way, to convince and persuade unbelievers, and make known to all the wonderful glory of God, and the only true way to honor and glory in his immortal kingdom. And in the State, if called in the halls of legislation to speak for the interests of a people, what power has that orator to guide and sway to measures of utility, who, well furnished on questions of public policy and duty, has at command the definite conclusions and the unfailing evidences and proofs of truth? He speaks with definiteness to the point in debate: and, with the clearness and cogency of unanswerable reason, sets forth his conclusions in the light of certainty: and they, who consult impartially the public interest, are convinced, and, by their concurrence, the affairs of the State are managed with safety and success.

Or, if he must contend with the perverse leaders of an ignorant faction, and fails of immediate success, he succeeds to plant the seeds of truth that shall bear a later harvest. Before his manly front and convincing appeals, the leaders of faction quail and cower. He steps between them and the misguided multitude, to show up the sophistry of the wandering harangues they substitute in the place of argument, and pin them down to their proper place of presumptuous ignorance or wilful falsehood. Their want of integrity becomes manifest; their substitution of their own personal aggrandizement in place of the public interests, stands reproved; and they and their measures, if upheld for the moment, receive the verdict of public condemnation at a later period. The advocate of truth thus triumphantly succeeds to impart the blessings of his wisdom to his own or a succeeding generation: and the triumph is forever recorded on the page of impartial history. Truth thus imparts to its possessor the power to labor most fitly and successfully for the welfare of his race: to set before them, more convincingly and persuasively, the true means and sources of their welfare.

But a still higher value belongs to the possession of truth, as the means of preparing us for an immortal life with God in his kingdom. In conforming our judgments to truth, we shall come to the teachings of nature and the teachings of revelation, that our minds may be filled with the knowledge of God. For we shall not have the truth with us practically, we shall not hold it in its highest and most earnest teachings, unless we view God as the sum and source of all spiritual excellence and happiness. He, the infinite Father of spirits, has created our spirits after the image of his own immortality: and he sets forth to us, in his works and word, the pattern of his own wisdom and goodness and righteousness and mercy, that we may conform our minds and feelings and aims to his, and fill our natures from his infinite fullness. Thus, at the fount of truth, we drink in the mind and spirit of God into our natures, and hold a fellowship with his Spirit, that gives witness to us of an immortal life with him in his kingdom. For Jesus, in coming to us as the Revealer of God and the Pattern of God, intending not merely to free us from the condemnation of the law, but to restore us to its great precept, hath said: "This is eternal life that they might know thee, the Only True God, and Jesus Christ whom thou hast sent." The very element and source of eternal joy to our souls in the kingdom of God, is taken in the truth, in the knowledge of God and Jesus Christ, in fellowship with them in mind, in spirit, in works: so that, as he lives forever in his own infinite fullness of knowledge, excellence and joy, they shall live also forever in the communion, which they begin here in his love through the truth, with him in his eternal kingdom.

The truth it is, that thus leads us to God and Christ in reconciliation and love in this life, and prepares us for an immortal life of increasing knowledge, love and joy with him in his kingdom.

I have thus enumerated the positive benefits, to be derived from procuring to ourselves the possession of the truth, as a treasure of great joy to our natures, as a means

by which we may benefit our race, and as our guide to
an immortal life in heaven.

Should we not pay then whatever price is necessary to
the possession of so valuable a treasure?  The treasure is
far more valuable to us, than the cost can be at any rate.
For the cost of mental toil, denial of sensual passions,
moral courage and humility, that may be exacted is, at
the worst, but a partial sacrifice and a temporary one,
which in itself is a salutary discipline for our natures,
while the truth procured by it, ministers positively and
largely to the welfare of our whole being, in all its relations,—and that to eternity.

Should we not then make the purchase?  If we withhold
the price and refuse, we necessarily forfeit all these high
and everlasting advantages; and, in mental indolence, in
the indulgence of sensuality, in cowering to the opinions
of the vile, in the vain boasts of pride, we shall become
the dupes of ignorance, error, and sin, and rove away
from the center of all truth and loveliness, like wandering
stars, into the blackness of darkness forever.

The precept which I have unfolded applies, I have said,
with special force to the life of the scholar.

The scholar has disciplined his mind to the processes of
study.  Shall he then suffer questions of deep and universal interest, on which he must act, to lie uninvestigated?
Shall he not rather apply himself to the task of settling
his mind clearly and firmly on the foundations of truth?

He can appreciate, to some extent from his own experience, the joys and advantages of acquiring truth.  Shall
he not follow on, then, to know the Lord and his works,
and to increase, at the fount of truth, the treasures of his
knowledge?

And, because of his advantages and opportunities, he is
expected to know the truth.  Shall he be content then to
utter among his fellow-men the fallacies that deceive, and
thus expose them to injury, and himself to detection and
contempt?  Shall he not rather strive to maintain the
reputation of an earnest and thorough champion of the
true, the right and the good?

My Young Friends, I have set before you a short precept of wisdom. Though short, it is comprehensive, and it guides you to your highest welfare. You can easily retain it in memory. Will you adopt it as a maxim of life? Will you put it into practice? You may find it difficult to do it always. But do it: and the gain will be yours. Do it: and its deep wisdom will appear to you in the happy experience of your souls, on the path of this life, and in eternity.

I may not have another occasion of speaking to you. I hope the many occasions, on which I have spoken already, may not prove in vain: nor the many lessons of instruction you have here received from your teachers. A review of the few years of your residence here, will serve to impress on your hearts lessons of thankfulness for the care and kindness of an overruling providence, and lessons of wisdom for your guidance on the ways of future life. You have lived to reach this goal. One, only, of your happy number has fallen from your ranks. Burnap is not with you to-day. He has fallen asleep in life's early morning. And over his grave you drop the tear of sorrow with the family, whose hearts are so saddened this day with their disappointment and loss. You have reached the goal: and again you are to start forth on a new career, to try, apart, the yet untrod paths of life. Have you not seen on your way already, that to let truth enter your understanding and heart, and bear the sway, is far better for your present peace and usefulness and your eternal prospects, than to wallow in the mire of sensual and earthly passions, and to cringe and bow, as slaves, for the flattery and favor of those around you who are addicted to like passions? Certainly you have, to your joy, if you have been faithful ; to your sorrow, if unfaithful. Go forth then, resolved, all as one, cost it what partial and temporary discipline it may, to be men of understanding and men of truth, for the honor of God and the benefit of your race, on this transitory stage of your existence. Then, happy will it be for you, when your days upon earth are ended, to have sent before you into heaven, and to leave behind you among men, joyful testimonies to your advocacy for God and righteousness; and, as you enter into the presence of your Judge, to hear from his lips the benediction of immortal joy: "Servants of God, well done."

Beloved pupils and friends, we bid you farewell.

## ISAIAH XXVIII: 17.

THE HAIL SHALL SWEEP AWAY THE REFUGE OF LIES, AND THE WATERS SHALL OVERFLOW THE HIDING PLACE.

THE prophet made this declaration to the rulers of Jerusalem, who sustained, as he declares, the character of "scornful men." They, it seems, who should have used their influence with the people for their holiness and spiritual welfare, were willing to stand up as opposers of the progress of divine truth, and as stumbling-blocks in the way of the salvation of Israel, by publicly taking the station of scorners of this prophet of the Lord. They were willing to deride the threatenings, which he denounced in the name of the Lord against sinners. The prophet declares, that they sustained their scornful spirit, by the vain imagination that they were secure from the threatened evils of death and hell. They had, in their own opinion, devised a way which would protect them from the evil: but the prophet assured them, that it was a refuge of lies; that they were hiding themselves under falsehood. He then announces to them, distinctly, the plan on which Jehovah would deal with the inhabitants of Jerusalem: that he would place in Jerusalem a corner-stone and foundation, tried and precious, on which those who in faith rested themselves for security would find protection; where they should not make haste, nor flee in the day of coming wrath: but that he would bring judgment, with the exact and even measure of the line and plummet, upon all others; and that the overflowing waters of judgment, like the deluge which had once desolated the world, would flow in on their hiding place and drown them in destruction. They who did not repair in faith to the Redeemer in Zion, he thus assured them, could resort to no refuge which would protect them from the holy vengeance of God.

This declaration in like manner assures you, my friends, that *there is no refuge, except the Lord Jesus Christ, which will protect you from the eternal wrath of God.*

In illustrating this subject, I will attempt to show,

I. That they, who are careless about their salvation, are sustaining themselves by some refuge.

II. That every refuge to which they betake themselves, short of the Lord Jesus Christ, leaves them exposed to the wrath of God. And,

III. That unless they speedily forsake every such refuge, they must be overwhelmed and destroyed by the judgment of God.

In presenting this subject to you, my fellow-sinners, my prayer to God is, that I may be enabled, in all fidelity and with sincere affection, to point out to you your imminent danger, and induce you to flee immediately to Jesus Christ for refuge, and to rest your souls in security on that Rock of Salvation, which God has placed in Zion for your deliverance in the coming day of judgment.

I remark, then,

I. In the first place, that all of you, who are at ease respecting your salvation, are quieting your fears by resorting to some refuge.

Fear is always excited in the mind of man, when he sees some great evil impending over him, and knows that he can resort to nothing which will afford him protection. Only strip him of every shelter, close upon him every way of escape, take away from him all power to remove the coming evil, and you pour at once into his heart the agitations of terror—a terror measured only by the extent of the evil that he is to suffer. The shipwrecked mariner, when on mid-ocean he sees the fragile ship that bears him, foundering, and soon to engulph him in the abyss of waters, if he discover no means of escape at hand or abroad, feels at once the terrors of hastening death. And if at that hour his soul is not buoyed up with some hope, he is open at once to the terrors of hell. And as he watches the rapid approach of the evil, the few moments that intervene, in which he can drink in the light and breathe the air of day, afford no relief to his heart. He is agonized with a despair that is to know no end, and, in the midst of his terror, he sinks in the abyss of the grave and hell.

Now it is on this general principle of our nature, that I argue, that every one must be filled with deep fear respecting the safety of his soul, or else must be quieting his fear by trusting in some refuge for the protection of his soul. And in order to show this, I will appeal only to one thing of which you are conscious. I will not ask, whether you believe in the threatenings of God, which glare upon you in such unequivocal and pointed declarations throughout his word; I will not ask, whether you believe in those affecting descriptions he has given you of the world of future punishment; I will not attempt to show you—independently of any declarations of the fact in the Bible—that your soul is in danger, and that your fears must be excited, unless you resort to some protecting refuge.

I appeal only to this one thing, of which you are conscious at this moment: viz. that your heart is estranged from God. This glorious Being, who made you, and on whose favor the soul is dependent for its happiness, is not the object of your affections. You are not seeking your joy from his favor and service. You are not sympathizing in his holiness and benevolence and justice with all the heart, and, in simplicity and love, surrendering yourself to his benevolent government. Your heart is fixed on other objects, which wholly separate you from all active and blissful communion in his love. You are thus, in the feelings and purposes of your heart, at actual variance with the design and object of his most holy and benevolent government, and are consequently trampling on his laws and authority.

Now this separation of the heart from him—this total insubjection to his benevolent government, is a fact which lies fully within the limits of your own consciousness. The thing is definite and obvious. It is no other than your own full and stubborn purpose of heart, to cleave to the inferior joys which you strive to find in your own personal and worldly and independent gratification. You need no declaration of the word of God to assure you of a fact like this, which comes so fully within the cognizance of your own consciousness. Whether you admit revelation, or pretend to deny it, this most alarming fact stares you fully in the face.

And this fact portends such danger to your soul, as must excite most serious apprehensions for your safety, unless you are resorting to some shelter, which you think will protect you from the evil. For it is obvious, that, with a heart thus continuing in alienation from God, and at variance with his holy law and righteous authority, there can be no peace to your soul in a coming eternity. For you can never escape from the vigilant eye, the almighty power, and the perfect government of this holy Being. And it is certain, that if you go forward forever with a heart thus at variance with him and his holy authority, you must for that reason be forever separated from all experience of his love, and lie under the full weight of his displeasure. And what misery must forever agonize that soul, that is to bear, through a long and hopeless eternity, the displeasure of a righteous and holy God, and an utter exclusion from all participation in the joys of his heavenly presence!

Now if you look only at your present separation from God and variance at heart with his government, you can see nothing else to flow from it but all this overwhelming anguish and ruin. If you hope to escape, your hope must come from some other quarter. It must come from something else, which serves you as a refuge from the impending evil. For, as to this variance with God in itself, it portends only everlasting ruin. You have persisted in it long. You have persisted in it madly, against the plea of your highest interests. You have persisted in it stubbornly, against much long-suffering and goodness on the part of your holy and justly offended Creator, while waiting on you for your repentance. You are persisting in it now. You are absolutely unwilling to give it up, and submit yourselves to God. And what can you expect from this astonishing contest with a righteous and holy Creator, but to fall under the everlasting sufferings of his displeasure? Nothing can meet you on this path but the everlasting ruin of your own soul—its eternal separation from all the joys which flow from holiness and the favor of God—its eternal endurance of all the anguish, which must come from degradation and sin and guilt, from an upbraiding conscience, a malicious heart, and the overflowing scourge of God's wrath. You cannot be quiet, then, in your present separation from God, unless you resort to something, as the refuge under which you would shelter yourself, and by means of which you hope to escape the impending evil. I do not say, that your soul is disquieted within you. I do not say, that you are alarmed with the apprehensions of the evil in question. But what I now affirm is, that if such are not your feelings, you are quieting yourself with the hope of some escape. What I have been endeavoring to show, and what I think I have succeeded in showing, is that, if you are quiet, it is not because you see no danger whatever surrounding your soul and threatening its destruction, but because you cling to something which you hope will protect you from the danger.

The inquiry therefore becomes as interesting to you as eternity, whether the refuge, to which you resort for quelling your fears, is one which will serve for your deep necessities, and protect you from the danger that threatens your everlasting interests? To assist you to discover · the truth on a point so vital to your well being, and to rescue you from every delusion of sin, I remark,

II. In the second place, that every refuge to which you betake yourselves short of the Lord Jesus Christ, leaves your souls still exposed to all this danger.

That refuge alone is valuable, which affords a sure protection from the coming evil. When this world was threatened with a deluge, every one to whom Noah preached had the opportunity, doubtless, in fear of the. coming evil, to build an ark for himself and household, which should ride over the face of the waters. At least, every one saw that no other species of refuge offered any protection against such an evil as a universal flood. And doubtless, whenever Noah uttered the threatening of God, his hearers resorted to some refuge to quell their fears. The first refuge, and perhaps the only one in their case, was unbelief. They did not believe that God would execute such a threatening. What had the world done to deserve it? Or, if they had offended their Maker, where should God find water sufficient for the submersion of a world? But, when the flood came, they were driven from this refuge; unless their unbelief followed them still, as they repaired for protection from height to height, until the last refuge was failing, and they could disbelieve no longer, as they were sinking under the judgments of heaven.

And so, in your present condition, it is just as easy to perceive that no refuge, on which you can depend, will afford any protection to your souls in a coming eternity, short of Jesus Christ. Christ is a sure refuge, for this plain reason, that in him God, your offended Maker, shows himself to you as willing to undertake with his own arm the work of your salvation. He has set apart his Beloved Son to the very office of bringing salvation down to the acceptance of just such beings and sinners as you. He has, in the crucifixion of Jesus Christ, voluntarily done all that was necessary for him, as a righteous king, to offer you, on your repentance and return to obedience, the free remission of your sins against his laws, and an admission to the joys of his favor. When the Lord Jesus, therefore, stands before you offering salvation,—offering, with the strongest proofs of sincerity, to take you at once and willingly under his protection and care, if you will only accept of him as your Saviour, and fully surrender yourself up to his care and government, there can be no doubt on your minds that this refuge is sure. The refuge is adapted to the very nature of the evil. The sinner, who, moved by a sense of the evil of his estrangement from God and exposure to his curse, will come and make full confession of his sin, and with a broken heart will trust all his salvation in the hands of Christ, and look to him alone for it, and enlist his heart in humble and thankful devotedness to his will and glory, is brought to a reconciliation and communion with his God, which shall go on as the days of eternity, and which no act of the government of God—not the solemn acts of final judgment and retribution—will ever dissolve or shake. For it is an everlasting reconciliation, and communion in love.

But every other source of deliverance, on which you can fasten a hope, is unavailing. In the first place, for this reason : that it leaves you still at variance with your Maker's government, and under his righteous curse—the very evils from which you need deliverance, and which threaten the eternal ruin of the soul. You may think of resorting to infidelity as your shelter. But, in that hiding place, you will not change your character or your relation to the infinite God. The revelation which you attempt to disbelieve, has not made you a sinner nor an enemy of God : it finds you such ; and on the basis of that fact, which lies within your consciousness, and must follow you, go whither you will in the universe, it has merely come on an errand of mercy, to set before you a Saviour for your deliverance. God has acted as your highest benefactor in bringing this volume of his grace to your hands, and he only asks you to believe and trust with all your heart in that fullness of grace, that offers to unite you to his love and holy kingdom. And to disbelieve this, to draw back from accepting a proposal like this, is surely to leave your hearts still in all their distance from God, and your souls in all their exposure to his righteous indignation.

Do you think to find a shelter in the belief of universal salvation ? But what if you try, and try hard, to persuade yourself of the safety of such a hope ? Will that belief bring your hearts off from your idols and sins ?

Will that belief bring you to repentance and hearty reconciliation and communion with God? Does not the searching eye of God, as it looks into your hiding place, see a heart there that is as insubmissive and rebellious as ever? and must not his holy indignation still pursue you, so long as you cling to a hope that alters not your character, but keeps you at distance from the surrender of yourselves to his government?

Or will you depend on mere external morality as your shelter? Will you hope for protection at the tribunal of God, because you conform to your own rules of righteousness? Because you act an honorable part before your fellow-men, and abstain from acts of direct injustice and cruelty, and do many things for the temporal welfare of your fellow-creatures? But while you rely on this, your hearts are still far from God, and not having entered into reconciliation with him, and become obedient to his holy dominion through Christ the Mediator, you are still the objects of his displeasure—the moral variance of your heart from the law of God still continues. And if you have no other hope for eternity, you go forward in your rebellion and sin against God, and can expect nothing but the fires of his vengeance.

Or will you trust in the intention you cherish, of coming to Christ for salvation at a future day? But, in this shelter, you still remain as you were. By this purpose of delay, no essential change is effected in your feelings towards God, or in his feelings towards you. There is no reconciliation, but rather a receding from it, in your greater insensibility and his greater displeasure. Your souls are still as open as ever to his consuming judgments.

Or will you trust to your convictions? Do you say that you entertain a clear and rational conviction, that God is good and just, and that you are a sinner; and do you think that a mere conviction of the truth, however deep and strong it may be, will save you? But if you rest in these convictions, without betaking yourself, as they urge you, in self-surrender to Jesus Christ for salvation, what change have they effected in your character or your relation to God? You are still dependent on yourself, and not on Christ, for salvation. And will the mere convictions of a sinner, who has fallen under his Maker's curse, and who still withholds his heart from surrender to the Saviour, avail to reconcile him to God?

Just so, if you will open your eyes to the nature of every refuge of which you have ever thought, or which you can devise, short of Jesus Christ, who died for your sins and offers to be your Saviour, you will see, that they leave you just where you were, without your approximating one step towards a happy and cordial submission to God as your only Lord and Saviour, or towards removing from your souls the righteous curse of his law.

In the next place, it is true of every refuge but Christ, that if you depend on it for safety, you not only retain essentially the same character and relation to God as before, but you also bind your souls to the same spiritual state more firmly than ever. The very act of depending on anything for your eternal happiness, binds you firmly to the object of your dependence; and, if that object be other than Christ Jesus, it leads you along thoughtlessly and carelessly in all your exposure, until the very evil comes upon you. For he who takes a shelter, goes into it for the very purpose of abiding the storm. And so long as he can think it secure, he will remain in it and await the consequences. If therefore every other refuge, to which you can trust for the salvation of your souls, but Christ, does not reconcile you and God at the time you enter it, it never will: it will but keep you from a reconciliation, just as long and as firmly as you depend on it for safety. All possible refuges other than Christ, therefore, bind you to your sins. They encourage you to go forward to the eternal world, in a thoughtless neglect of all your spiritual duties towards God, and all the consequences of a continued rebellion. And what can be expected from such refuges, that lead you to an utter carelessness about all your contrariety to the holy government of God? A rebel, made willing to adhere to his rebellion through all the goodness and holiness and grace, that are beaming on him from the throne of God! made willing to adhere to it, without regard to the consequences! made willing to adhere to it, till this life is closed, and to adhere to it through the anguish of death, and to go with it into the presence of his Maker! Can anything come of such reliances and hopes, but the agony of eternal sin and guilt and despair? Must they not leave you unprotected in the great day of God's judgment?

But still again. Other refuges, on which you depend for the safety of your souls, must bring on you the additional *guilt* of *slighting all the love of Christ*. They not only leave you still in a state of alienation from God in your hearts; they not only encourage you to go forward in such a state to eternity, with a careless presumption: but in choosing to resort to them, rather than go in confidence to the Saviour as your only hope and righteousness, you bring on you the greater guilt of slighting his love and mercy. He is able to save you from your sins, and to bring your souls to the everlasting enjoyment of God's favor and government. He has given you the most convincing and melting proofs of his willingness to do all that is necessary for your redemption to God. He has in compassion visited this world, and surrendered up his life on the cross for you, that he might protect the government of God while offering you salvation. And he is before you with his offer, calling upon you, as lost sinners, to depend on him for the salvation of your souls. He only asks you to reject all other hopes of salvation, and with all your heart give up yourselves to his protection and love. Why will you not try this Friend of sinners? Why will you not repose all your hope and salvation in his keeping, and accept from him the pardon, the communion with God, the sanctifying grace, which he offers? Why will you not depend on him for everything necessary to your deliverance and redemption, and joyfully surrender your souls to him wholly and forever? It is love and mercy in him that asks you to do it, love and mercy, that has wept tears of sorrow and sweat drops of agony for you already, and that will never fail you, if you will rely on it. Will you, rather than bring your hearts to submit to such love and mercy, draw back to other hopes and refuges for eternity ; hopes and refuges, that have no other tendency or effect, than to keep your souls in all the pollution and condemnation of sin ? Oh, what an unfeeling requital is this of his love ! To resort to any expedient to quiet yourselves in sin, rather than give yourselves up to such a Benefactor and Saviour. To go away from him in your guilt, and rush on the horrors of eternal death, rather than fly to his arms for deliverance, and humbly accept of pardon and every grace as his gift. There is not a single other refuge, to which you cling for quieting your fears, but you show in it all this strength of unwillingness to come to the Saviour. Infidelity, universal salvation, external morality, conviction, intentions about the future, self-righteousness, confidence in yourselves or others, everything else on which you can fasten a hope, while this Saviour is nigh, is but a pretext for shunning him, for keeping your heart from him, and for refusing him the joyful surrender of your souls. And what has this blessed Saviour done, that you should be so offended in him—so strongly offended that, rather than be beholden to him for your salvation, and go willingly and penitently to accept it, you will hide under any shelter you can find, though you die for it eternally ? Can there be any safety in those refuges, which serve only as pretexts for cherishing all this hardness of heart towards Christ ? If you are resting in any such, no matter what it may be, however fair and specious it may appear to you, you are cherishing all this guilt and hardness of heart against God the Saviour ; and when the floods of divine wrath, which are coming, shall sweep over our guilty race, they must flow in on your hiding place, and, if you continue in it, overwhelm you in destruction. To this thought, I would now direct your attention,

III. In the third place : that, unless you speedily forsake every such refuge, you must be destroyed by the judgment of God.

There is a day of judgment coming. The Almighty Ruler over us is a holy and righteous God, whose authority we have all trampled on, whose law we have all broken, and to whose righteous penalty of endless death we have all subjected our souls. If he is a good Being, and seeks the happiness of his moral kingdom; if he is a righteous Being, and wishes to enforce his good laws and make his authority respected, and thereby deserve the confidence of his subjects, the sinner will not be left by him to go on unpunished, nor will this guilty world be suffered to go forward in its sins, and still live, as it is now doing, upon his abused benefits. A reconciliation must soon take place, or these abused benefits will all be withdrawn, and the guilty left to perish in eternal want and pain.

The presages that there is a day of coming wrath for sinners, meet you on every side. Your own consciences whisper to you, that God must come down in his wrath on the guilty, if he is a holy and righteous Being. Your own fears suggest that, while your hearts are at variance with God, there can be no safety. Your solicitude to cling to something as your refuge, shows that you wish protection from some possible, some probable evil. Connected with all these warnings from within you, there are warnings from without. The angel of death is flying over this guilty world, and sweeping its generations away from all the light and privileges they here enjoy, bearing the souls that have not loved God into his holy presence, to receive from him their eternal retribution. The Lord himself hath spoken by the mouth of all his holy prophets, and has declared that he is coming to execute judgment. But louder than all other warnings, more convincing even than all the threatenings of his wrath, is that great act of his mercy in laying with his own hand in Zion a foundation, solid as the everlasting rock, precious as the salvation of the soul, that sinners might repair to it freely, and escape the storms of coming vengeance. Nor can I conceive of a more alarming testimony, than is given in founding on this Eternal Rock all

the hopes of this probationary life. For, if God has provided for us a refuge like this; if he has given up his
Beloved Son to the agonies of crucifixion, to make atonement for our sins, and serve us the purposes of a righteousness in law; if he has done an act like this, in order
to afford us a means of deliverance, he sees that a storm of
vengeance is at hand, which shall sweep over all the unreconciled of our guilty race. He sees that equity and
righteousness to his kingdom require of him, that he
should bring down on the impenitent and unreconciled a
judgment and wrath, from which there can be no escape
through eternity. And the very offering of this refuge,
shows that this day of wrath is at hand. If the evil might
be delayed, and delayed as long as sinners might choose;
if he felt not obliged, as a God of justice, to appoint some
time to execute judgment, but was at liberty to defer it,
and defer it forever; he would not have sent Jesus Christ
into the world, to bear the atonement of our iniquities.
Such an indifference to executing judgment, as is supposed, viz. that he has no determination ever to enter
upon its execution, is totally inconsistent with taking any
steps of mercy in the way of deliverance. What motive
could he possibly have for offering his Son as a Redeemer
to sinners, if he had not a design to judge the world in
righteousness, and if he were not moved by mercy to
make a provision of possible salvation for sinners, who
were so soon to come up, in view of the universe, before
his judgment seat, and receive their endless retributions?

The very provision and offer of this refuge shows, that
the mercy of a righteous God can extend no other deliverance to you, and that when this offer is withdrawn he
must, if it have been neglected, execute judgment and
wrath, that extends through a hopeless eternity and over-
whelms the soul in the pains of eternal death. And all
this wrath is speedily coming. "Behold," said this Saviour,
when he closed the volume of inspiration, (and these are
the last words, which in that holy book of his mercy he
leaves vibrating on your ears,) " Behold I come quickly."
The day of respite, the day for deliverance, ye prisoners

of hope, is short.  These hours fly swiftly.  These scenes of redemption are soon traversed.  The cry of mercy is, "To day."  You must choose your refuge speedily.  One only hope is set before you; and that is tried, sure, precious, and freely offered you.  Jesus Christ is now willing to undertake for your salvation, if you will surrender your soul to his care and government.  Renounce every other hope and surrender yourself at his feet, and he will receive you and protect you in the coming day of judgment, and lead you up to the joys of everlasting holiness. If you have trusted in any other refuge, you have no time to lose.  You cannot detain yourselves there with any safety to your souls.  If you remain in it, you are lost. The judge is at the door.  When you leave this house of your pilgrimage, you are in his presence.  You look up, and lo! the great day of his wrath is come.  The refuge in which you trusted, is found to be a refuge of lies.  It never brought God and you to a reconciliation in love. It only hardened you in presumption.  It only helped you to slight all the love and mercy of the Saviour.  And now the flames of consuming vengeance must reach you. The only opportunity of reconciliation is past.  The Judge is come to take vengeance on all that know not God and have not obeyed the gospel.  His eye of omniscience will find you out, and pour the light of insufferable brightness on all your guilt.  His heart of mercy cannot now forgive you.  His heart of holiness and righteousness must cast you off to hopeless misery.  And his arm of Almighty power will imprison you, in your wretchedness, beyond all escape.

In vain will you contend with the Almighty in judgment.  There will be no refuge from his wrath, when he shall have withdrawn the only refuge his mercy could grant, and have risen up with the attributes of omniscience and almighty power to execute judgment.  Other refuges in which you trusted will be swept away, and your souls, unprotected, unreconciled to God and his holy government, must suffer the everlasting punishment which sin deserves and his righteous law denounces.

The subject which I have been illustrating, shows the careless sinner that he is in danger of losing his soul, and the convicted sinner that he can find no safety but in immediate submission to Christ.

Careless sinner, you have placed your reliance on some other foundation than Christ Jesus. Though you may speculatively believe in his person and offices as a Saviour, and think that you can have salvation in him, yet you do not repair to Him with an all-reposing confidence that brings you as a sinner, self-condemned and in despair of every other hope, at his feet to renounce your pride and selfishness and sin, and surrender yourself joyfully to him, to be saved only through his righteousness, and live only to his praise. He is not practically your chosen refuge— the one to which with all your heart you cling. You have repaired to some other shelter, in which you can indulge your chosen ways and refuse the self-denial and the cross of Christ. You have entered it, in order to abide the storm. You depend on it, and are at ease. And unless something shall arouse you, you will remain in that hope, till you perish with it beyond the power of redemption. I invite you, then, to solemn consideration. You are acting in this life, whether you know it or not, with reference to the interests of your soul. You have now an opportunity to secure its salvation. You may go freely and cast it with full surrender on the care of Jesus Christ, and find in him that solid peace which arises from hearty reconciliation with God, and that protection in the day of coming judgment, which will shield you from the curse of the violated law and elevate you to everlasting glory. Why, then, think of resting any where short of an actual surrender of your soul to Christ Jesus? Wherever else you place it, the storms of vengeance are to fall. Every other shelter is to place you amid the flames of retribution, without relief and mercy. And will you thus needlessly keep away that soul from the Saviour? Will you throw it into the fires of eternal judgment? What, in the wide universe, calls on you to make this eternal sacrifice of your soul, when your way is open directly to God? Give up that hope, which you cannot indulge without the guilt of suicide to the soul. It only deludes you with a false peace, and leaves you exposed to eternal ruin. It keeps you away from God, your duty, your happiness; and only nourishes your pride, your sensuality and selfishness. Relinquish it at once. Do you fear to be without a hope? But you are in reality now without God and without hope. Will it make it any the worse, if you come so far to yourself as to see your real state of wretchedness? Will it place you any further from heaven, or any nearer destruction than you really are, to feel the truth that you are a condemned sinner, in absolute want of all things for your salvation, and that you must cast yourself on the mercy of Jesus Christ alone, or perish? Unless you consent to take this very place, there is no hope for you. Every semblance of one, to which you cling, is but a delusion that keeps you away from Christ and hardens you in your pride and selfishness. Act then, in view of the judgment of God and the necessities of your soul. Slumber not in any delusion. Flatter not yourself in your own eyes. Let the fear of God be before you. "For the Lord shall rise up as in mount Perazim, he shall be wroth as in the valley of Gibeon, that he may do his work, his strange work; that he may bring to pass his act, his strange act. For I have heard from the Lord God of Hosts a consumption, even determined upon the whole earth."

But the sinner, who is thoughtful and convinced of his need of salvation, has a deep interest in the subject which I have been illustrating. He is shown, that he can find no safety but in an immediate submission to Christ Jesus, his only Saviour and Lord. I know not whether there is one sinner here that carries within him a thoughtful and anxious heart to day. Yet every heart knoweth its own bitterness, and in many a bosom anxieties and convictions often spring up, which are not directly disclosed to man. And if any one before me is thus pining away in his sins, with secret convictions and apprehensions which he is striving to suppress, to him I will address myself. You have, my fellow-sinner, at least ascertained one fact,—that, notwithstanding everything to which you may have looked for safety, your soul is still in danger; exposed to the terrors of a guilty conscience, and the condemning sentence of your final Judge. You are wandering shelterless, and find no solid rest for your soul. But there is no safety in remaining where you are. Your conviction and fears, will never make a refuge for you. There is no hope for you but one, and you must flee with all your heart to that refuge. This is your first duty, your immediate duty, and the longer you delay it, the more do you resist your own conviction and the strivings of the Spirit of God. The longer you delay it, the greater is the danger, that your deceitful heart and the wiles of the Adversary will lead you to fall back for hope and quietness to some refuge of lies. Come then at once to Jesus Christ, that you may obtain true rest and happiness to your soul. Come just as you are. You cannot render yourself any better or more deserving by delay. You must come in all the shame of your guilt and poverty, if you come at all. He is willing to receive you, if you will but renounce your sin and pride at his feet, and fully give up your soul to him, to receive from him your righteousness, sanctification and redemption. He is that High and Holy One, who sways the scepter over the universe, and who became a man of sorrows for the very purpose of offering you his salvation. He has put on the aspect and the very feelings of humanity, in order to come the nearer to our hearts. You may go and surrender yourself to him, with all the fearless confidence you would to any benevolent and righteous man, who should offer you his protection on any emergency. Only he is a thousand fold more pure in his righteousness, and more ardent in his benevolence and compassion; and he is calling upon you, in an emergency as great as your everlasting condemnation to the wrath of God. He is that man, who shall be as a hiding place from the wind and a covert from the tempest. Oh! let him draw you to his throne with the cords of his humanity and compassion. Give up yourself to him, whatever sacrifices it costs you, and take to your soul freely the joys of his salvation.  Depend on him, from this hour and through life, as the Saviour to whom alone you look for salvation; for whose favor you will forsake all things; to whose praise alone you desire to live; and in whose righteousness alone you would be found in the coming day of wrath.  In this very way, Paul accepted of his Saviour. In this very way, he pressed forward through life in the Christian race, and threw himself over the goal at last as a victor, and laid hold on the crown of everlasting life and glory.  " What things were gain to me, those I counted loss for Christ.  Yea! doubtless, and I count all things but loss for the excellency of the knowledge of Christ Jesus my Lord: for whom I have suffered the loss of all things, and do count them but dross that I may win Christ and be found in him, not having mine own righteousness which is of the law, but that which is through the faith of Christ—the righteousness which is of God by faith,"—" the righteousness " which God, the Judge of all, will acknowledge in the last day, and in which he will accept the redeemed into his everlasting kingdom!

Who is there here, that will thus accept the Saviour? Who will thus enter into reconciliation with God?  Who will thus prepare for the judgment seat of Christ?  Who will thus escape from the prison of despair, and enter into the inheritance of endless glory? Methinks I hear one and another say, with trembling yet confiding faith, 'I will.' Take that resolve, returning sinner, with all thy heart! Jesus is ready to receive thee to the refuge of his grace, and thou wilt never be ashamed of closing with his proposal of salvation.

---

EPHESIANS, V: 11.

Have no fellowship with the unfruitful works of darkness; but rather reprove them.

WORKS of darkness, literally, are those deeds of sin, which men would blush to commit under the light of day. But the desire of concealment, which throws so many crimes, actually, into the night, characterizes, to some extent, every species of overt iniquity ; and on this ground, all this class of actions are properly denominated " works of darkness "—unfit for the light of day.

The apostle knew that his converts at Ephesus had once been addicted to such conduct, and that they were still surrounded by the children of disobedience, who were indulging in such iniquities ; and, in the text, he gives them counsel respecting their behavior towards these workers of iniquity. Have no fellowship with their deeds. Never join them in their sins. Never encourage them by example. Never allow yourselves to do that, which they can plausibly allege in their own justification ; " but rather reprove them." Let your conduct stand forth as a sentence of condemnation against their sins. Let your opinions be known to carry with them a holy indignation against their crimes. Reprove them. Go, bear the indignation and grief of your hearts into their presence ; and tell them—when no other eye sees them but yours and your Maker's—tell them their faults to their face. Carry the expostulations of love to their ears, and, with all the persuasion you can draw from the word of Christ, claim a hearing.

Such are the directions of the apostle to Christians, who were surrounded by the sinful deeds of the wicked—

not only to shun the fellowship with them that would be ruinous to themselves, but to carry to them the reproof that might lead to their salvation. I learn from the words, therefore, a duty which belongs to the friends of God and virtue in all ages, when surrounded by the crimes of the wicked—THE DUTY OF REPROOF.

In pursuing the subject, I would point out some of the *methods*, in which you may with propriety reprove the wicked for their sins, and mention some *considerations which may serve to enforce this duty.*

Among the methods, in which you may with propriety reprove the wicked for their sins, I specify the following :

I. By refusal to comply with their enticements.

The slightest species of reproof that can be given to sinners, arises from the refusal to unite with them in their crimes. When they are grown so bold in iniquity, as to solicit the followers of Christ to come down from the height of their profession and hopes, to unite with them in their sins and follies, the mildest reproof that can possibly be given is, to return to their solicitations a prompt and decided negative. Unless the Christian can give so slight a reproof to a sinner, as to say '*no*' to his enticements, the sinner will never fear reproofs from his example or his lips. Nor is there any impropriety in using with sinners this species of reproof. They have no claim on you, surely, to unite with them in their deeds of folly. You are lords over your own conduct, and may make your own choice, without saying why or wherefore to any but your Master in heaven. In the exercise of your unalienable rights, you may throw a flat denial in the face of every enticing sinner; and by it effectually say, 'Go thy way. When I have need of thee, I will call for thee. Obtrude not on me thy sinful schemes. Take the reproof my denial gives thee.'

II. You may reprove the wicked, by an *example* opposed to their practices.

A still stronger reproof is thus conveyed to the wicked, by the light that is reflected upon them from examples of piety and virtue. The man who always carries with him

into their society the stern front of unyielding virtue;
who is known by his uniform conduct to bear in his breast
sentiments of abhorrence and indignation towards crime;
who shows himself so firmly attached to the government
of God, and the schemes of divine benevolence, as to
repel even the approaches of their solicitations; speaks,
with silent and impressive eloquence, the language of
reproof to their consciences. Incomparably more is done
by the heavenly light attending such reproof, than can be
by all the reproofs of the tongue without it. The wicked
see in such examples the mirror, that reflects the glory of
the Deity, the authority of his law, the excellence of
virtue, the deformity of sin. They stand

> " Abashed, and see how awful goodness is."

And in the midst of such exhibitions of character, they
pass on themselves the verdict of condemnation for their
sins.

Nor is there any impropriety in bearing to the wicked
this form of reproof. Your right to obey the God of
heaven, to show your loyalty—no man can wrest from
you. You need only be loyal and be virtuous among
your companions, and the living reproof is carried home
to their consciences. As it has been eloquently remarked
of our republican country, that her very existence carries
up a reproof to the throne of tyrants, and a refutation of
all the arguments by which they would uphold arbitrary
rule, so the very existence of stern piety and virtue is
itself a stinging reproof to the wicked, and a loud condemnation of their guilt and folly.

III. You may reprove the wicked, by direct address to
their consciences.

The highest form of reproof, is that of bearing to the
wicked the direct expression of virtuous grief and indignation, which their conduct excites in your souls. When,
in refusing communion with them in their evil deeds, or
in exhibiting before them virtuous examples, you tacitly
convey reproof to their consciences, it may not be so
apparent to them that you design particularly to reprove

them for their ways ; and they may neglect, on their own part, faithfully to make an application to themselves of a reproof, which they share in common with many others. But when, in the spirit of meekness that disarms opposition, you go to the sinner, and pour into his ear the recital of his crimes, the complaints of injured virtue, the warnings of interceding grace; his conscience owns, in you, a messenger of God, come to administer the righteous and merciful reproofs of incensed, yet forbearing love. This direct address is reproof, that singles him out to his own conscience; and forces him to draw off his attention from the guilt of others to his own, with the irresistible application, "Thou art the man." He views his crimes through the unprejudiced feelings of a friend to virtue. Conscience is against him, and with his re- prover: and there arises a mighty struggle in his mind betwixt the opposing powers of sin and virtue ; a struggle which must end, either in the awful victory of guilt over conscience, or in the victory, forever blest, of conscience over guilt.

Nor is there any impropriety in using this most power- ful and most salutary form of reproof. Your tongues were given you for use; and though there are certain bounds of propriety and wisdom in the use, with respect to the age, and station, and character, and circumstances, of those whom you address, of which God has given all of you, I hope, reason and common sense enough to judge ; yet these limitations of wisdom form no argument against the legitimate use. To what use can they better be appropriated, than to doing good? Some may make too much of their tongues in this matter ; but others too little. Yet no man can deny you the right to use, for the benefit of others, this glory of your frame. You should, therefore, stand firm in this liberty wherewith God your Maker has endowed you.

With this view of the proper methods of administering reproof, I would now turn your attention to *some of the considerations, which should inspire you with resolution to perform the duty.*

1. You have on your side the *authority of God.* God said, through Paul, to his children at Ephesus, while surrounded with the crimes and iniquities of the Gentiles, and says in effect to his children in all ages, respecting the iniquitous among whom their lot is cast, " Reprove them." He has issued forth his warrant to all his friends on the earth, to be reprovers of the vicious. He has bidden them take the counsels and warnings of his word, and administer the reproofs of his offended, yet waiting love, to those who are his enemies. The command has reached your ear. " Reprove them," by every method of wisdom and love. With the warrant of his authority, you are safe. He will protect you and bless you, while on his errands of mercy ; and give you a mouth and wisdom, which no adversary will be able to gainsay or resist. Carry home the power of religion to their hearts. " Who will harm you," if, under his authority, " ye be followers of that which is good?" Will you shrink before his enemies? Shall a face of flesh and blood move you from your purposed obedience to God? How, from so humiliating a vanquishment, can you return to the throne of grace, or appear at the throne of judgment, and face the God of all power? Have faith in God ; and be strong to reprove his enemies.

2. You have on your side the *examples of all the wise and holy.*

God and all his faithful servants have ever acted as reprovers of sin. God, in the laws of his government, the arrangements of his providence, and the messages of his word, is engaged in administering solemn reproof to his enemies. The Lord Jesus, the high pattern you propose to copy into your lives, during his embassy to earth, and while dwelling among the enemies of God, was no idle spectator of those sins, by which they were wounding infinite purity and goodness, and ruining themselves and others. He took the part of God against an evil world ; and resisted all its temptations and offers ; and held before it the unsullied light of his example and precepts, to show its deformity. He addressed to its hardened sons the

reproofs of indignant love,—not consulting to please himself, but to perform his duty,—till he could cry, with the
prophet, unto God his Father, "The reproaches of them
that reproached thee, fell on me." The Spirit of grace,
in the mission he is accomplishing, is engaged in reproving
a guilty world of sin, and in carrying home to the consciences of individual sinners the stern rebukes of God's
unbending word. You are countenanced in reproving
sin, by all the faithful servants of God; by Enoch, Noah,
Abraham, Lot, and all the patriarchs; by Moses, Elijah,
Isaiah, Ezekiel, Daniel, and all the prophets; by Peter,
James, Paul, and all the apostles; by all the friends of
God, from the foundation of the world to this day, whose
bodies are deposited with us, whose souls are in heaven,
and whose memories are embalmed in the records of the
Church; and by all, in every place on earth, who are now
the followers of Christ in sincerity and truth: in whose
lives and on whose lips dwells the law of truth and kindness. All this cloud of worthies, with the great God at
their head, have arrayed their example before you, while
surrounded by the filthy conversation of the wicked, to
have no fellowship with them, but boldly to reprove.
Will you not then associate yourselves with this company
of the worthy, in their noble deeds? How can you
expect to meet their approbation, or share in their
triumphs, if you enter not with them into their labors
of love?

3. You have on your side the *interests of the Church.*

How long will it take the professed followers of Christ,
to learn that they cannot maintain a neutrality in the
world? that the enemies of God *are* enemies? and that
the mere attempt at neutrality is a concession made them,
next to base submission? Oh, how humiliating to be
governed, and trampled on, and triumphed over, by the
enemies of God,—when a decided fidelity, and a bold
reproof administered to them for their sins, would lift you
high above their power, and put ten thousand to flight!

The Church of God is not capable of flourishing, except
as she embosoms within her that energy of holy purpose

and example, and speaks forth the word of God in that tone of boldness, which administers reproof to the negligent, the worldly, the vicious, the hardened, who surround her, and who assail her peace and welfare. Arrayed in this glory, she strikes dismay into the host of her foes; she spreads abroad the conquests of her King; and even collects the vanquished with joy around her standard of Eternal Life. The time of her reproofs is the time of her safety and her triumphs. Within her borders is purity, light, hope, joy; and without, terror, dismay, shame, submission. Even they that despised her, come bending to her, calling her, the City of the Lord, the Holy One of . Israel.

Yield not up, then, the everlasting interests of religion and the Church to the follies of man. Assert the honor of your high calling, and boldly carry reproof to the enemies of Zion. Self-defense, the first law of nature, and defense of Christ's cause, the first law of Christianity, unite to call you to this holy purpose, and to arm you with a vigorous resolution.

4. You have on your side the *welfare of sinners themselves*.

The works of sin and darkness to which they addict themselves, are unfruitful in anything but evil. They are ruining themselves and their companions in guilt: for the wages of sin is death. They will not escape, unless they are reclaimed from their sins and errors. They are searing their consciences, blasting their reputation, destroying their comforts, and plunging their souls in eternal flames: and how shall they be recalled to virtue and to happiness, if they are neglected, unrestrained, and unreproved by the friends of God? Where is their hope, if none possess disinterested love enough, to address to them the reproofs that are necessary to their salvation? A sinner unreproved, grows bold in iniquity. A sinner unreproved, spreads wide the contagion of sin. He is daily adding to his guilt, and fitting himself and others for more aggravated woe. You are then guilty of a cruel neglect of his welfare and influence; if, while knowing his faults, and knowing how freely they are published and censured behind his back, and knowing how they are bringing down on his soul the insupportable judgments of heaven, you do not, at once, bear into his presence the rebukes and counsels of Infinite Love. The Scriptures impliedly charge this cruelty on those who neglect the duty, by the form in which they enjoin it: " Thou shalt not hate thy brother in thy heart: thou shalt in any wise rebuke thy neighbor; and shalt not suffer sin upon him."

But, when you administer the faithful rebukes of love to sinners around you, you are seeking by necessary means the high object of "saving their souls from death, and hiding a multitude of sins." Their feelings may be wounded, while stung with a view of their deformities and the indignations of virtue ; but you are only probing, to heal ; you are but administering the necessary medicine, to effect a recovery.  Their consciences, even at the time, and forever afterwards, do justice to you, in testifying to your self-denying kindness ; and if, subdued and melted by your reproofs, they are recovered to virtue, their hearts will forever bless you, as the kindest of benefactors. Hundreds now on earth are joyfully walking, arm in arm, the way to the heavenly Zion, who once met each other in the unpleasant relation of reprovers and reproved, and were mingling over reproved guilt their tears of bitterness.  And thousands now in glory are praising God, for those kind benefactors who, overlooking the trials they might meet with from ingratitude and guilt, dared, unsolicited, to address to them the rebukes of Infinite Mercy.

The very welfare of sinners, then, here and in eternity, demands of you fidelity in this duty—demands that you have no fellowship with them in works of darkness, but that you boldly reprove.

In view, then, of the methods in which you may convey reproof to sinners, and of the considerations which encourage and embolden you to do it, I would call upon all the friends of God among you *to perform this duty.*

There is always a sufficient call for its performance in this world of evil. You need not go back to the ancient heathen of Ephesus—you need not go abroad to benighted Pagans—you need not search out the dark portions of this Christian country—you need not, probably, look beyond the limits of your own neighborhood—to find those who are engaged in the unfruitful works of darkness. It is your lot, as it has been of the Church in all ages, to be surrounded by the wickedness of blinded sinners. Travelers with you to eternity—without God and without hope—they imperiously demand of you a faithful discharge of this duty.

"Be strong and do it." Let no leaven of iniquity among yourselves, corrupt with inefficiency the whole mass. Let no root of bitterness spring up to defile many —to hide the light of example, and stifle the voice that would administer reproof.

"Be strong and do it." Fear not the sneers of the impious, or the displeasure of the reproved. The God of Israel and the hosts of the wise are with you, the interests of Zion and of sinners are with you, in the performance of this duty.

"Be strong and do it." And Zion shall arise. The glory of the Lord shall compass her, as with walls of fire. Her enemies shall be subdued into contrition. Converts shall be multiplied as the drops of the morning. Joy shall be awakened on earth and in heaven over reclaimed and forgiven sinners.

In view of this duty, and the considerations which urge it upon the friends of God, I may surely *warn the workers of iniquity, to receive reproofs with humility and gratitude.*

You are reproved by the word of the living God. You are reproved by your own conscience. And, if you are not that hardened scorner, who mocks at all things serious, you may be favored with the reproofs of man. Remember, that he, who in love reproves you, is a friend —a true friend—a tried friend—whose love has broken through many obstacles to meet you with its warnings; and who brings to you the appeals of truth and soberness

—who comes, commissioned of God, and countenanced by all the good and wise, to urge the interests of true piety, and to seek the salvation of your soul.  I adjure you by the living Saviour, trifle not with reproof.  It is one of the last remedies of divine forbearance.  Unless you are humbled by it before God, I am compelled to say, you are fast ripening for ruin.  Slighted reproofs accumulate the stores of divine wrath.  He that *will not* receive severe remedies, and who *cannot* be restored by mild ones, *must die!*  Oh! hear it, ye that sport yourselves in your own deceivings, on the borders of eternity, —hear it: it is the last, kind warning of injured, insulted *Mercy*—" HE THAT, BEING OFTEN REPROVED, HARDENETH HIS NECK, SHALL SUDDENLY BE DESTROYED, AND THAT WITHOUT REMEDY!"  Sinners, there is awful *meaning* in those words of God!

I. KINGS, XVIII : 17—46.

THE portion of sacred history, to which I have referred, is an account of the cause of Jehovah* against Baal, tried before Israel at the altar of sacrifice on Carmel.

This trial was instituted by the prophet Elijah, in behalf, and under the direction, of Jehovah. The circumstances, which gave rise to the trial, were these: Three years before, Elijah, offended with the great sin of Ahab in introducing the service of Baal into Israel, had solemnly sworn to that monarch, that there should not be rain or dew in the land any more, except at his word. He then left the presence of Ahab, and withdrawing from the land of Israel, lived in concealment at Zareptha, in Zidon. But now, the famine which arose in consequence of the drouth, pressed sorely on all the inhabitants of the land; and Jehovah, remembering mercy towards his afflicted people, ordered the prophet to leave his concealment and appear at the court. "Go, show thyself unto Ahab: and I will send rain upon the earth." With this command and promise of God, directing and upholding him, he was emboldened, not only to face the incensed monarch again, but to require of him, as the condition on which the mercy of the rain should be

---

*In the treatment of this subject, I prefer to use the specific name, Jehovah—as employed in the original Hebrew. Our translators have put in its place the generic title, the Lord, in every instance in the Old Testament but four: following, instead of the original, the Septuagint version ; the work of Jewish translators, who, in their superstitious reverence at that period for the unpronounceable name, Jehovah, neither introduced it nor translated it, but substituted the latter title for it.

granted, that he should give an opportunity for a public trial, before the people, of the cause of Jehovah and Baal. The account of his appearance before the monarch, is thus stated : (v. 17, 18, 19:) " And it came to pass, that when Ahab saw Elijah, that Ahab said unto him : Art thou he that troubleth Israel ?  And he answered, *I* have not troubled Israel ; but *thou* and thy *father's house*, in that ye have forsaken the *commandments* of the Lord, and thou hast followed Baalim.  Now, therefore, send and gather to me all Israel unto Mount Carmel, and the prophets of Baal four hundred and fifty, and the prophets of the groves four hundred, which eat at Jezebel's table." This was a bold summons to address to an offended monarch ; but there was infinite power back of the prophet : and starvation by famine, or deliverance through this hated prophet, was the only alternative set before the king : so the summons is obeyed, and the opportunity presented for Jehovah to establish his authority over the hearts of his people, and prepare them to receive the blessing.  (v. 20.) " So Ahab sent unto all the children of Israel, and gathered the prophets together unto Mount Carmel."

The national assembly is convened on Carmel.  The mountain range known by that name, rises gently from the plain of Esdraelon to the height of fifteen hundred feet, and runs a few miles to the northwest ; when, sloping down into a promontory, it dips its foot in the waters of the Mediterranean.  Covered over its whole sloping and rolling surface with a rich soil, it is, in usual seasons, adorned with a luxuriant vegetation, from which it derives its name, Carmel,—a vineyard or fruitful field ; and, for its graceful form and rich verdure, it was set forth as an image of beauty and fertility by the Hebrew poets. But now, scorched by the drought of three years, its excellency is faded.  Here, on this mountain elevation, on the north-eastern side, probably, which looks towards Jezreel, the city of Ahab, and towards the brook Kishon flowing at its base, the vast assembly are gathered. Ahab, the king, in his pavilion with his attendants ; the prophets of Baal, on the one hand, and Elijah, the prophet of Jehovah on the other,—the opposing advocates ;—and, at a respectful distance around and below, the thousands of Israel who are to witness the trial and abide the judgment pronounced from heaven.

Let us now look at the trial, directing our attention, particularly, to the point that was in dispute ; the method agreed upon for conducting the trial ; the process of conducting it ; and the judgment obtained, with its effect upon Israel.

I. The point that was to enter into trial, and on which the issue rested, was stated by Elijah at the opening, when before the people he entered his complaint. (v. 21.) "And Elijah came unto all the people." With slow and dignified step, his flowing mantle about him, the prophet leaves his station near the king, and advances towards the multitudes of Israel, that his voice may be more clearly heard by all the parties. (v. 21.) "And he said,—How long halt ye between two opinions? If Jehovah be God, follow him : but if Baal, then follow him." He complains of their halting, like a lame person, from side to side, between Jehovah and Baal ; as if it were a matter of indifference which they followed as their leader ; as if they might manage to keep in favor with both and offend neither. He asks them how long they will allow themselves to continue, as they have done in their past history, to keep wavering and fluctuating between two opinions so utterly at variance, as whether the God they ought to worship is Jehovah or Baal : and he proposes that, now, in presence of the advocates of both deities, they bring this question to a decided issue,—whether they will choose, as their God, Jehovah only and forever, following him with all the heart in their worship, conduct and hopes ; or whether, forsaking him, they will take Baal, and Baal only, and transfer all their interest and hopes forever to his care.

The question turns on the truth and righteousness of the claims of Jehovah or Baal : whether the self-existent and eternal Jehovah, who brought their fathers out of Egypt through the hand of Moses, with tokens of Almighty power, and established them on their land, should be acknowledged as their God: or Baal, the great heavenly luminary, the sun, whom the surrounding nations at that period, Phœnicia, Chaldea and Moab, worshipped as the generative principle of life. Whether they should follow Jehovah, in the rites of worship and the commandments he had given through Moses, or follow Baal, after the custom of the nations, in the impurity practised in the groves, and the cruelty of sacrificing their children in the fires.

This question was calmly proposed and submitted by this solitary prophet of Jehovah, in presence of the numerous prophets of Baal, who felt themselves strong in the royal patronage of the queen, their fellow-countrywoman and foster-mother, and strong in the countenance of Ahab and the people, whom they had flattered in their sins and led away from the pure service of Jehovah. Yet, opposed by such fearful human odds, Elijah that day felt strong in the truth and righteousness of his cause, and in the presence and power of the living God.

The question now submitted to the people, was received by them in silence. (v. 21.) "And the people answered him not a word." This was one point gained, to have the people receive a question, which so much reflected on themselves, with silent acquiescence, as if willing to hear the cause and abide the issue.

II. The prophet next proposes to Israel a method of trying in their presence the cause of these conflicting deities, and obtaining a decisive judgment on their opposing claims: and this method is, to test the ability of each to answer the prayer of his servants. (v. 22—24.) "Then said Elijah unto the people, I, even I only, remain a prophet of Jehovah: but Baal's prophets are four hundred and fifty men. Let them therefore give us two bullocks: and let them choose one bullock for themselves, and cut it in pieces, and lay it on wood, and put no fire under: and I will dress the other bullock, and lay it on wood, and put no fire under: and call ye on the name of your gods, and I will call on the name of Jehovah; and the God that answereth by fire, let him be God."

The method of obtaining judgment proposed by the prophet, is reasonable and fair. Surely if one deity, when called upon by his servant to prove his claims, shall send down fire from heaven upon his own sacrifice, and the other shall not, then it will appear which one is the true God; with which one is lodged the treasury of all power; which one can defend his own honor, and hear and bless his servants; and which one, being inattentive to both, is feeble and false, and altogether unworthy of worship and confidence. In regard to the sacrifices, too, all the favor asked by Elijah is, that, as he is alone, poor and without human patronage, and the prophets of Baal are many and enjoy the patronage of royal wealth, the latter should be at the expense of furnishing the victims: while to them he would grant the choice of their own victim, and the opportunity of sacrificing first, with all the advantage they might hope to derive from the length of time in their favor.

In proposing this method of trial at the altar, the prophet stood committed for the honor of his God before the people, if they accept his offer. But he has, as appears afterwards from his prayer, an order from Jehovah, and he has sufficient faith in his wonder-working presence, to warrant him to *risk all on the result.* In the case of ordinary men, however, not endowed with prophetic gifts or favored with immediate revelations from heaven, the example cannot be pleaded as a warrant or permission even, to try the Lord by appeals to him for *miraculous* interposition. He will be tried and proved by the supplications of his people at large, only in reference to the promises he has made, and those ordinary works of his providence and grace by which he accomplishes them.

But here now is a prophet standing before Israel, directed of Jehovah, strong in the faith of his wonder-working presence, desiring to call back the descendants of Israel to him, the God of their fathers; and before all, he puts at issue the question between the claims of Jehovah and Baal, on the judgment to be declared by fire from heaven, in answer to prayer which each party is to offer at the altar of sacrifice.

The method of trial proposed to the people, met their approbation: as it is said, (v. 24.) "And all the people answered and said, it is well spoken." Surely, if the prophet of Jehovah objects not to make this trial of his God, it becomes the people to abide the issue, nor suffer the prophets of Baal to withdraw from the contest by refusing the challenge.

The method of conducting it being settled, the process of trial now ensues. Elijah, sustained by the voice of the whole people, turns to the prophets of Baal, and calls upon them to take their part in the trial first. (v. 25.) "And Elijah said unto the prophets of Baal, choose you one bullock for yourselves and dress it first: for ye are many; and call on the name of your gods, but put no fire under." This direction was in accordance with the proposal which the people had accepted; and gave full scope for the many priests of Baal, by beginning with the day, to consume what time might be necessary to a thorough and satisfactory trial. However much they may have hated the situation in which they were now placed, yet as they were bound and held by the voice of all Israel, they could not refuse to enter upon the trial of their cause, without giving it up at once as defenseless, and bringing down the rage of the people upon themselves, as deceivers and the authors, as Elijah claimed, of the calamities that had come upon Israel.

Accordingly, they take upon them the trial of the cause of Baal, after this sort. (v. 26.) "And they took the bullock which was given them,"—i. e. either furnished by the people without their expense, or the one which the judges among them had selected and brought to their body—"and they dressed it, and called on the name of Baal, from morning even until noon, saying, O Baal, Hear us."

For four hours or more, the people of Israel stand in the scorching rays of a summer sun, that is burning the world with drouth, and hear four hundred and fifty prophets of Baal vociferate, in a horrid jargon, the vain repetition, "O Baal, hear us, O Baal, hear us!" What think they, at this time of high noon, of Baal? What mercy has he on his worshipers; what regard to his own honor; what care of his public servants; what ears to hear, or heart to feel: that he will allow all his prophets to unite so long in calling on his name, in vain? They shout; they cry; (v. 26.) "but," says the account, "there was no voice, nor any that answered."

Failing of success, as noon arrives they grow more furious and frantic. "And," the history proceeds, (v. 26,) "they leaped upon the altar which was made." How little respect to their god and his altar have they, thus to leap up, and trample upon the unburnt sacrifice! No doubt, at this hour of trial, the sight of their own victim was a torment. No doubt they wished in their hearts to trample both the victim and altar into the dust, that both might disappear from the sight of the waiting people: but they only set forth themselves as frantic madmen, who in vain kindle up the fires of passion in their own hearts, to deceive a people waiting to see a material flame descend from heaven to burn up the victim.

But these prophets have already consumed much time, and the prophet Elijah, now that their fury is at its height, as if desirous to hasten the process and relieve the waiting people, suggests some reasons why, perhaps, their god does not hear them: reasons which, though they burn and scathe the false prophets and their god, may open the eyes of Israel to the folly of heeding such delusions. For sarcasm, like the lancet, proves a salutary instrument, when it saves the whole body, at the expense only of a deadly fungus fastened on its life. (v. 27.) "And it came to pass at noon, that Elijah mocked them, and said: cry aloud: for he is a god,"—i. e., you say he is—"either he is talking, or he is pursuing, or he is on a journey, or peradventure he sleepeth and must be awaked."

Israel, I imagine, who had been taught, through Moses, ideas, which could not have been wholly effaced, of a God who made heaven and earth; who is ever present in all his works and with all his creatures; and who never slumbereth ; Israel must have seen the ridiculous folly of these priests, in the dilemma to which they were now brought by the opposing prophet of Jehovah.  For their Baal either will not or cannot hear.  If he will not, at a time when his honor and service are all at stake, and are now become the ridicule of the opposing party, surely he can claim no more the respect and confidence of the people.  If he cannot; if he is prevented, as men often are, by previous engagement in conversation or amusement in the chase, or by absence on journeys, or by sleep,— is it not ridiculous to be waiting in vain at his doors with petitions and wants, to which the people can as well attend themselves?

It would seem, therefore, that these prophets, unanswered by their deity, must have given up the trial of their cause at this time as utterly hopeless, when they saw both their god and themselves become the ridicule of the whole assembled multitude.

But the maddened and phrenzied worshipers of false gods, usually attempt to make themselves objects of compassion by self-inflicted cruelties; as if, knowing themselves to be astray, they would punish themselves enough to purchase of others sympathy and impunity in their sins.  This device was still left as a last resort.  So these prophets, in their straits, now strive to turn the tide of ridicule, by attempting to arouse sympathy and compassion.  (v. 28.) "And they cried aloud and cut themselves, after their manner, with knives and lancets, till the blood gushed out upon them."  But these appeals to compassion cannot turn away the thoughts of the people from waiting for the approving signal from heaven : and so, as they gash their bleeding persons, they seem as if only anticipating the pains and penalties of defeat, and as having begun with their own hands the work of their execution and death.

But to give them every advantage, the prophet Elijah still longer delays to enter upon the trial of the cause of Jehovah ; and the prophets of Baal, as if to continue a folly they know not how to cease, and render themselves still more ridiculous, continue their vain incantations till the time of evening sacrifice. But it was carried to that length and satiety, that not only their god would not answer, but even their fellow-men would not regard them any more: as the history states. (v. 29.) "And it came to pass, when mid-day was past, and they prophesied until the time of the evening sacrifice, that there was neither voice, nor any to answer, nor any that regarded." No voice nor answer from above, as was before stated, nor, as is now added, any that give their attention more in the assembly of Israel.

The time was now come for Elijah to try the cause of Jehovah; for the people, disgusted with the false prophets, were ready to give their undivided attention to his offering, nor suffer, as at an earlier hour they might have done, the false prophets to seize some portion of the fire as it fell, and claim it as their own. (v. 30.) "And Elijah said unto all the people, come near unto me. And all the people came near unto him. And he repaired the altar of Jehovah that was broken down." That broken and neglected altar, which once was honored with the service of Jehovah, was now again to be consecrated to his service, and honored by the tokens of his presence. But that was not the altar he was to take for the trial. He builds another for the purpose. (v. 30.) "And Elijah took twelve stones, according to the number of the tribes of the sons of Jacob, unto whom the word of Jehovah came, saying, Israel shall be thy name. And with the stones he built an altar in the name of Jehovah." An impressive lesson to those sons of Israel who are thronging around the prophet: to remind them of that patriarch head, who was blessed by Jehovah, and by the wrestling angel named Israel or 'power with God,' and to set before them the obligation of their being unitedly consecrated to the service of Jehovah, Jacob's God. To render the trial beyond the power of any deception, as to fire, and make more signal the interposition of Jehovah, he takes the following measure of precaution. (v. 32.) "And he made a trench about the altar as great as would contain two measures of seed;" i. e., the superficial extent of which would require, if strewed with seed for planting, two seahs or third parts of an ephah, equal to more than a half bushel of our measure: a very broad trench around the four sides of the altar. (v. 33.) " And he put the wood in order, and cut the bullock in pieces, and laid him on the wood and said, Fill four barrels with water, and pour it on the burnt sacrifice and on the wood." The water, it may be remarked, might have been taken from the brook Kishon, which flowed at the base of Carmel, and which, fed by the springs of this mountain range, had not yet wholly ceased to flow, after the long drought. (v. 34, 35.) " And he said, Do it the second time. And they did it the second time. And he said, Do it the third time. And they did it the third time. And the water ran round about the altar. And he filled the trench also with water." Twelve barrels of water were thus taken to the altar by these descendants of Israel, at the command of the prophet, to make sure and signal the interposition of Jehovah, the God whom Jacob worshipped.

The time had now come for Elijah to call on Jehovah, to defend his own glory and cause, by sending down fire to consume the sacrifice. (v. 36.) " And it came to pass, at the time of the offering of the evening sacrifice, that Elijah, the prophet, came near and said." He drew nigh the altar, all Israel intent to hear and witness. The prophets of Baal were silent, (or, if continuing their incantations, by their hoarse and faint murmurings adding only to the dignity of the prophet) and, in a calm, rational, confident manner, he addressed this prayer—a model of faith and devotedness—to the God whom he worships. (v. 36, 37.) " Jehovah, God of Abraham, Isaac and of Israel, let it be known this day that thou art God in Israel, and that I am thy servant, and that I have done all these things at thy word. Hear me, Jehovah, hear me, that this people may know that thou, Jehovah, art God, and that thou hast turned their heart back again." He appeals to his God, as Jehovah, the Being of infinite perfection; the God who, by his promises and faithfulness in the past to Abraham, Isaac and Jacob, stands engaged to uphold his cause in every age; he pleads with him to grant the decisive token of the fire, for the sake of upholding his own honor and service in Israel. The prophet, in his plea, would merge himself and all the surrounding people of Israel, as mere subordinates, that Jehovah would put honor on his own name and service, by upholding his cause in the hands of his prophet, and causing Israel to turn back in their hearts from the service of Baal, with acknowledgment of his newly manifested glory and claims.

In this signal prayer,—full of faith in God, and breathing a pure desire for his glory,—the prophet has touched the heart of the self-existent One; he has set in motion that living energy, that originates, upholds, and sways at will, all power and might within this vast creation.

The prayer is uttered. The prophet is silent. All Israel expectant, await the signal. The prophets of Baal,—dusty, bleeding, ashamed and forgotten,—are looking from their disfigured altar and victim askance toward the altar of Elijah. Ahab trembles lest the poise should turn, to sink his flatterers and elevate his faithful reprover. When lo! judgment is declared; the contest is decided; Jehovah and his prophet are victorious!

(v. 38.) "Then the fire of Jehovah fell, and consumed the burnt sacrifice, and the wood, and the stones, and the dust, and licked up the water that was in the trench." What signal power, that consumes not only the wood and victim, but every vestige and memorial of those who would call in question the power and majesty of Jehovah!

The effects of this declaration of judgment are seen, in the immediate decision of Israel to take Jehovah as their God, and in their fulfilling, at the command of the prophet, the trying duty, required in the law given to them through Moses, of executing the false prophets. Israel are moved to declare for Jehovah. (v. 39.) "And when all the people saw it, they fell on their faces: and they said, Jehovah, he is the God; Jehovah, he is the God." Bowed down to the earth in fear and reverence, all acknowledge that he is the God who upholds his cause in the earth, who has power to reward his servants and punish his enemies: that he, and not Baal, is the God they must henceforth follow. The whole assembly of Israel are thus swayed back from Baal to Jehovah, and with loud voice declare that they will follow him as their God. But they have taken their vow; and now a trying duty meets them, at once to test their adhesion and loyalty. For, according to the national law that Jehovah had given them through Moses,* "the prophet or prophets that shall speak to Israel in the name of other gods, to turn them away from Jehovah their God, must be put to death." To the execution of this trying duty, the prophet now calls them. (v. 40.) "And Elijah said unto them, take the prophets of Baal: let not one of them escape. And they took them: and Elijah brought them down to the brook Kishon, and slew them there." Thus they, who had led off Ahab and Israel into open idolatry and sin, and had provoked the vengeance of Jehovah against his people, to smite them with drought and famine, were effectually put to silence. They should never more lift up their voice to cause Israel to offend, neither should their blood, soon to be washed away, with their rolling bodies, by the swelling torrents of Kishon into the sea, be allowed to pollute the land of Jehovah.

And now is the hour of mercy and relief to suffering Israel, who have vowed unto the Lord and begun obedience to his law. The prophet, who had once retired from the land announcing the judgment of drought, and had now come with the promise of mercy; and who, having this power with God in his hands, had authority with the king and all Israel to assemble them to this trial: having succeeded to gain over the heart of Israel, and silence the prophets of Baal, now announces good tidings. He bids the king refresh himself unsparingly: for there is a sound of abundance of rain, that is to remove the stints of famine. He gets him to the top of Carmel, and bends in silent prayer. He sets his servant to watch the western sea. Again and again the servant passes from his

---

* Deut. xiii : 1, 2, 5 : xviii : 20.

post of observation to the prophet with no tidings. At the seventh time, he announces a cloud arising from the sea, to appearance of the size of a man's hand. He sends the servant forthwith to bid Ahab prepare his chariot and descend from the mountain with the people, before overtaken and stopped by the swelling mountain torrents. The cloud expands in every direction; it grows dark with its stores of winds and waters: and when Ahab and the people and the hurrying prophet have found shelter in the city of Jezreel, it pours its reviving floods over the parched earth, and causes joy to the thousands of famished Israel.

Such is the history, as briefly as I could present it with justice, of a memorable day in Israel, on which Jehovah allowed Elijah his prophet, whom he had sent to them with a promise of relief, to institute, as preparatory to that mercy, a public trial of his cause, now come into conflict with Baal, against that of the idol: in order that, to all the demonstrations of his power and goodness in the past, which had now become fruitless in the presence of these servants of Baal, he might add new evidences, to regain the hearts of Israel, and to silence their troublers; and thus be acknowledged in his judgments and mercies, as the God in whom Israel should trust, and whom alone they should serve.

Among the lessons to be derived from the proceedings of that memorable day, I will mention the following:

1. Jehovah, the God of Israel, proved himself, on that day, to be the only God that is worthy to command the homage and service of our race. He is the one, who spake to the patriarchs; who gave laws and commandments to Israel through Moses; who brought into that nation his only Son, and through him caused the word of repentance and forgiveness to be published to the nations, preparatory to a day appointed, in which he will judge the world in righteousness; who, in that long series of his dealings with Abraham and his seed, from the call of Abraham to the close of the mission of Christ and his apostles, caused this word to be prepared and published, as his

book of instruction, to guide all the nations to the knowledge and acknowledgment of his glory and his claims.
He, on that day when his claims came into contest with
Baal, the god of surrounding nations, came forth from the
hidings of his power, at the call of his faithful servant:
and, from the secret store of his treasures, poured forth
from heaven the fires that swept from earth the victim,
the wood, and the very altar itself of the sacrifice that
called in question his power. On that day, when the
question was tried, whether he or Baal, whether he or
any opposing deity, was to have the preference, he
showed himself the living and true God; who has control
over the powers of nature and the course of events in the
creation, who had withheld the rain as a judgment, and
granted it again as a mercy, upon Israel. He, the ever-
living God, remaineth the same in all generations; holding in his hands the resources of everlasting strength: to
maintain the worship and service he inculcates in this
book, and to fulfill all its promises and threatenings.
Jehovah, made manifest by signs in Israel, made manifest
in the flesh in Jesus Christ—Jehovah, the author of the
Bible, then claims our faith and obedience, to the exclusion of all others. On the heights of Carmel, he showed
himself strong to defend his cause, and to put to silence
all his adversaries. Let us hear the lesson, which for all
ages he inculcated that day; that none can contend with
Jehovah and prevail: that none can forsake his worship
and service, without rushing on his judgment: and that
none should experience his mercies, without turning back
to him in their hearts. Let us then, in imitation of Israel
that day, turn to Jehovah, before all the accumulated
testimonies of his power and faithfulness, with reverence,
exclaiming from the heart: 'Jehovah, he is the God in
whom we will trust, he is the God whom we will obey:
so shall we triumph in his strength, and be refreshed with
his mercies.'

2. Another lesson inculcated in the trial on Carmel, is
that of the essential difference between the worshipers
engaged in a false, and in the true religion. We see this

difference strikingly exemplified in the. prophets of Baal
and the prophet of Jehovah, as they were tested in this
trial in regard to their worship. A false religion has not
the support of truth ; its votaries are astray from the only
true God ; they act as before the people, rather than as
before a deity ; they seek their own honor and emolument,
at the expense of sin in the people ; and, when put to the
test as to their religion, they rest not in the truth of their
cause, but on working their own passions into frantic
madness to affect the people, on loud vociferations, unmeaning repetitions, or extravagant actions, to absorb attention ; or in cruel woundings and penances of the flesh,
to excite compassion : and all, as a vain substitute and
show of religion, while astray from the only true God,
and while given to the sins and lusts that fill the world
with unrighteousness and woes. Such were the prophets
of Baal in their worship; such are all the idolaters, who
have ever established a religion and service of idolatry
in the earth ; and such too are they who, creeping with
their idolatries into the service of Jehovah, have dared
to set up idols in his sanctuary. They have all imitated
these practices of Baal's prophets on Carmel; substitu-
ting for knowledge, truth, and the pure desires of piety
and benevolence, their public shows before the people,
their ridiculous ceremonies, their extravagances and penances, their indulgences of the people in sins for gain and
emolument. How different Elijah, the prophet of the
living God! He is calm and dignified, reposing on the
truth and justice of his cause. He calls on God in a
rational manner, as a being who has power to hear, and
who has made promises in the past, to uphold the faith of
his people. With a pure and firm purpose, to consult the
honor of Jehovah, and the advancement of his cause, both
in himself and in Israel, he makes that his plea, with
earnestness and simplicity, and without repetition. He
is calm in his feelings ; putting his unshaken trust in Jehovah, to whom he breathes the sincere desire of his heart
that he will hear his prayer and fulfill his request. This
is accordant with a heart of firm faith and pure obedience,

that brings honor upon God in presence of the multitudes, and gains from him audience and favor at the altar of devotion.

Let then this striking example be a test to us, whether we are in error or in the truth, in respect to practical religion. Let us ask ourselves, whether in religion we set up ourselves and our interests before the people as supreme, or whether we merge our persons, our interests and our all, in the honor of God and the advancement of his cause.

3. Another lesson taught us at the trial on Carmel, is the power which may be employed by an individual child of God to advance his cause in the earth. Elijah stood that day on Carmel as a solitary servant of God. Against him were arrayed the four hundred and fifty prophets of Baal; the king of Israel, their protector and friend; and the whole multitudes of Israel, committed to these idolaters by their compliances. What had he to rest upon, that he should attempt to uphold and advance the cause of his God against this overwhelming torrent of idolatry? First, he had faith in God, as a Being of infinite and unchanging power, who had begun a plan of grace in our world which, by promises irrevocably spoken, he had pledged himself to carry forward in every age. And before that God, in whose breast were locked up the secrets of the future, and with whom were the issues of all power in the creation, he felt that he might come nigh to plead and prevail. Though the past was now unalterable; though the present was dark and discouraging; yet on the future, that lay concealed with God, he looked with faith and hope, as open at his almighty bidding to immediate issues of good. Next, he was furnished with a powerful plea that he could present to Jehovah. He was an obedient friend to his cause. He desired to have Jehovah honored in him and through him as a servant, and honored before Israel, and by Israel as his people. He bore in his heart this pure desire to merge himself and his surrounding fellow-creatures in the cause and honor of Jehovah, which cause and honor carry with them the blessedness

of God, and the highest good of his vast kingdom to eternity. He was thus furnished with a plea that does not fail to touch the heart of God. He stood up as a true and devoted servant of his, breathing before others, in the great congregation, the pure desire that he would honor himself while his cause was in so feeble hands, and while his honor was concerned with so many around; and the plea avails. So the faithful servant of God, who labors for his cause, whether in public or in private, when he brings this pure plea before God, tries him and proves him on a point nearest his heart, and will not fail to have audience. Once more, the prophet that day asked for an interposition of direct almighty power in the fall of fire from heaven, that was competent as a means to give honor to his cause, to turn back the hearts of his people, and silence his foes. Still God has in his hands the treasury of almighty power: and if he does not now allow his friends to ask for direct miracles to be wrought, to sustain a cause sufficiently based on that evidence already, yet he is open still to be tried, in all the applications of his almighty power in his works of providence and grace. Still he may send, at the earnest request and upon the pure plea of any faithful servant, that providential dispensation, and that working of his word and Holy Spirit, which will advance his cause in the earth; which will turn the hearts of men to acknowledge and serve the Lord, and which will put to silence his enemies. Yes; this wonder-working power in the spiritual world, like the rod in the hand of Moses, is in the hand of that believing and devoted child of God, who breathes, at his throne of grace and into his ear, the pure and fervent desire, that he would uphold and extend his cause and honor his name in the earth.

Let no one then feel himself weak who can in true faith call upon God for help. The humble believer, without office in the Church, unknown to fame, who in his little sphere of action seeks to honor God in faith and obedience, can in prayer touch the heart of God, in behalf not only of the immediate circle in which he lives and moves, or the Church with which he is connected, but of friends, and laborers for God and souls, in any part of this wide extended globe. My brethren, do you know this privilege? I fear we sometimes crush our spirits, by feeling that we have some great thing to do ourselves in order to advance the cause of our God, and must do it alone. Look then to the privilege granted you in prayer. Go, cast your burden on the Lord, and ask him to bring in the aids of his Spirit and might, to accomplish your desires for the advancement of his glory and kingdom. Go to the heart of infinite love. There touch the springs of all good success on earth. The earnest prayer of a righteous man availeth much. Elijah was a man "subject to like passions as we are;" yet, at his prayer, the rain long withheld in judgment from Israel, descended again to bless the earth.

Finally: The trial on Carmel teaches us that God will put to silence all the adversaries of his cause and people. With him is all power; and, by the tokens of his might, he can confound and put to shame all his adversaries. He can send down the fire of his Spirit, to re-consecrate his forsaken altars, and to regain the hearts of his revolted people to follow him and walk in his precepts, and, by the revival of his own honor and cause, overawe and put to silence all opposers. He can, in his wrath, commission the sword to destroy. And by mercy, or by wrath, he will silence all his adversaries; and that speedily. The wicked man may flourish awhile. He may set up his cause and find his patrons, in the earth. He may flatter himself with his devices, and content his heart in his iniquities. But his day of trial is coming. And where then will be the might in which he trusts? Who of all his idols or friends will hear or save; when Jehovah, that is mightier than all, shall come forth to execute judgment? He shall be taken away in his iniquities. The sword of the Lord shall devour him in anger. And the places that knew him shall know him no more forever.

My friends, hearken to the warning that comes from the heights of Carmel against espousing any cause opposed to that of Jehovah. The Bible represents on the earth the cause of Jehovah: the book that utters his voice; that speaks his will; that breathes forth the promises of his mercy and the threatenings of his justice,—behind which, to guard and fulfill, lie concealed awhile the resources of that everlasting strength, which upholds and guides all the movements of this vast creation. If, in your heart and life, you discard the authority of this book; if, in your intercourse with others, you attempt to put down in their minds its authority; you engage in a controversy with the living Jehovah, and must meet the fate of those who contended against his authority in the days when he was giving out these oracles with the testimonies of his miraculous power. Act not such a foolish part on this short stage of life, to fall forever under condemnation. Imitate rather the good and holy Elijah. Take Jehovah for the God whom you will only and forever follow. Seek and obey the instructions of his word. Maintain the honor of his name and worship. And, with faith and love in your hearts, and in humble, earnest prayer, ask him to promote his cause in your hands, and to shower on the parched world around, the blessings of his grace. So will you live and die the happy servants of God, the honored benefactors of mankind.

MARK XVI: 19—LUKE XXIV: 50-53—ACTS I: 4—14.

THE sorrows of the Crucifixion were past. An interval of forty days had now elapsed since the joys of the Resurrection. During this interval, Jesus did not lead about the band of his disciples, as their constant companion, as he was wont during the days of his public ministry. He appeared to them on certain occasions only ; and, in some instances, by express appointment of time and place. His personal appearances took place so often, before so many concurring witnesses, in such varied circumstances, and with such recollections of the past in his conversations, as to afford many infallible proofs, that this was indeed Jesus, alive again after his passion by resurrection from the dead.

This interval of forty days had brought them now near the Pentecost—the fiftieth day from the second of the Passover, called the Feast of Weeks ;—a feast day, on which they were to receive far richer gifts than the first-fruits of the wheat harvest, which were then wont to be gathered—on which they were to receive their first heavenly gifts after the coronation of Jesus, in the descent of the Spirit upon them at their inauguration into office, the first fruits of the great spiritual harvests that Jesus was to reap on earth from his sufferings.

At this time of full proof of his resurrection and of near approach to the festival, he convened them together by appointment, and met them in their assembly. "Being assembled together with them," is the introductory account in the Acts, as given in our translation. This meeting took place within the walls of Jerusalem ; but it would seem that, instead of being continued at the place of their gathering, he soon led them to the height of Olivet, and held his conversation with them by the way. For Luke, in his Gospel, says, that "he led them *out* as far as to Bethany,"—out of the city to the borders of Bethany, on the Mount of Olives,—implying that, having assembled in the city, they took *this walk, before the Ascension:* and, in his history of the Acts, he says, that, " when he," Jesus Christ, " had *spoken these things,* he was taken up;" and consequently he must have *reached* the place where he ascended, *at the time of closing the conversation* For Luke adds, that, " then,"—immediately after the event,—they, the disciples, returned to Jerusalem, *from the Mount of Olivet.*

Jesus had met them by appointment a short time before this interview, on a mountain in Galilee, not unlikely the elevated Tabor, as he was seen by a few of them a short time before, near the sea of Tiberias: and there, where his glory had been prefigured, he then proclaimed his approaching elevation to all power in heaven and on earth, and commissioned them to preach the Gospel to all nations.

But now is he immediately to take possession of his power. And at Jerusalem he meets them once more, that he may have his final interview with them on earth, and give them instructions as to their approaching inauguration into public office. He walks with them through the familiar scenes of his past ministry. He goes with them down the vale of Jehoshaphat, he crosses the brook Kedron, he passes the garden of Gethsemane, he ascends the height of Olivet to make them witnesses of his glorious Ascent to the Throne.

In this conversation by the way, he reminded them, first of all, of what he had said to them, on that sad night of the Passover, about his Father: that the Father had promised to send down to them the Holy Spirit, when he had left; that it was expedient for them that he should go away ; that, by going away, he should see that the Spirit was sent down ; and that the arrival and presence of this Comforter would more than make amends for the want of his bodily presence. He reminded them, too, of the prophecy of John the Baptist, when he announced of the coming Messiah, " I baptize you with water, but he shall baptize you with the Holy Ghost." By recalling to their minds these heavenly promises, first proclaimed by John at the ford of Jordan, and more fully unfolded by himself, in his discourse on the night of his and their sufferings, he gave them now clearly to understand, that they were soon to receive the promised gift of th'e Holy Spirit : and the direction which he gave them was, that they should hold themselves in readiness for the gift, and, for that purpose, should remain together, waiting for the blessing in the posture of faith and prayer, at Jerusalem. He " commanded them that they should not depart from Jerusalem, but wait for the promise of the Father, which, saith he, ye have heard of me. For John truly baptized with water "—with this outward washing he initiated his disciples into the expectation of the kingdom, and inaugurated *me* into the office of proclaiming the kingdom— " but ye shall be baptized with the Holy Ghost not many days hence." Ye shall be inaugurated into your office of witnessing for me, as I was to my ministry, by the descent of the Holy Spirit.

By thus announcing the promise of the Father and the prophecy of John as soon to be accomplished, and directing them to wait at Jerusalem for the accomplishment, their curiosity, it seems, was excited on the old subject of the temporal kingdom of Israel. For Luke immediately adds, " When therefore they were come together ;" —*i. e.*, when, excited by curiosity, they had gathered, as a body, more closely together around his person—a gathering of the body at the time more closely, for they were already on their last walk with Jesus, and could not assemble around him afterwards—when thus excited, they asked of him, saying, " Lord, wilt thou at this time restore again the kingdom unto Israel ?"

The idea of the re-establishment of the kingdom among the sons of Israel, in greater splendor than in the days of Solomon, by the person of the coming Messiah, was the prevalent opinion cherished among the Jews at that age. This opinion, shared in likewise by the twelve, concerning Jesus during the days of his ministry, had been disturbed and shaken, in a great measure, from the time of his public condemnation and crucifixion. On the day of his resurrection, if we may gather the general sentiment of the disciples from the speech of Cleopas, they were astonished, but could scarcely recover from the blow given to their hopes in regard to the temporal deliverance and glory of Israel. "Our rulers" have "delivered him to be condemned to death, and have crucified him." "We trusted it had been he who should have redeemed Israel." 'But now he is come to life again, and we are astonished; yet how can he, whom both Jews and Romans have condemned, gain the power and opportunity, that he once had, on his way of miracles, to take and wield the kingdom?' But on this occasion the promises of Christ about the future, and his directions that they wait at Jerusalem a short time for the coming of the Comforter, revive at once their hopes, that he will yet establish his power over the people; and their curiosity is excited to know, whether he will take this opportunity to restore to Israel the temporal rule and authority, long passed over to Assyrians, Babylonians and Romans. "Wilt thou at *this* time restore again the kingdom to Israel?"

Jesus, in his reply, turned off their thoughts from the time of the kingdom, as a matter they would better understand from events in the future, than they now could from any mere declarations; and bade them, in effect, leave that question for the Father to settle by his providential authority and control, and attend rather to the duties which were more immediately to occupy their labors, and for which they were to be strengthened by the promised gift of the Spirit. "It is not for you to know the times and seasons, which the Father hath reserved in his own power,"—*placed*, *fixed* by his own authority. But what will enlighten you far more into the nature of the kingdom, and your duties in it, "Ye shall receive power, after that the Holy Ghost is come upon you, and you shall be witnesses unto me, both in Jerusalem, and in all Judea, and in Samaria, and unto the uttermost parts of the earth."

This, if we except his parting benediction, was his last speech with them on earth—a speech, in which he led forward their views to the work which he would have them execute on the earth as his witnesses: that they, who had seen his past acts of mercy and power, should proclaim him as the Messiah and Saviour at *Jerusalem*, the seat of his most violent persecutors and murderers; in all Judea, in Samaria—at that day hated of the Jews— and to the utmost bound of the world.

The Saviour, with the band, had now reached the height of Olivet, east of Jerusalem. They stood together, it is supposed, on the central one of the three eminences which, ranging from north to south, crown that mount. Here, as they took their last look of his familiar and beloved countenance, he was standing before them, with uplifted hands, pronouncing upon them his benediction and farewell. "He lifted up his hands and blessed them." And as the words of blessing and well-wishing to their welfare are sounding from his lips, suddenly, his countenance being still fixed on theirs and theirs on his, he begins to rise from the earth; he ascends into the sky; a cloud of glory rolls under and around him, as a sustaining and ascending chariot; he is borne upward beyond their sight; he enters—as the glorious vision would indicate, and the message he soon sent down certified—the heavenly world; he there takes a seat, as head over the whole creation, at the right hand of God. "And it came to pass, while he blessed them, he was parted from them." "While they beheld, he was taken up, and a cloud received him out of their sight." "He was carried up into heaven." "He was received up into heaven, and sat on the right hand of God."

The eleven were looking earnestly upon that ascending cloud, tracing the pathway of their glorious Lord towards the house of his Heavenly Father, and were transfixed, with adoring wonder, in the same position, after he had gone beyond the reach of their vision ; when, suddenly, their attention is arrested by an appearance at their side. " While they looked steadfastly towards heaven, as he went up, behold, two men stood by them in white apparel." These were messengers, sent from heaven with the very first tidings from their ascending Lord, to satisfy their minds more fully in regard to the exalted throne to which he was gone, and to leave the message on earth, that its inhabitants are to see him at a future day returning in like power and glory. Whether these messengers, whom the sacred historian calls " men," were in reality men, sent from the ranks of the redeemed in the heavenly world, as Moses and Elias had been on the mount of transfiguration ; or whether they were sent from the angelic orders, all of which are to accompany the Saviour, when he shall come again in the glory of his Father, is not certain from the language. For they are called *men*, in reference merely, it may be, to their personal appearance : and such an appearance we know to have been borne by angels, on their visible embassies to the earth in the earlier ages. So, on the day of his resurrection, two angels, clothed in white, appearing as young men, were seen by the women, as they came to the sepulcher, sitting within, at the place where the head and feet of the Lord lay, to announce his removal by resurrection. But as the disciples are thus suddenly turned towards these heavenly visitants, they hear from them this message : " Ye men of Galilee, why stand ye gazing up into heaven ? This same Jesus, which is taken from you into heaven, shall so come in like manner as ye have seen him go into heaven." This is an extraordinary and heavenly announcement of the place whither the Lord is gone, and of the certainty and glory of his future return to the world, at the completion and close of his kingdom of grace on the earth.

'Gaze up no longer, in astonishment and doubt as to the future, whether he shall come immediately back, or whether he is lost to you forever. Look forward in faith and hope to another coming of your Lord, in like glory, in the clouds of heaven. He now takes the throne to rule, to guide, to save ; he will come in the glory of the throne, to gather his people to himself and to his Father in heaven, and to separate from among them all that offend and do iniquity.'

Thus were the band parted from the sight of the Lord, on whose instructions they had so long attended ; whose miracles of divine power and compassion they had so often witnessed ; and whose kind and patient labors for their spiritual welfare had so deeply won their love. They cannot now ascend with their Lord, to see him in his heavenly glory, and rejoice before him there : they have a work left for them to do in his behalf on earth. So they leave the mount of his benediction and Ascension, and, broken off from longer earthly intercourse with him, bearing with them sweet memories of the voice they shall no more hear, the face they shall no more see in the flesh, they go to the place appointed them, to wait together for the promised presence and baptism of the Holy Ghost. " Then returned they unto Jerusalem from the mount called Olivet, which is from Jerusalem a sabbath-day's journey." " And when they were come in," [to the city], "they went into an upper room, where abode both Peter and James and John, Andrew, Philip and Thomas, Bartholomew and Matthew, James the son of Alpheus, and Simon Zelotes, and Judas the brother of James." These eleven are particularly enumerated by Luke in his history of the Acts, to identify the witnesses of the Ascension with the constant attendants of the ministry of Christ, to whom he had now given instructions in regard to their apostleship. " These all," it is added, " continued with one accord in prayer and supplication, with the women and Mary the mother of Jesus, and with his brethren." Thus, when her son as to the flesh had ascended, Mary, the mother, now under the care of John, with her remaining children now believers in Jesus, is, with the band, to await the gifts of the coronation ; and the women from Galilee also, the other Mary that loved much, and Salome his aunt, the mother of James and

John, who attended him to minister to his wants and to those of the band, still continue their ministrations: and now, that their Head, to whom they were so deeply attached, is gone to the Father, they are all united in one sentiment of love and hope to draw nigh the throne of grace, and wait for the promised blessing. They now, in constant supplication, look with a livelier faith to the Heavenly Throne; and to it they raise all the affection and confidence inspired by the past instructions, the promises, the faithfulness of their now ascended Advocate and Lord.

From this account of the Ascension of Jesus, we may gather the following topics of instruction.

1. This historic account proves the reality of the exaltation of Christ to the throne over the whole creation.

I mean, that it supplies a link in the chain of evidence, which is necessary to render that evidence complete, and, without which, it might be embarrassed with difficulties. For, although the voice of prophecy foretold the ascent of Christ to the throne, after his earthly mission,—"The chariots of God are thousands of angels: the Lord is among them. Thou hast ascended on high, thou hast led captivity captive, thou hast received gifts for men, yea, for the rebellious;"—though Christ had repeatedly *foretold* that he should leave the world, and go to the Father; and proclaimed on the mount of Galilee, "All power is given to me in heaven and on earth";—and though, on that mount, the *Father, from the cloud of glory*, had proclaimed him his well-beloved Son, and caused his glory to be prefigured: yet, to render this prophetic evidence complete, some facts, it is clear, must have taken place, after the resurrection of Christ from the dead, in regard to the *disposal of his human nature*, to accord with these representations, and show that they were founded upon historic truth and reality. With these *facts*, the historical record just examined directly supplies us: and as these facts are properly attested, the chain of evidence is complete. Or, if it is objected that the narrative is not recorded directly by the apostles themselves, the eye witnesses, but by Mark and Luke only, yet these historians, most intimate friends of the apostles, must have received the information directly from them; and their narrative, when published, must have been acquiesced in by those of them who were living: and the apostles themselves *indirectly* give us their own testimony, in what they state, in three epistles at least, of the exaltation of Jesus, and his design to re-appear on earth at the close of the Gospel dispensation. The evidence, therefore, is complete.

There have been those who have seemed stumbled at these very facts; who think this particular portion of the history not accordant with spiritual ideas. But whether there is any offense truly given to spiritual ideas in this account, and whether such an opinion should make us hesitate at all in regard to the testimony of eye witnesses, may appear on further consideration. What, then, is in reality more fully accordant, I would ask, with all the prophetic and Scriptural representations given of the mission of Christ on this earth, or with its nature, than that it should thus terminate by the ascension of his human nature, out of our world, to some exalted sphere of visible glory at the head of the heavenly world?

If God is a spirit, everywhere present, yet his creation is finite. And the human nature of Christ, after his resurrection from the dead, must have a locality somewhere— a residence in some place in the universe. This is certain, from his having a finite soul resident in the body. And if he left this world in human nature for some other sphere in the universe, a departure from the world in any place must be by ascension.

Now there are only three suppositions possible in the case; one, that, after his resurrection, he should still remain in body and soul on the earth perpetually; another, that his soul should be again separated from the body, never again to cleave to any; and a third, that his soul, still in union with the body, should leave this world for some other sphere in the creation—one of highest exaltation, as represented in revelation.

But it will not be pretended that he has remained in bodily presence on the earth perpetually. How, too, could it be consistent with the representations of the supreme glory to be given to Christ, as the reward of his humiliations, that he should still remain forever on this earth after his resurrection? Is this a place—here, where opposition and enmity and reviling ever met him,—this scene of humiliation, a place of residence consistent with the representations of the honor and glory to be given him by the Father? But, again, if he disappeared by the separation of his soul from his body, what would that be but to have undergone temporal death *again?* For, if our Lord showed himself alive after his passion, and allowed the disciples to handle him, and see that he was not a spirit, but had flesh and bones, it is clear that he united soul and body, and could not have disappeared by separation of the soul from the body, without the death of the body. He must then have laid down his body to see corruption; and how would that harmonize with the Scriptural representations, or with the nature and design of his mission to lay down his life *once only* for the sins of men. What then remains, in the nature of the case, as any probable disposition of the human nature of Jesus after the resurrection, than that very one which this historical account supplies: that Jesus,—alive from the dead, both body and soul, leaving our world, without dropping that body in death, but with a miraculous change merely passing upon it to transform it into a spiritual body— ascended in glory, in presence of his disciples, to heaven, to a visible headship there over the angelic world and the redeemed—to the throne of universal dominion, the throne of the Father? Nothing more need be supposed in this case, than what is perfectly consistent with the narration; that, as in the case of Elijah and of those who shall be alive at his second coming, his body, as he ascended, was changed into a spiritual body.

Consider now, with these probabilities of the case, the evidence which the narration supplies. The eleven disciples are all before him on Olivet. They hear him talk of what he will send down to them, from the throne, in a few days. He blesses them, with uplifted hands. He begins to rise from the earth. A cloud of glory, which had ever in this world represented the presence of the Deity, seems as it were re-enàcting the scene on Tabor, and proclaiming to the witnessing disciples, in symbol, that the Father, well pleased, was welcoming him as a Son, to his *own glory*—as, indeed, it is represented that he shall hereafter come again, seated on a cloud, in the *glory of the Father*. Still more to confirm them as to the elevated station to which he ascends, two heavenly messengers come, and audibly announce that their Lord has ascended to heaven, and that there he shall remain till he shall descend to the world again in like glory.

Jesus, then, by ascending from the earth after his resurrection, it is obvious, took the universal throne—the throne of God—a visible headship over all the principalities and powers of the heavenly world, and shines forth before all, in the brightness of the Father's glory, in the express image of his person. So that, as he left this world of his humiliating mission, he was there, for his faithful obedience and sufferings in the cause of God among men, crowned with honor and glory. And angels—who celebrated his coming on earth with their heavenly songs, who aided him in his fearful agonies with their sympathies, who contemplated with wonder the place where he lay entombed, who remained after his ascent, to assure the disciples whither he had gone, and of the interest felt in him and his cause in the heavenly world;—angels, on that day doubtless, went up with him in the cloud of glory and seated him on the throne over all, and willingly and joyously obeyed the decree of the Eternal Father, when bringing his Son as heir into possession of the government of this lower world: " Let all the angels of God worship him."

2. In this account of the Ascension of Jesus we are taught, that he desired still to promote the welfare of his disciples on earth, when ascended to his throne of glory.

43

How could it be, after all he had done for the cause of God among them, and for their spiritual welfare, that he should for one moment forget their welfare, when he went to his own joyous rewards? His heart was proved too compassionate and true, amid the toils and sufferings and death of his ministry, ever to be absorbed in his personal glory, so far as not to be affectionate and true towards them still. Therefore, when about to be exalted out of their humble state, and to go to his Father's throne, he engages to send down to them a powerful Comforter, the Spirit, to supply the place of his bodily presence; he bids them wait on him, with confidence that through the Spirit they shall be strengthened for the duties and trials of their office : and, as he leaves the earth, his last look is upon them; his hands are lifted up in blessing; his heart is directed to them in assurances of good will, in wishing them to fare well in their earthly course.

But without now tracing the history of his providence over them after his departure, in which we might perceive the fulfilment of his promises and blessings, can we not see, in this very conduct of his at the time of his departure for the throne, that he expected, (and wished them also to expect,) that he would still effectually provide for their strength in duty and trial, and cause the blessing he pronounced to abide effectually with them, as an unfailing spring of grace and joy to their souls.

He appointed them, indeed, a great work, hazardous and difficult; of reproving a guilty world for sin against God, and calling them to repentance, and of preaching and proclaiming him to the human race as a Saviour; and to begin their mission at Jerusalem—the place where resided his most powerful and most implacable enemies, who had effected his crucifixion; and who would be ready to assail, with murderous hatred, any attempt to revive his cause again among the people. Yet it was a great object, to save souls and redeem them to the kingdom of his Father, for which he had cheerfully laid down his own life, and in which they might well hazard theirs. But he would not send them in their weakness; forth unfurnished, unprepared. He would have them wait on him for the Spirit, to impart wisdom and strength and mighty works, to convince and reprove the world, and give success to their testimony. He would see them, as they waited at Jerusalem for the baptism of the Spirit, abundantly supplied with power and might from above. They should reap the first fruits of the spiritual harvests, that were to be gathered from his sufferings—the early and latter harvests of the world. And wherever they went, the blessing he left was to abide upon them, to cheer and sustain their hearts. Thus did he teach us, in his care for the disciples whom he left for a while still in the world, that his followers in all their duties and trials should wait on him for strength and blessing: that, on the throne over all, he is still as regardful of their wants, as though he were toiling with them amid the cares of this life, and that if, in compliance with his directions, they wait on him, he will grant them, if not the *wonder-working powers* of the Holy Spirit, yet that enlightening, sanctifying, comforting influence from his presence, that will be sufficient to uphold and strengthen them amid all their earthly duties and trials.

3. The Ascension of Christ to the Heavenly Throne, has taught his followers to rise in their affections and hopes, from worldly to heavenly things.

When he was on earth, and laboring in the midst of the band of his disciples, they were continually looking forward to some great change in their *worldly* condition; expecting to see their master on the throne of the *earthly* Israel, and to be sharers with him in his *temporal power and glory.* These expectations seemed irrecoverably lost on the day of his public condemnation and crucifixion, and were scarcely revived again on the day of his resurrection. 'For how shall Jesus now rise to power over Israel, hated and condemned as he has been at their hands?' But from the time they saw him on Olivet, ascending in glory from their sight, to occupy the heavenly throne, promising his blessings from thence; and heard the angel witnesses proclaim, 'he who has ascended now to heaven will come again at another day in like glory;' they cease longer to gaze upward for his re-appearance to bodily vision; they cease longer to look up for his immediate return: as if he were lost to them forever, they worship him together as their ascended Lord, they return to Jerusalem with joy and thankfulness, waiting, in supplication, on the Heavenly Throne, as now the object of all their faith—the source of all their expectations and joys.

The ascent of their Lord seems to have led their thoughts and hearts at once to a throne higher than any earthly, and to joys more pure and lasting than those of this world. Jesus, the friend and instructor whom they had followed, they now see has gone up before them to heaven, carrying with him all the affection and love he had manifested to them in life and in death. Their views and feelings are now raised beyond the objects of sight, which are temporary, and exalted in faith to the invisible throne of all might and dominion in heaven. There now is Jesus, a forerunner for them in their own nature: and they know that he will there provide them their eternal mansions. There is Jesus, their high priest and advocate, crowned with all power: and now they may confidently ask anything in his name; for if they do, he will do it for them, "that the Father may be glorified thereby." There is Jesus, their Friend, and with him, their affections and hopes have ascended to the throne; and all their duties and trials in this life they cast on his providence and grace; their eternal joy they expect to derive from him, when he shall come again, in the glory of that throne, to take up with himself all his redeemed to an eternal abode with him and his Father.

Whether the little band at Jerusalem, immediately after his Ascension were led at once, and before the Pentecost, to all these views of hope and expectation from the throne of heaven, we may not indeed be certain. Yet they soon were; as is obvious from the fuller description the apostles have left, of the speedy spiritualizing and exaltation of their hopes. And it is certain that the *means* which the Spirit of God made effectual to this end, was the exaltation of Christ above this world to the throne of heaven. And on this *means* the apostles relied, to elevate the affections and hopes of their converts. " Set your affections on things above, where Christ is at the right hand of God." " Our conversation is in heaven, from whence also we look for the Saviour, the Lord Jesus Christ, who shall change our vile body, that it may be fashioned like unto his glorious body."

My Christian friends, let us then,—as we see Christ, having taught and suffered as our Saviour on earth, ascending, after his resurrection, from this earth to the heavenly throne,—feel that that throne is now accessible to us, in all our wants, and notwithstanding our guilt and unworthiness: because Jesus is there, our Great High Priest, before the Father, having entered the holy sanctuary with the blood of sprinkling and with intercession, to save to the uttermost those who come to God in his name : because Jesus is there, admitted to the Heavenly Throne itself, as the immediate Head and Lord of All. Let us treasure up all our affections and hopes with him, the Forerunner of his people and their highest Friend, who has gone to prepare them a place in his own love and the love of the Father to eternity. And let us, while we remain in this world, so cleave to him in faith, so breathe from his Spirit the spirit of love, so walk in his precepts, and so labor in his cause, that, on that final day of his coming to receive his people to himself, we may meet him with joy and not with grief—that we may behold his eyes beaming on us with love, his hands raised over us in blessing, and hear from his lips the sentence of eternal joy and welcome, " Come, ye blessed of my Father, inherit the kingdom prepared for you from the foundation of the world." O! what a glorious reward for the patience and labors of the saints on earth—patience in hope, and labor in love—thus to be exalted with the exalted Saviour to the kingdom of the Father, and to rejoice in their presence and love forevermore!

## THE WISDOM OF GOD IN THE APPOINTMENT OF TEMPORAL DEATH.

---

HEBREWS IX : 27.

IT IS APPOINTED UNTO MEN ONCE TO DIE.

OUR present life is soon to terminate in the night of death and the grave. We began our existence amid the graves of those who have preceded us ; and soon, leaving our stations to those who come after us, must we lie down, with all our predecessors, in the vast cemetery of the dead. This world—our birth place—the scene of our privileges, toils and trials—is also our appointed sepulcher : and, populous as it ever is with life, it is still more so with death, into whose silent chambers all the generations of man successively pass.

This common lot of humanity proceeds from the appointment of the Creator. Such is the conclusion of *reason*. For, if there is a Creator of our life, he, surely, must be its supreme disposer. If God has given us existence, he, evidently, has ordained the nature of that existence, the laws of its support and duration, and the causes of its earthly termination. Such, also, is the assertion of *revelation*. No assertion can be clearer than that in the text. For, though impersonal in its form, it leaves no doubt on any mind as to the person to be understood, from whom the appointment proceeds. " It is appointed unto men once to die."

The necessity of death, which is common to the race, we are to regard, therefore, as founded in the voluntary appointment of the Creator. Yet the appointment is not arbitrary. It is founded, doubtless, in reasons of wisdom and goodness.

There can be no doubt that the occasion for the appointment arose out .of the sin of our first progenitor and his race : so far, at least, as to the adoption of this *particular manner* of removing man from this world ; and that, if Adam and his race had continued holy, the removal would have been made in a different manner. But as the appointment was one to be adhered to universally,—even in case of the followers of Christ, who are forgiven and released from all condemnation and punishment,—it is obvious, that such appointment of temporal death is not identical with condemnation and punishment, any more than is the other appointment,—which is said, in the context, to follow death—that of a day of universal judgment.

There must, therefore, be other reasons, which lie at the ground of appointing such a particular evil as temporal death to our race, and not the simple one that justice, in punishing sin, requires it : more general reasons of wisdom and goodness ; and these are the reasons into which we will now inquire.

Nor can such an inquiry on our part be presumptuous, if conducted with a proper spirit and in a proper manner : with a desire to increase in the knowledge of God, and to see more of the wisdom and. goodness of his ways ; and with a careful reliance on the teachings of his word and providence, for our instruction.

I observe, then, that the wisdom of God in appointing temporal death to our race will appear obvious to us, if the three propositions, which I am now to state, are ascertained, on inquiry, to be founded in truth.

I. That the plan of providence, begun with man and his race, forbids his immortal existence here upon the earth.

II. That his removal from the earth, if necessary, must be effected in the mode, either of a supernatural change, or of temporal death. And,

III. That, of these two ways of removal, death, considered in its bearings on the present and future state of man as a sinning race, has several advantages which would be lost, upon the plan of a supernatural change.

These propositions, if sustained, go no further, it will be seen, than to show the wisdom of this general plan of procedure with our race,—of removing all its generations from the world in this one way of temporal death. They enter not into reasons for the variation of time and manner in the removal of individuals by death, nor deny that there may be subordinate and special reasons which regulate these also in wisdom. But of the wisdom of the general appointment of temporal death to our race, we are now to judge ; and let us enquire,

I. Whether the plan of providence, begun with man and his race, admits of his immortality here on the earth?

That plan may be considered in its relation both to the *animal* and the *spiritual* nature of man : yet in neither respect does it proceed on the ground of an immortality to his life here on the earth.

The *animal* nature of man was not fitted to continue forever.

For his body is composed of materials, which in their nature are corruptible ; its organization, in relation to the forces which exist on the earth, is frail and destructible : with its powers of digestion and circulation, it is dependent on the productions of the world for its nutriment, and is designed, not only for his individual existence, but for the increase of his species. It is no part of our inquiry now, why he was originally constituted in this manner, for we are speaking only of the dealings of God with a creature thus made. But certainly, this constitution of things was in irreconcilable variance with allowing him and his increasing species an immortality upon the earth. For how were all the individuals of his constantly increasing race to escape forever those adequate causes of destruction to the body, which arise out of the very nature of his residence, and which increase with the increase of his species? Such causes exist in the various chemical, mechanical, and other forces, which are constantly acting on the globe, and among which man is to live and move ; and they may arise from the limited extent of the means of nourishment afforded by the earth, and must so

arise whenever the race, by the supposition forever increasing, have so far outstripped these means as to impose
the necessity of starvation somewhere.

In the nature of things as at first constituted, therefore,
we come to the necessity, either of a change in the bodily
constitution of man and his system of life upon the earth,
or of its non-continuance here to eternity. Either man
must cease to be man, or the plan of continuing him and
his constantly increasing species immortal on the earth
must fail. In this way we reason respecting all the animal
creation under man, that their immortality itself is out of
the question : and, so far as man has an animal nature, I
see not why the reasoning is not perfectly applicable in
respect to his immortality on the earth. Nor do I see
how the fall of man can be supposed to have any bearing
upon this reasoning, or invalidate its force at all. For we
are speaking now, simply respecting the necessity of a
removal of man from the earth ; not of the mode of his
removal. This might have been effected, had Adam and
his race continued holy, at any moment by a supernatural change of the body and translation.

But that a necessity of providing another state of being
for the immortality of man, was founded originally in his
animal constitution, I think is taught, in most explicit
terms, by the apostle Paul, when assigning the reasons for
a change in the body at the resurrection he says, that
"flesh and blood cannot inherit the kingdom of God"—
that "a corruptible body doth not inherit corruption"—
that "Adam," referring here to the account of his creation in Genesis, "was *made* a living soul"—drawing the
breath of life like the animal creation,—*i. e.*, constituted
by his Creator with a life in a natural body, that is animal
and corruptible. And the history states that Adam was
favored at the first with a tree of life, whose leaves he
might apply to heat or invigorate a frame susceptible, in
its nature and from surrounding forces, of injury or
decay.

But if we turn from a survey of man's animal nature,
and consider his *spiritual* nature, the truth of our observa-

tion will be still more apparent,—that it is necessary to provide for his immortal existence elsewhere than in this world. The essential facts, connected with his spiritual nature, are these : that he is subjected to a state of moral discipline and probation here, is held accountable to his Creator for his conduct, and is to reap the results of his trial during his subsequent immortality.

The fact is indisputable, that the human species have always commenced their existence here under such an order of things as probation. Adam, the father of the race, did; and all his posterity do now. Such an ordering of things may be necessary—let such a nature at the outset commence acting, either in a holy manner, like Adam, or in a sinful manner, like his posterity—to its confirmation in holiness, or to its recovery from sin. But, however that may be, such a plan of dealing with man's spiritual nature in this world is settled ; and, things being as they are, the question simply is, whether they do not give rise to the necessity of the removal of man. Now, on this plan of dealing with man, it is obvious, that there must be a close to the probation of each individual, by retribution in reward or punishment; that this cannot take place in the world, so long as the plan continues of making the world the trial-place for the species; and that, to constitute it other than their trial-place, involves the necessity of the removal of a part or the whole of the race from the world ; *i. e.,* the impossibility of their immortal existence on the earth. Each step in this process is so evident in itself, or so founded on that which precedes it, that there can be no doubt as to the conclusion.

But let us review it. I said that there must be a close to the probation of each individual, by retribution in punishment or reward. Is not this position, with which we begin, a self-evident truth? The probation must come to a close, or be continued to eternity. But there is an absurdity in supposing a probation, which is to decide an eternal state, to be continued to eternity. That would destroy the eternity, for which the trial was designed. That would be equivalent to asserting, that a thing is designed for eternity, and is not designed for it, at the very same time: which is a contradiction in terms. But let us look at the particulars of the case.

The probation of man, as now constituted, has reference to the species as commencing their spiritual existence and action in sin; deserving punishment; and receiving the offers of redemption through Christ:—a probation, in favor of their repentance, which is to have its issues in eternal retribution. Nothing is plainer now, than that to continue those, who remain confirmed in impenitence and sin, forever amid the many undeserved privileges and blessings attendant on this state of trial, would prevent the eternal retribution of deserved punishment from taking place; and that, to continue the followers of Christ forever amid the imperfections, toils, struggles and sorrows of this state of trial, would equally annihilate the result of an eternal retribution in the rewards of grace.

Since then there must be a close to the probation of each individual of the race, at some time, by his entrance on the necessary results of rewards and punishments, we come to the next step in our reasoning: that this entrance of individuals upon eternal retribution cannot take place in this world, so long as the plan continues of making it the trial-place for the race. For if the race continues going forward in numbers, if new individuals are constantly coming forward upon probation, then, to continue the world still, as a trial-place for them, involves the necessity of continuing a system of providence, which is adapted to probation—a system, which distributes privileges and trials, blessings and chastisements, indiscriminately to all, and which is inconsistent with a state of full retribution in rewards or punishments, to any who remain here.

We come, then, in our next step, inevitably to the result, that it is impossible—on the present plan of providence—to attach an immortal existence to the race on the earth. For as man must close his probation in retribution, and, as this close cannot take place by continuing him on the earth, so long as this world is made the trial-place of his species, it follows that if his existence is continued here, the world must cease to be a place of trial: but now there is no plan which can be adopted with the world, when it ceases to be the trial-place for man, which does not necessarily interfere with the possibility of continuing the race upon it.

The world at that era, we may suppose, may be entirely destroyed, or swept of all its inhabitants ; or it may be made the residence for a totally new order of beings ; or, if used for man, it must by the supposition be made a place of retribution. No other plan is conceivable. But, if the world is entirely destroyed, or entirely swept of its inhabitants, or made the residence of another order of beings, either plan would involve the entire removal of the race. Or, if made a place of retribution for man, it must be made, either a place of punishment for the lost,— and that would involve the necessity of removing the redeemed out of it ; or a place of reward for the redeemed,—and that would involve, by necessity, the removal of the lost.

On every possible disposition of the world, therefore, removal in part or in whole is necessary. The continuance of the species here forever, is impossible.

If then, there exists a necessity for the removal of man from this state, founded in his *animal* and *spiritual* nature, we inquire—

II. Whether this removal must not be effected, in the mode either of a supernatural change of body and translation, or of death and a subsequent resurrection ?

For it is obvious, in the first place, that the removal of the race to their scenes of residence in retribution, must be attended with some important change in their physical constitution, to adapt them to their new residence and their new condition. There are two reasons for this, both adverted to in revelation, which I would particularly notice. One is, that when mankind enters upon a state of retribution, there can be no propriety in the further increase of the species. For that would be to place new individuals, with their animal and spiritual nature, at the very commencement of their existence in opposite states and worlds of reward and punishment.

But another and still more important reason for such a change, is that the body should be then fitted for an immortal and incorruptible state.

Now, though the present physical constitution of man is too frail and perishable, and the subject of too many wants, for such a state, it does not follow, on the other hand, that in order to exist imperishably, man must be absolutely disembodied, and entirely divested of a physical constitution. That, indeed, would leave no alternative but simply temporal death.

For a physical body, for aught that appears, may be composed of such materials, and constructed in such a manner, and placed in connection with such a world, as that, when animated and energized by a living spirit, it should be forever beyond the reach of any secondary causes of dissolution. And a body,—if constituted of materials and held together by laws of life, which no chemical or mechanical forces existing could destroy or crush, and, if dependent on no external materials for supply, or on none but such as are unlimited as light or space,—would be justly called strong and immortal, and be fitted for an endless existence. There would be no forces existing in the universe, adequate to its dissolution or destruction.

If, then, the removal of man from probation to the scene of his retribution requires a change in his bodily constitution, or if, to use the terms of Scripture, "the natural body" which man has here is unfitted for the world of retribution, and he is to have, while resident there, a "spiritual body," then it follows, in the next place, that the removal of man to that state must be effected, either by means of an instantaneous supernatural change, or by means of death.

For man comprises, in his constitution of being, a spirit in vital union with a body. And in order to be invested with a spiritual body—the body in which he enters on retribution,—there must be, either a severance of his spirit from the body, or there must not. If there is a severance from the body, then temporal death takes place; and, in order to enter on the world of retribution, there must be a subsequent re-union to his body, made spiritual—which is resurrection. But if there is not a severance of his spirit from the body, and life continues, then, in order to enter on his eternal state with a spiritual body, it is necessary that, while the union of soul to body still continues, there should be an instantaneous and supernatural change in the composition and organization of the body itself, transforming it, as in the case of Elijah, from the natural into the spiritual.

This is the only alternative which exists, and between which the choice lies as to a general and common plan of procedure, in respect to the removal of man from his present to his future and immortal state.

We are prepared now to enter upon the consideration of the third and last observation, by which I would show the wisdom of God in appointing temporal death to our race.

III. That in consequence of the sin of man, and the plan adopted for his redemption, death has many advantages, as a mode of removal, above that of a supernatural change.

This observation is applied, not to every form of probation, which might be supposed to be adopted with man, or to that which was originally adopted with Adam; but to that which now exists—in which man commences his spiritual existence and action in sin, and is put on trial, with reference to recovery and redemption. Taking the facts of human probation as they are, the comparison turns on the application of the two possible modes of removal from the present state, and the bearings they respectively have on the existing and future state of man.

Now, it must be conceded that the removal by death occasions pain more or less intense. In the separation of the body from the soul, there is necessarily involved the painful sensations which we call the pangs of death. Yet there is nothing else to render departure by death any more painful than departure by a sudden and miraculous change. For, by the supposition, all other things remain the same; and consequently, whatever other sources of painful emotion are attendant on departure out of this state of probation, besides the mere sensation of dying, must equally attach to either mode of departure. The trials of separation from the world and our kindred, and the emotions of the soul in entering on its future lot,— whether gathered from sin and the condemning power of the law, which now constitute the sting and venom of death, or from deliverance and joy granted through Christ,—must be essentially the same. By the appointment of death, therefore, as the mode of removal, all the amount of evil, that is necessarily added to the endless existence of man, consists of the few pangs of sensation which attend it.

But even these pangs are probably counterbalanced by the superior joys attendant on a subsequent resurrection. This is indeed a conjecture: but a conjecture highly probable. All the analogies of the present state, which arise out of the greater pleasure received from the restoration of any gift after it is lost, than from its continued possession, strongly favor the supposition. These joys, if superior, are justly set off to counterbalance the animal pangs of death: for they are offered to all, in this state of probation, and they are the ultimate possession of all, who would not, on either method of removal, equally lose all future blessedness by an impenitent life.

If, then, all the evils which necessarily attach to temporal death, are merely the short and momentary pangs of sensation which attend upon it, and if these even are counterbalanced to every individual, who would not equally lose the joys of immortality on either plan, it clearly follows, that it is wise and best to adopt that particular plan of the two, which most favors the ends which God in his goodness is seeking to accomplish, in his dispensations to our race. Now that death is the plan which most favors those ends, is evident from the following considerations.

1. Temporal death, by the pangs with which it ushers the race into their state of retribution, serves to remind the living, in a most affecting manner, of the eternal death which sin deserves.

Since mankind are sinners, and the plan of divine goodness towards them in this state of probation is, to favor their humility and repentance, and their resort to the Redeemer for pardon and life, it is surely most consonant to such a design, to give them in his providence some impressive testimonies to their ill desert; to strew around them some striking tokens of the evil they have incurred, and from which they need deliverance; to deal out to them some drops and prelibations from that cup of his wrath, which is hereafter to be poured out without mixture upon the heads of the wicked. This serves in this life the purposes of warning, chastisement, correction. He has done this, to some extent, in the pains he calls us to experience in all our way in life. But what more impressive or more appropriate testimony could be given, than to place around the portals of our entrance into eternity the bitter pangs of death? There is nothing witnessed or experienced in the present state, which so vividly represents to us the terrors of final ruin and punishment, as dying:—it is dying, and dying, yet never dead!—nothing which so much attests that such a state awaits those, who refuse to yield to the spiritual influences and salutary discipline of this life. Placed as these pangs are at the gate of eternity, through which we must inevitably pass, they cry out to us through this whole life, to fly in our guilt to the Redeemer for salvation, and shun the pangs of the second death—the eternal death of the soul.

The prospect of death, indeed, may not be so pleasant to our feelings, as would be the idea of an easy transition into eternity by an instantaneous and miraculous change: but it is more conducive to our spiritual welfare; better adapted, in conformity with the plan of God for our salvation, to keep us impressed with a sense of the great evil we deserve,—to keep us humble and lowly before God, and at the feet of our Redeemer, all the days of our appointed time until our change comes.

2. Again, death by separating the dead from our sight, serves to conceal from us a future state, and throw us on faith.

The method of God's goodness toward us in this life, is to guide us by his word and by means of faith; and, by imparting sufficient testimony about the future to serve us for motives of encouragement and strength, to make us mainly intent on our present duties; and, by keeping us strictly to a temperate, sober and godly life, to train us up for holiness in his kingdom. Now it is well for this end, to throw us by his dispensations of providence on faith, and to draw us intently to his word for our instruction, there to receive from his Spirit, his admonitions, reproofs, directions and counsel. Since then, it is the method of his Spirit to guide us to salvation by means of his word, it cannot favor the design, to call back the dead to us to report to us their state and condition. Neither can it, to have heaven and hell opened as it were to our sight, by the miraculous change of those around us, and their visible flight from us to their different abodes of joy and sorrow. We might, indeed, be greatly agitated to see a friend at our side suddenly transfigured into a form of glory, and with transports of joy on his countenance betokening his leave of us, as he ascended on a chariot of fire to the heavens. We might be greatly agitated to see another transformed into a body of darkness and shame, and to hear him pouring upon our ears the groans of perdition, as he was driven away from us by the breath of the Almighty. We might be greatly agitated, by looking thus over the borders of the eternal world, and seeing the eternal condition of our friends. But would these agitations of sight administer to our faith? Would they send us, with greater anxiety, to the word of God for instruction, to receive from him the lessons of life? Plainly, a providence which leaves the bodies of men with us at their departure, and conceals from sight their disembodied spirits, which sets the seal of death and the grave upon all the transactions of the future world, which bids us leave all our departed friends to God's keeping, and learn all our duty and welfare from his word—this is that which best serves to nourish in our hearts a filial faith and obedience, and to secure the end of our faith, the salvation of our souls.

3. Again, death, by the causes which precede it, usually gives warning of our approaching removal from the world, and thus favors particular preparation.

All we know of death is, that the union of the animating soul with the body, depending on certain conditions of the body, ceases when, from any causes, those conditions are destroyed. This may take place from various causes; but, according to the order of providence, it is a process by natural causes; and the event is consonant, in this respect, to the general economy of events in the world. Its approach, therefore, is usually indicated by its causes, and the opportunity is presented—the warning given—for particular preparation. But this could not be, on a system of immediate change and translation. I am not prepared to state all the consequences of such a system, in which it might be said of every one, at his departure, that, like Enoch, he was not found, for God took him : but one thing is certain, that, suddenly, in a moment, in the twinkling of an eye, by the fiat of the Almighty,—as it will be true of those who survive at the sound of the last trump,—the friend now at our side, or the absent friend whom we were expecting to return, would exchange his mortal for an immortal clothing, and wing his way from the earth to his fixed abode for eternity.

Now, if this were a perfect world, and every one in it were perfectly and constantly prepared in all his concerns, both temporal and spiritual, to leave it at any moment, it might not make so much difference, whether any warnings were introduced into it of approaching removal. But, imperfect and sinful as this world is, where so much is left at loose ends in temporal and spiritual matters, where most are disposed to put off all preparation for eternity, and where those who think of preparation are so prone to forget it and be surprised, it is a mercy to the world and all that are in it, that there should be warning administered, to favor special prepara tion—that some intimations should be given beforehand that our departure is nigh—that some messenger should arrive before our removal, crying, ' Set thine house in order, for thou must depart.'   Such a herald and fore-runner precedes death, in disease.   His signals are seen in the emaciated form, the haggard eye, the hectic flush. His presence is felt, in the various pangs he administers by his touch.   He withdraws men from the busy occupa-tions of life.   He leads them into the chamber of retire-ment.   He opens their ear to discipline, that they give up their transgressions ; that, on the borders of the eternal state, they prepare to leave the world with the least pos-sible injury to the interests or feelings of their fellow-men, by any neglect of duty to them,—with the least possible dishonor to God, which may arise from neglect of inter-course with him in prayer and faith.

One consideration more only, I will add.

4. That death, by reserving that which is supernatural in the change to the future, affords the opportunity for a more illustrious manifestation of the glory of God at the last day.

On either plan of removal, the individuals of the race must be removed at successive periods of time, in order to provide room for their successive generations ; at least, until that day, when the world ceases to be the trial-place of man, and the race is to extend no further.   But if the individuals of the race, successively, were transformed and translated to their respective places of retribution, the affairs of this world would end, simply in the co-tem-poraneous transformation and translation of the particular generation who were, at the time, on this stage of life. The general resurrection of all mankind from the dead, that most stupendous and impressive scene of God's power, *could* not take place.   And the general summoning of mankind to a public judgment, though it were pos-sible, would not seem so consonant to the previous dis-pensation, which had placed all, with their spiritual and immortal bodies, in their abodes of full and perfect retri-bution.

Now, if this world were a perfect world, and all its inhabitants passed from it into eternity without any grounds for impeachment of their conduct, or without any impeachments cast by them on the conduct of God, their Ruler; if all mankind, and all other beings acquainted with them, were perfectly satisfied of rectitude in all the transactions of men, and of God towards them; there might, indeed, be no occasion for a judicial trial, like that of the general judgment. But it is a sinful world. Complaints against men, and complaints against God, have been loud in it, and have been wafted, in sighs or curses, up to heaven through every generation. It is a divided world. Some have taken up the Lord's side, confessed the wrong, and justified God, and consented to accept and follow the Redeemer, whom he has sent, through much tribulation. Others have held out against the Lord and his Anointed, and opposed his friends, and hoped to triumph in their cause. There must then be a judicial trial and a settlement, in order to give peace to God's disturbed kingdom—to vindicate his character, and protect his trusting friends. Now, if it were *possible* to do this on the plan of the successive transformation of men, and their successive translation into the abodes of final retribution, it could not be so *appropriately* and so *impressively* done, as on the plan of removal by death. By such a removal, though men successively depart this life, they do not enter at once, with their spiritual bodies, on the full and complete glories or miseries of their final state. They are reserved for a day of open and final judgment. And when that day arrives, all will be in harmony and keeping with so important a transaction, and make an impression on every heart too deep for eternity to efface! The Judge will descend in the clouds of heaven. The heralding trump of the archangel shall sound loud and wax stronger, till the very dead hear and awake from the dust of the earth. Before the Judge, now seated on his throne, shall be assembled all the nations of men. There will he make manifest to the assembled race and to a witnessing universe, that all his ways are equity and truth ; that his friends are worthy to receive the Almighty protection and blessing he is to extend to them ; that his enemies deserve the irrevocable curse, by which he is to consign them to the everlasting fires of vengeance. O ! on that morning of awakening from the dust of the earth, and witnessing such a process, what an eager attention shall enchain every eye to the Judge ; what clear conviction burst in light on every conscience ; what deep emotions thrill through every heart ! How manifest on that day will be the power and the righteousness and the grace of the Saviour ! How will he be glorified and admired by all that have believed and trusted in him ! ' Lo ! this is our God ! we have waited for him, and he has delivered us.' How will he silence all his enemies, and bring them to shame, when, stripped of all their pleas and complaints, they fall down before him, self-condemned, speechless, and in despair !

Such are the considerations, which show us the wisdom of God in appointing temporal death to our race : that it is impossible, on the plan commenced with man, that he should possess an immortal existence upon the earth ; that his removal from this state, if necessary, must be effected in the mode, either of a supernatural change of body or of death ; and that, in consequence of the sin of man, and the scheme of redemption established for his recovery, death, in its bearing on the present and future state of man, has several advantages in it, as a mode of removal, above that of a supernatural change ;—such as, by its pangs serving to impress on the living a sense of their ill-deserts ; by concealing from their view a future state, to throw them on the word of faith for their guidance ; by the warnings it gives, through its causes, of its approach, to favor their special preparation ; and, by reserving the restoration of the body by supernatural power to the future, to afford an opportunity for a more impressive manifestation, at the last, of the glory of God in his dealings with our race.

The view we have now taken of death, as appointed by our Creator in wisdom, admits of a practical application ; with presenting which I will close.

Is it appointed unto men to die? Then, let every one make the application to himself:—'*I am included* in this appointment of heaven. *I too must die.* I cannot live here always. I must depart hence into a scene of retribution. I cannot hope to depart like Elijah, in a chariot of fire. I must bear the pangs of death, and leave this body in the corrupting grave, not to resume it till the resurrection. Am I *prepared* for so great a change? I must leave this my birth-place, the scene of my earliest joys and latest hopes. Have I idols here that I cannot forsake? I must go through the shadows of death, into the presence of God. Have I chosen a portion in him and his heavenly kingdom, for which my heart pants? My Creator tells me, I must die. Am I prepared? Let the question be ever present till I can answer it with satisfaction. Am I prepared? Let it follow me till I die. *Am I prepared?*'

Again: is the appointment that men should die made by the Creator in wisdom? 'Then I am not to repine, that such a lot has fallen to me, and to my friends around me. I must bow down at the feet of my Sovereign, and submit to the appointment, that I know and see to proceed from his wisdom. I should fall in with its practical designs. Come, let me survey death! I can see in it terrors, but they are the terrors of overshadowing mercy to the living. I can learn a lesson here, that nothing else this side eternity can impart. I see my ill-desert shadowed forth in this emblem of the second death, and I fly to my Redeemer, who has the keys of death and hell, for my deliverance. Come, let me survey the dead! They are stiff and cold in their last slumber. Their spirits have departed! But where? I see them not. If I call, they will not answer! Yet, amid this deep silence of the dead, I hear the voice of heavenly wisdom bid me, ' Go, search the Scriptures. In them ye have eternal life. They are they which testify of the world unseen, and of the way to reach its never ending joys.' Come, let me survey the doomed to death! Disease is preying on his frame. His life is wasting away. His Lord has announced

that he must now depart.  These moments of lingering
mercy are given, for the poor trembler to make his peace
with man and God.  Let me look at the triumphs of
death in the world.  He has borne every generation
away to his shades!  He has peopled all his domains with
his victims.  But I will not quail before his power.  I
will not despair of the cause of God.  I will wait, in hope,
till the end shall come.  Then shall the conquering
Redeemer mount his chariot of glory.  Then shall he
appear a second time, bringing full salvation unto them
that look for him, and trampling his foes in the dust.

The appointment that men should die, *is* made by the
Creator in wisdom.  Then, if I concur with the designs of
that wisdom, I am forever safe, forever happy.  If I do
not, I am not, and cannot be, either safe or truly happy.'

---

CHRONICLES XVI: 29—PSALMS XXIX: 2—XCVI: 9.
WORSHIP THE LORD IN THE BEAUTY OF HOLINESS.

THE Psalmist thus gave utterance to the feelings of a pious heart. In Jehovah, the God whom he worshiped, he saw a Being worthy of the religious homage of all. The joy he took in the honor of this infinite Being, inspired the ardent desire to have others honor and serve him too; and that desire was breathed forth in the imperative call: "Worship the Lord."

Nor was he indifferent to the *kind of worship* which men offer, or the *manner* in which they pay their devotions to Jehovah. The spirit and manner of their devotion, he comprised in one word—holiness—the quality which characterizes the being and the ways of Jehovah himself, and which should characterize the persons and the offerings of his worshipers, if there is to be maintained, in the relation between the worshiped and the worshiping, the loveliness and beauty of unity and cordiality of feeling. For holiness is the crowning excellence of the Infinite One:—which sets him up, as the pattern of supreme loveliness and the fount of supreme joy to his intelligent and moral creation. Holiness, therefore, becometh the being, the presence, and the house of the *Lord* forever; and they, who enter his house and come into his presence to pay him their offerings, must come with 'holiness to the Lord' inscribed on their thoughts and feelings, if they would be appropriate and becoming in their devotions — if they would taste the loveliness and joy of pure and acceptable worship.

The words of the Psalmist then present two thoughts, which claim our attention and obedient regard;

46

I. One, That we worship God; and—

II. The other, That our worship be characterized with the lovely and acceptable spirit of holiness.

1. There is an imperative duty, binding on us all, to worship God.

Think for a moment on this great subject, and, in presence of the great Jehovah, whose creatures you are, ask yourselves whether you are not held fast, by righteous and most affecting obligations, to pay him supreme homage. There is a God in existence, an infinite Being, who presents himself before you in the glories of a perfect character. Is he not, though unseen, ever present with all—though unfelt, ever upholding all,—and by his works making known to all his eternal power and godhead, passing before all in the glories of his righteousness and goodness and truth? Who then can be justified in confining his views to this world and his fellow-creatures; as if there were no God in existence, and as if these glories of his character were all a blank and unmeaning void? Who should not rather inquire diligently after him, and seek his presence, and bring him those offerings of reverence and respect that are due to his glorious name?

Again: This glorious Being is our Creator and King. Has he not interested his infinite heart in your welfare, by giving you a rational and moral existence, capable of communion in his love? and established a providence and moral government over you, to guide you to the sure and permanent sources of your happiness in himself? In respect to his providence:—his fatherly hand, though unseen, is constantly presenting to you its free and bounteous gifts to attract you to his love, or administering to you the rod of necessary discipline to correct your faults. And shall you, in your constant dependence and wants, look alone to things in his creation for your supply, in neglect of him, the ever living Fountain and Source of all? Should not the constant care of his heart bring us rather to his presence with thankful acknowledgment of his care and love, and with the offering to him, in return, of our most devoted service? And in his moral government :—does not his voice, though unheard by the outward ear, whisper in your conscience of a law of love towards him and your fellow-creatures, which he guards with the authority of rewards and penalties?  And does not that voice, once uttered aloud on Sinai, still prolong its fearful tones through revelation, in the command, "Thou shalt worship the Lord thy God, and him only shalt thou serve?"  Will you then dash all the hopes and joys of your existence against the penalties of his government, by refusing him your homage, or will you reverence him as your Sovereign, and seek in your devotion to him the high and everlasting rewards of submission and obedience?

But again: This glorious Being, our Creator and King, being especially mindful of our deep necessities as sinners, is now offering himself to our acceptance as a Redeemer and Sanctifier.  As a Redeemer, has he not done much for you in your sins to call you back to his presence?  In the person of his Son, he has veiled the dazzling glories of the Godhead, that would consume us with their overpowering terrors, and has come nigh in the form of humanity, to seek us in our guilt with the sympathies of his heart, and to stand between the penalties of Heavenly Justice and our souls, that the lightnings of vengeance, which he could sustain, might strike on his person and leave us safe and unharmed in the arms of his forgiving mercy.  And now, in the earthly sanctuary, he offers himself as the refuge and hiding place of the guilty, who would in him obtain reconciliation with God and eternal inheritance in his love and kingdom.  Will you then withhold your hearts from the calls and offers of such mercy, to brave alone the penalties of Heavenly wrath?  Or will you accept that mercy with all joy, and, with the offerings of penitence, thankfulness, devotedness, bow down with heart-worship before the Lord your Redeemer?  As a Sanctifier too, he meets you in the sanctuary of worship, in the person of the Holy Spirit, who comes to enliven and bless with his presence the means of instruction he has furnished, in his own inspired word, the sanctified talents of his living people and ministry, and the ordinances of prayer and praise he hath appointed for the utterance of the feelings of devotion. And while he is present to call sinners to repentance, and to train up believers in the holiness that is to fit them for his spiritual kingdom in eternity, will you refuse to come into his sanctifying presence and feel its power—will you neglect these only opportunities of salvation? Or will you not rather cast in your lot with his people, will you not unite with them in seeking the grace that alone fits the soul for heavenly joy—in worshiping God the Spirit, in spirit and in truth—in worshiping this living source of holiness and salvation?

Are you not placed under bonds then from which you cannot escape, are you not held by cords of power you can never break—to worship God?—bonds and cords of his own infinite excellence, his care of you as creatures in the use of his providence and authority, his mercy towards you as sinners, in Christ Jesus and through the Spirit of grace.

But our obligation to worship God is not the only thought set before us in the exhortation of the Psalmist: we turn now to the other, that

II. Our worship of God should be characterized with the lovely and acceptable spirit of holiness. This thought, the Psalmist sets before us in the concluding words of the text: "in the beauty of holiness."* This thought then I would now present more particularly to you, as claiming your practical regard, viz. that holiness is that quality, which constitutes the true excellence and beauty of divine worship: without which that worship is necessarily an offense to a correct spiritual taste; and by which that

---

* I am not ignorant that some give to the closing Hebrew word the sense of sanctuary, as if the exhortation were intended to call the Jews to worship God in a certain place, rather than in a certain manner—in the beauteous tabernacle, rather than in the beauteous spirit of holiness. Yet, though it is capable of that rendering, and though that rendering is suggested by the translators of our common version in a marginal reading, I am satisfied with the sense they have preferred to give to it and have introduced into the text,—viz. holiness,—the quality that characterizes the worship offered.

worship, whatever else is imperfect in it, is ever commended to such a taste as lovely and acceptable.

But before we consider this bearing of holiness on the excellence of divine worship, let us fix more precisely in our minds the idea of the moral quality denoted by the word holiness. The primary sense of the English word is that of wholeness, entireness, soundness, to which the Hebrew, corresponds, as consecrated—sacredly, entirely;—and it is applied not to the intellectual, but to the moral character; not to the understanding, but to the heart—the seat of the emotions and purposes; in order to denote that purity of feeling, that integrity of purpose, which estimates things and treats them according to their worth and importance, and which especially regards as inviolable those rules of conduct, on which the welfare of intellectual and moral beings depends, such as truth, righteousness, charity. This wholeness of character, as the word means, considered as a voluntary state, is the devotion of the whole being to that which is morally good, and separation from that which is morally evil. It is whole-souled piety towards God; whole-souled charity towards man; and whole-souled abhorrence of that which worketh evil towards either.

Now that this whole-hearted devotion is necessary, in order to render the worship of God truly excellent and acceptable, is conclusively proved by that sense of fitness and propriety, which inheres in our moral natures and which enables us to judge as to what is becoming and appropriate, in the relation of things one to another.

Consider then, either the Being to be worshiped, the design for which his worship is established, or the particular parts of service belonging to that worship; and judge whether its true moral beauty and excellence depends not on holiness or whole-heartedness in the worshipers.

Think then of the *Being* approached in religious worship: the Lord—or Jehovah—the eternal, immutable, and infinite—the all-knowing, the all-powerful, and most holy —the Creator and Ruler of all—the Redeemer and Sanctifier of his chosen. Love to the welfare of his moral creation occupies his whole heart; concentrates his whole wisdom in counsel; sways his whole power in action; keeps him firm in his uncorrupt truth and righteousness; makes him strong to hate all iniquity and frown it away from his presence; and renders him the fountain of eternal confidence, love, and joy to the kingdom, who in holy consecration yield themselves to him as his obedient people.    How then shall we approach this Being?  Who shall come into his presence with acceptance?  Who shall ascend his holy hill with the offering that is due to his name?  Who unite his heart to the heart of Jehovah, in the loveliness of sincere unity, in the joy of pure communion?

Truly, there can be no pure and acceptable approach of one being to another, except on the basis of spiritual resemblance—unity in thought, feeling, action.  For what agreement can pure benevolence have with supreme selfishness; what communion, light with darkness; what concord, Christ with Belial?

If then you approach the most high and holy, come with your whole mind and heart consecrated to him and his cause of righteousness and truth.  Yield your whole souls in willing obedience to the control of this King of righteousness.  Commit your whole being to the care of his redeeming and sanctifying grace.  This will bring you into true and cordial union with him and his plans of righteousness and grace.  This will render your reverent and humble communion with him, sweet and attractive to your own hearts, lovely and acceptable in the sight of men and angels, and accepted in the sight of God.  For thus you withdraw yourselves from the vanities and pleasures, that set up their rival and idolatrous empire against God; that debase and disappoint; that fill with sin and wretchedness.  You unite your hearts and sympathies to Him, who is the fount of eternal holiness and joy to his servants.  You take your proper place before him, as humble, devoted, obedient children, that would forever be united to his excellence and loveliness, and would gather thence your eternal supplies of knowledge and love and joy. You worship him in the beauty and loveliness that pertains to his character, by sharing in that character in your own humble measure, and desiring to grow up into that character more and more forever.

Consider, next, the *design* for which the public worship of God is instituted, and see how necessary it is to the fitness and excellence of that worship, that it be offered in holiness.

The design of instituting public worship in our world, doubtless was to make it a means to a further end, to make its forms the means of paying our spiritual homage to God, and of aiding his spiritual dominion in our own hearts and in the hearts of others. So was it with the forms of worship, instituted in Israel through Moses. So is it with the simpler rites of worship, introduced into the Church of Christ through his apostles. The design was, that we might wait on God to honor him with the expressed homage of reverence, submission, confidence, thankfulness, and joy ; and to obtain from him, for ourselves and others, the gifts of his instruction, correction, benediction, on our way to his eternal kingdom. It was that his people might honor him, as the Sum and Source of all Excellence, and be furnished by him unto every good word and work in his kingdom.

How then can the public worship of God be truly excellent, and made, in accordance with its design, truly lovely and acceptable, except as it is offered in holiness? The spirit of holiness renders the service truly a means of *honoring God.* For it is an honor to God that is due to his glorious character, that we accord to him the reverent adoration, the submission, the confidence, the joy of our hearts. And this honor is truly rendered to him by those, who come to him in the heart worship of a holy character, that beats, in its humble and imperfect measure, in sympathy and unison with his character. For how shall the heart, that loves benevolence and purity and righteousness, look up to the infinite God, shining forth in the full glory of those perfections, otherwise than with emotions of supreme respect and reverence, that truly accord in devotion with the homage which the lips utter? How shall such a heart not feel the sweet and powerful ties, which bind its interests to his supreme throne, and give beauteous meaning and sincerity to the utterance of submission and confidence,—submitting all things cheerfully to his dominion, and confiding all to his perfect care? How shall not such a heart feel the preciousness of all its experience of his Almighty care, and utter pleasant songs of thankfulness? And how, in looking up to the boundless treasures of wisdom and love on which it now feasts, and hopes to feast forever as its inexhaustible portion, shall it not swell with rapturous joy, while saying, in sincerity and truth, unto God, '*Thou* art *my* God, my portion, and strength forever?'

The spirit of holiness in the worshipers also renders their service, according to its design, a means of *obtaining*, for themselves and others, *spiritual blessings from God.* For "them that honor God" in their worship, "he will honor; and they that despise him shall be lightly esteemed." They that come before him as partakers in his own spirit of holiness and love, and that come, in accordance with the design of worship, to obtain grace to help them in their needs, make their appeal to a heart that loves the same cause as they, that loves it more intensely than they ever can, and that is ready to sympathize with them in their desires to have that cause advanced, in their own hearts, and in the hearts of their fellow-creatures. These shall, in their worship, receive the blessing from the Lord, and obtain righteousness from the God of their salvation. For they have clean hands and pure hearts, and lift not up their souls to vanity; but, in the beauty of a pure trust and hope, wait on the God of their salvation for every good in this life and in that which is to come.

If, then, you would appear before God in the spiritual beauty of the worship that honors him and secures his blessings, you must worship him in righteousness and true holiness. Otherwise, as you take the forms of honoring him on your lips, you will only mock him with heartless ceremonies; as you outwardly ask his blessing, you will inwardly provoke his curse.

Once again, I ask you to consider *the parts of service*, which engage our attention in the public worship of God, and to judge, whether the true excellence and beauty of that worship does not depend on the spirit of holy devotedness in the worshipers?

That worship, as appointed in the earthly Church, consists essentially,—under all the circumstantial differences of order, arrangement and manner, which it admits,—of the reading of the word of God, of instruction and exhortation from that word by the living ministry, of address to God in prayer and song, and of benediction from the God of grace and salvation.

How, then, will you wait on God in the public *reading of his word?* and in the dispensations of that word by the *living ministry?* What is appropriate and acceptable? What is unbecoming and offensive? One thing is clear, that, in these parts of the service, *God draws nigh to men*, to speak to them in tones of authority and mercy. For, however imperfect the voice of the human reader in uttering that word, or however inadequate the methods of the human preacher to set forth the full meaning of that word in his instructions,—whatever means and agencies intervene in this part of divine service between God and his worshipers,—yet the word read is his: the living, faithful ministry of that word is his; he takes this method to come nigh to men; to meet them in his sanctuary with reproof, counsel, correction, instruction in righteousness. He addresses them with the power of his invisible Spirit, and with words of truth and grace, on the great subjects of his glory and their welfare here and in the world to come. That still small voice from him that is enthroned over all, rises clear above all the human agencies in the scene, and bids every one that hath an ear, hearken to what the Spirit saith to the collected congregation. How, then, will you here meet God, on his throne of instruction? Would you turn away your face from the words and instructions of an earthly father? Would you sit listlessly, or compose yourself to sleep, before an earthly ruler, delivering to you precepts of authority?

Would you amuse yourself with vain thoughts, when words of life and death to you hung on his lips? Surely, the great Jehovah is despised, if you thus treat his instructions. The rude and insulting offense is given, that treats his presence and words of life as less valuable than the momentary indulgence of sloth or vanity or amusement. No: we are to turn our hearts to his words of instruction; we are to feel that we are present before God; and to say, each from the heart, ' I will hear what the Lord God shall say unto me. I will turn mine ears to instruction, and seek for my soul the way of life from God.' We are thus to meet God speaking to us through his word and ministry, in the spirit of attention and obedience, if we would act in a manner appropriate and becoming the service—if we would appear lovely and acceptable before the God we worship.

In addressing Jehovah in *prayer* and *sacred song*, how can our worship be appropriate and acceptable, unless offered in a spirit of holiness, with a mind and heart attentive to the honor of God and the spiritual welfare of his creatures? In approaching his throne of majesty with our adorations, confessions, petitions, intercessions and thanksgivings, whether in prayer or in song, we take upon ourselves to speak unto the Most High God: and before that throne is Jesus, the Mediator of the New Covenant, who hath died for us, the just for the unjust, that he might bring us nigh to that throne with acceptance. However humble and imperfect the language in which we breathe out our thoughts and feelings to God; yet the privilege is, in this part of service, extended to us most freely, to call on the name of the Lord, that we may be saved and obtain audience and favor with the God of our salvation. The throne of the Heavenly Majesty is nigh; the way of approach is open and clear; and even the sinful and unrighteous have a righteousness provided for them to shield them from wrath, when they come in faith, and fix their attention and hearts on the things of God. How, then, when his people meet him to breathe out their hearts before him, shall we treat rightly this hearer of prayer and praise ?   Would you turn away from the opportunity, to indulge in the idle doze, or to amuse yourself with companions as thoughtless as yourselves? Such neglect of the great Jehovah at the hour he meets you for audience,—how unbecoming and offensive must it appear to his eyes of purity, how unbecoming and offensive even to your own eyes, should they be once opened to see the reality !   But how appropriate and lovely is the sacrifice of prayer and praise, when, beyond the outward form, that a thoughtless mind might abuse, there lies deep in the heart the consciousness that God is present : and there ascend, from its inmost recesses, emotions that seek their true utterance in breathings of prayer and praise to his most holy name !   How lovely and acceptable before God, to treat him with whole-hearted devotedness, as our pardoning and covenant-keeping God, our Refuge and Friend in life's changes, our Saviour in death, and in the world to come ; to say to him, as his people have ever done, " Forgive my iniquity ; uphold me with thy free Spirit ; lead me into the land of uprightness ; make me joyful in thy countenance ; and I will now and forever utter the memories of thy great goodness !"

It is thus, and thus only, by true devotion in the house of God, that you are prepared, at the close of service, to receive, in all thankfulness, his high and holy benediction. For while that closing service is performed, how unsuitable and offensive is the impatient hurry, the thoughtless noise, the vacant stare, that treat it as an unmeaning ceremony —that proclaims indifference to the great Jehovah, whether he utter a blessing or a curse.   But how appropriate and lovely is the spirit of that whole-souled worshiper, who stands, in attentive silence, to hear God pronounce through his earthly servants his benediction ; who, as it is uttered, sends up to God the silent ejaculation, that it may fall and rest on his heart, ' Bless me, even me, O my Father !'

If, then, you consider the essential parts of the divine service in their meaning ; or the great design for which that worship has been instituted ; or the character of the

Being who is worshiped ; is it not obvious that the true excellence and beauty of divine worship depends on its being offered in holiness?  And when you consider the obligations that bind you to draw nigh to God in religious worship, is not the duty which the Psalmist proposes to you worthy of your thoughtful and obedient regard : " Worship the Lord in the beauty of holiness "?

There are two thoughts which I would suggest at concluding : that we keep our worship in the earthly sanctuary pure ; and that we here fix our hope on the glories of an eternal worship in heaven.

Let us keep our worship in the earthly sanctuary pure. Here we now meet God on our way to the throne of judgment and the recompenses of eternity.  We here halt from time to time on the way ; to refresh ourselves with joy in his presence ; to gather strength to endure and overcome the trials and temptations incident to this probationary state : and to quicken in our hearts that spiritual life that fits the soul for heavenly rest.  When coming before God on such an errand, with such interests dependent upon him, surely it becomes every one to draw nigh him in sincerity and truth.   Let us, then, my friends, as we engage in the worship of God here, ever banish from us every unworthy thought and feeling, every disturbing care, all levity of manner and behavior, and wait upon him in all the loveliness of a serious, thoughtful, obedient and joyous faith.  For surely it were a lovely spectacle—the image of a heaven upon earth—to see those, who come up to the courts of the Lord, all realizing the presence and glory of the God that is worshiped ; according to him, from full and earnest hearts, the honor that is his due ; and seeking, in every part of the service, to obtain his heavenly grace on themselves and others ! Oh ! shall it ever be?  Shall there ever come from the Lord the day of power and glory, that shall set up that heavenly scene everywhere on the face of this now polluted world ?

Finally, let us fix our hope on the glories of an eternal worship in heaven.  That is a lovely and blessed world, where all hearts yield to God the honor and obedience that are his due, and pour out eternally their thanks and praises for-his inexhaustible love and kindness. That is the land of uprightness; where dwell the perfectly pure and devoted, whose vision of God grows eternally brighter, whose full-hearted love never droops, whose deep-toned praises never tire. Oh, shall we ever reach that blessed world? Shall we ever mingle in its praises? Let us give all diligence, in this our earthly pilgrimage, to make our calling and election sure. Let us now draw near the Lord, and learn here on earth to engage our hearts in those blessed employments. So shall an entrance at length be ministered unto us abundantly into that ever-lasting kingdom of our Lord and Saviour Jesus Christ! So shall Cherubim and Seraphim bear us up to his presence, to unite with their throngs and with all the hosts of the ransomed in the pure and glorious worship they ever offer at his throne!

Oh, *shall* we ever reach that blessed world? *Shall* we ever mingle in its exalted praises?